# THE EUK      ᴌRS

Martin Gilbert is one of the foremost historians of the 20th century. In 1968 he succeeded Randolph Churchill as the official Churchill biographer, writing six volumes of narrative and editing eleven volumes of Churchill documents. He has also published a definitive history of the Holocaust and twelve historical atlases, including those on British, American and Russian history. Since 1962 he has been a fellow of Merton College. He was knighted in 1995.

## Books by Martin Gilbert

### THE CHURCHILL BIOGRAPHY

Vol III *The Challenge of War, 1914-1916*
Vol III (documents in two parts)
Vol IV *The Stricken World, 1917-1922*
Vol IV (documents in three parts)
Vol V *The Prophet of Truth, 1922-1939*
Vol V *The Exchequer Years, 1923-1929*
(documents)
Vol V *The Wilderness Years, 1929-1935*
(documents)
Vol V *The Coming of War, 1936-1939*
(documents)
Vol VI *Finest Hour, 1939-1941*
Vol VI *At the Admiralty, 1939-1940*
(documents)
Vol VI *Finest Hour, May-December 1940*
(documents)
Vol VI *The Ever-Widening War, 1941*
(documents)
Vol VII *Road to Victory, 1942-1945*
Vol VIII *'Never Despair', 1945-1965*

### OTHER BOOKS

*The Appeasers* (with Richard Gott)
(Phoenix Press)
*The Roots of Appeasement*
*Britain and Germany Between the Wars*
(documents)
*Plough My Own Furrow: the Life of Lord Allen of Hurtwood* (documents)
*Servant of India: Diaries of the Viceroy's Private Secretary* (documents)
*Sir Horace Rumbold: Portrait of a Diplomat*
*Churchill: a Photographic Portrait*
*Churchill's Political Philosophy*

*Churchill, A Life*
*In Search of Churchill*
*Auschwitz and the Allies*
*Exile and Return: the Struggle for Jewish Statehood*
*The Jews of Hope: the Plight of Soviet Jewry Today*
*Shcharansky: Hero of our Time*
*Jerusalem: Rebirth of a City, 1838-1898*
*Jerusalem in the Twentieth Century*
*Final Journey: the Fate of the Jews in Nazi Europe*
*The Holocaust: the Jewish Tragedy*
*First World War*
*Second World War* (Phoenix Press)
*The Boys: Triumph Over Adversity*
*Holocaust Journey: Travelling in Search of the Past*
*A History of the Twentieth Century* (Three Volumes)
*Letters to Auntie Fori: 5000 Years of Jewish History*

### ATLASES

*Recent History Atlas, 1860-1960*
*British History Atlas*
*American History Atlas*
*Jewish History Atlas*
*The Arab-Israel Conflict: Its History in Maps*
*First World War Atlas*
*Russian History Atlas*
*Jerusalem Illustrated History Atlas*
*Children's Illustrated Bible Atlas*
*Atlas of the Holocaust*

# THE EUROPEAN POWERS
## 1900-1945

Martin Gilbert

PHOENIX
PRESS

5 UPPER SAINT MARTIN'S LANE
LONDON
WC2H 9EA

A PHOENIX PRESS PAPERBACK

First published in Great Britain
by Weidenfeld & Nicolson in 1965
This paperback edition published in 2002
by Phoenix Press,
a division of The Orion Publishing Group Ltd,
Orion House, 5 Upper St Martin's Lane,
London WC2H 9EA

Phoenix Press
Sterling Publishing Co Inc
387 Park Avenue South
New York
NY 10016-8810
USA

A CIP catalogue record for this book is
available from the British Library.

Printed and bound in Great Britain by
Butler and Tanner Ltd, Frome and London

ISBN 1 84212 216 9

FOR HELEN

# CONTENTS

# ILLUSTRATIONS

## Acknowledgments

The author wishes to thank the following for supplying photographs:
The Radio Times Hulton Picture Library 1, 4, 5, 9, 12, 13, 14, 15, 17, 18, 19, 20, 26, 33; The London Electrotype Agency 30, 36; The Osterreichischer Nationalbibliothek 8, 10, 11, 23, 27, 28, 29, 31; Keystone Press Agency Ltd. 22, 32, 34, 35; Edmark, Oxford 37, 38; Camera Press Ltd. 16; Helmut Laux, Frankfurt 21; Mirrorpic 24; Imperial War Museum 3; Fox Photos Ltd. 25; P. A.-Reuter 7; Messrs. Vickers 2.

## MAPS

*All the maps were specially prepared for this volume
by Martin Gilbert*

# PREFACE

THIS HISTORY of Europe describes many violent and unpleasant events. It refuses to speak of unity where there is no unity, or of progress where progress is absent. On the broad plain of history the river flows in a wide, smooth sweep towards the sea: all is progress, visible and irreversible. But there are also, if one looks closely and carefully, side currents, eddies, cataracts and whirlpools, where no such easy, comforting movement can be discerned. It is of such a turbulence that I write: of fifty years when civilized, democratic, and industrialized nations lapsed into the barbarism of two continental wars; when the hopes and aspirations of gentle, cultured people were swiftly, disastrously, and, for many, finally dashed into tiny fragments; and when evil, done not only by soldiers but by civilians, grew and flourished and overflowed.

This volume gives a glimpse of the enormity of the horrors which Europe witnessed, and of the strange and often muddled men who created those horrors, or failed to stop them until, for many millions, it was too late.

The American reader may be puzzled by so much violence. His own land has hardly known—certainly not since 1865—excesses of cruelty. Yet every system can collapse, every democracy tumble, every instinct of humanity and justice fade away unless citizens, however humble, show vigilance and care. I hope the European example will serve as a vivid warning of what dangers lurk under the calm surface of prosperity and progress.

MARTIN GILBERT

1966

Progress is not a law of nature. The ground gained by one generation may be lost by the next. The thoughts of men may flow into the channels which lead to disaster and barbarism.

H. A. L. Fisher, *A History of Europe*, 1934

Without having improved appreciably in virtue or enjoying wiser guidance, mankind has got into its hands for the first time the tools by which it can unfailingly accomplish its own extermination. That is the point in human destinies to which all the glories and toils of men have at last led them. They would do well to pause and ponder upon their new responsibilities. Death stands at attention, obedient, expectant, ready to serve, ready to shear away the peoples en masse; ready, if called upon, to pulverize, without hope of repair, what is left of civilization. He awaits only the word of command. He awaits it from a frail, bewildered being, long his victim, now—for one occasion only—his master.

Winston Churchill
*Shall We Commit Suicide?*, 1924

# UNITED EUROPE: A VISIT TO THE CELESTIAL CITY

IN 1900 Europe was the world: the nations of Europe, covering between them only a small percentage of the earth's surface, seemed capable of whatever task might be demanded of them in commerce or war, in any part of the globe.

The Europe that wielded such power and knew such confidence had been created within the previous hundred years. Few of its nations could boast even a century of political unity. Germany and Italy had each consisted of many rival states before 1850; Austria and Hungary had been constant and embittered enemies; France had been torn between the constitutional extremes of absolute monarchy and "red" republicanism. Russia and Britain had their own internal troubles. In Russia popular discontent seemed likely to lead to revolution. In Britain a similar sense of impending unrest culminated in the Chartist agitation of the 1840s. The agitation died down but the dissatisfaction remained. Skeptics forecast the downfall of the British monarchy before the end of the century.

By 1900 all this had changed. Europe appeared to have settled her internal problems. Each state boasted of its stability and took for granted its strength and permanence. German unity, sealed by two victorious wars, against Austria in 1866 and against France in 1870, had resulted in the establishment of a centralized, autocratic state structure, carefully fostered for twenty years by Bismarck, the first Imperial Chancellor, and skillfully manipulated after 1890 by the young and ambitious emperor, Wilhelm II.

France, having recovered financially from defeat by Germany, accepted a republican form of government as that which least divided the warring political factions. The French Republic began in a negative way: she was neither a military regime nor a monarchy, neither a theocratic state nor a socialist one. But by 1900 she had developed positive qualities. She was strongly anticlerical and equally hostile to imperial adventures; she was parliamentary in structure and encouraged vigorous political debate in Parliament and in the Press. She also encouraged innovation in art and architecture. She was sufficiently active in her own interest to have entered in 1892 into a defensive alliance with Russia.

Russia remained autocratic, but Nicholas II was a moderate, reforming emperor who tried to satisfy, but if necessary to restrain, radical demands and pressures. Russia's peasant-slaves had been emancipated since 1861. They had become peasant-proprietors; cautious, conservative supporters of the autocrat.

England saw between 1850 and 1900 a growth of imperial power and a consolidation of parliamentary government that were unparalleled in Europe. Her navy was supreme on the seas and could transport her armies wherever they were needed. The stature of her monarchy had grown and republicanism disappeared. Her commercial power seemed unrivaled even by the growing industrialization of Germany. This dominance was symbolized by Queen Victoria. She came to the throne in 1837. In 1876 she accepted the title of Empress of India. In 1897 she celebrated sixty years of rule. By 1900 her children and grandchildren had married into almost every royal family in Europe. Even her soldiers thought of the Empire as belonging to the Queen herself, crying, in Rudyard Kipling's words:

> Hands off o' the sons o' the Widow,
> Hands off o' the goods in 'er shop,
> For the Kings must come down an' the Emperors frown
> When the Widow at Windsor says "Stop!"

Another European monarch had ruled for almost as long as the aged queen. In 1867 Franz Josef of Austria-Hungary had seen his two nations brought together into a close and powerful union. He had become Emperor of Austria and King of Hungary, symbolizing in his person the serenity and permanence of Europe's largest continental empire. As the nineteenth century reached its end Franz Josef had been on the throne for fifty-two years.

Europe knew internal security in 1900. It had also accepted an

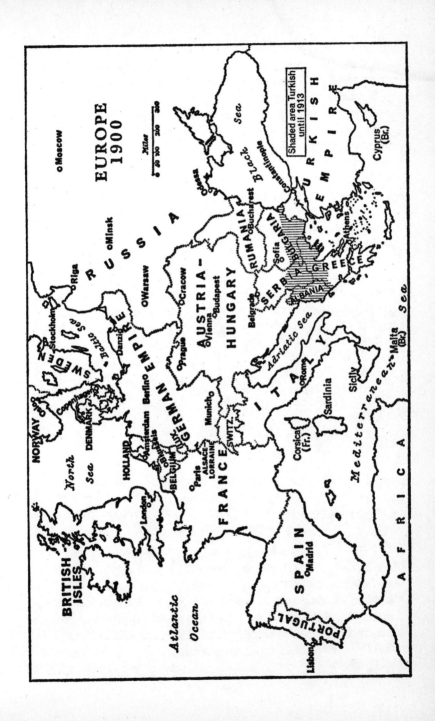

overseas burden. The romance of empire had prompted great expeditions and annexations. Much of the non-European world formed part of the European empires. Portugal, Belgium, Britain, France, and Germany ruled large tracts of Africa; Britain ruled India;[1] the Dutch controlled the East Indies. South America was free from European imperial ambition, having thrown off the mantle of Spanish imperial power early in the nineteenth century. Only Cuba and Puerto Rico in the Caribbean Sea, a few strips of African coastline, and the Philippine Islands in the Pacific remained as a reminder of the once all-powerful Spanish Empire.

One distant country still lay open to European ambitions: China. In 1895 Japan had defeated China, and Chinese weakness was thus revealed to the world. The European powers, fearing an eastern imperial rival, combined to stop Japan taking too great advantage from her victory. Until 1895 Europe's policy in China had been that of the "Open Door," allowing traders of any European nation to do what trade they could in whatever part of China they chose. But with China's weakness exposed Europe's ambition grew. The "Open Door" policy was abandoned in favor of "spheres of influence," essentially a political rather than an economic concept.

Germany was the first nation to seize a national concession; Russia, Britain, and France followed. Each began by demanding exclusive use of a Chinese port; then each pushed inland. There seemed no reason why the nations of Europe should not achieve as complete a control over China as the British, alone, had achieved over India. Europe could use technical power unknown to China; it could ship vast quantities of men to the East and could arm them with the most formidable weapons.

The Chinese resented Europe's intrusion and feared European ambitions. On 20 June 1900 the German Minister in Pekin was murdered and the Chinese began their siege of the European legations. The siege lasted for nearly eight weeks. As no news reached Europe other than that of the murder of the German Minister and the start of the siege, it was angrily and falsely assumed that the legations had been destroyed and all the Europeans in them killed.

The Chinese Imperial Government had originally hoped to con-

---

[1] The Portuguese ruled the coastal towns of Diu and Goa; the French were sovereign in the ports of Pondicherry and Mahé.

trol anti-European sentiment, but the Anti-Foreign Society (or "Boxers") had grown in four years from an extremist group to an all-powerful organization. The Boxers believed that neither sword nor bullet could hurt them. They declared their aims in a widely publicized proclamation:

"Foreign devils have come with the doctrine of Christianity. . . . They have attracted the greedy and avaricious as converts. . . .Telegraphs and railways have been established, foreign cannon and rifles manufactured, railway engines and electric lamps the devils delight in. . . . Foreign goods and property of every description shall be destroyed. The foreigner shall be extirpated. . . ."

The Boxers had murdered a number of missionaries, and had destroyed European cathedrals, factories, banks, and desecrated graves before they besieged the legations. With this sudden acceleration of violence the European troops in China were at once organized to march on Pekin, to rescue the besieged Europeans.

On 7 August 1900 a German general was appointed commander-in-chief of the European forces in China: the American, Russian, French, Austrian, British, German, and Italian governments all provided contingents to join with the Japanese forces.

On 13 August the British force entered Pekin and on 26 August the Celestial City surrendered. China was forced to accept European traders and spheres of influence. Thus Europe imposed its will on the Orient. Though it had needed the assistance of Japan and America, it regarded its victory as primarily a European one.

The European expedition came just in time to save the Europeans in Pekin. But, despite the victory, most of the European residents remained nervous of Chinese violence and unconvinced of the rapidity with which European help might come if it were needed again. More attention was in fact paid by Europe to investment in Japan. But there was no thought of conquering Japan, which was so powerful that in 1902 Britain thought it worthwhile to become its ally. China, seemingly so divided and clearly defeated, failed to sustain the interest aroused by the expedition or to attract traders into its interior.[2] The conquest of Pekin had been in vain.

Empire-building proved an arduous and unrewarding task for the

[2] European concessions were confined to the coastal regions, and in particular to Shanghai. It was not until after the Communist revolution of 1949 that the European extraterritorial rights in Shanghai were abrogated.

ambitious men of Europe. But the possession of empire gave the imperial nations of Europe a feeling of power and permanence which, however ill-founded, reenforced the confidence sprung from internal stability. Although the actual benefits in terms of trade, profits, and political control were small, the prestige of empire was paramount. The sickness, the bad climate, the poor communications, and the hostility, or apathy, of the local populations were not a sufficient deterrent to the lure of imperial sentiment and romance. It was not the politicians, soldiers, or traders, but the novelists of empire, who were keenest in championing imperial sentiment.

# ☆ 2 ☆

## THE BRITISH EMPIRE IN FAMINE
## AND WAR

THE LARGEST EMPIRE in 1900 was the British, an empire, it was said, on which the sun never set. Its color on the map was an imposing red, but the uniformity of the color hid a multiplicity of problems. In both India and South Africa the glories of empire were somewhat tarnished by 1900.

India was never the "gold mine" that people in Europe imagined it to be. A few individuals grew rich in trade and commerce, but the government of India was more concerned with political problems than with economic profits. It was able only with difficulty to balance its annual budget. It had to struggle every year to offset the expenditure on public works and the maintenance of a large army against the income from land revenue, a salt tax, and a charge on government-sponsored opium sales. In 1900 income from land revenue fell rapidly as a result of widespread famine.

Famine struck over a wide area in 1896 and by 1900 as many as two million people had died of starvation. All the resources of the Empire—private charity, government activity, and the exertions of individual officials were put at the service of the stricken subcontinent.

In 1898 a new Viceroy, Lord Curzon, was sent to India. His arrival coincided with an outbreak of plague which added its own severe mortality to that of the famine. In one week alone 5,725 people died of plague in a single province, Bombay.

Lord Curzon fought government inefficiency and challenged apathy in whatever branch of administration it was to be found. He intervened personally whenever he felt that the slackness or bad

7

policy of a civil servant was holding up needed reforms. He introduced land reforms whose aim was to lessen the tax burden that lay upon the peasant, and thus make it possible for the peasant to resist the ravages of drought and scarcity. He saw that the land tax pressed so heavily upon the peasant that when drought came he could not call out reserves of foodstuffs or capital, and that when his fields dried up his life was in jeopardy.

Curzon had no illusions about the ease or luxury of imperialism. Of those Englishmen who had died helping to organize relief during the first onrush of famine in 1896 he said: "These men did not die on the battlefield. No decoration shone upon their breasts. No fanfare proclaimed their departure. They simply and silently laid down their lives, broken to pieces in the service of the poor and the suffering among the Indian people."

But in England the sacrifice of courageous British officials passed almost as unnoticed as did the death of two million Indians. The Indian Empire was taken for granted. Men assumed that it was powerful and prosperous. While administrators of every rank labored to make life at least tolerable for as many Indians as possible, most people "at home" found the problems of Empire tiresome.

But one imperial problem grew so large, eclipsing even the horrors of Indian famine, that it entered into the conscience of Britain and aroused interest and anger throughout Europe.

The Boers of South Africa, descendants of the Dutch settlers, had won their independence from Britain in battle in 1881. They had formed two Republics, the Transvaal and the Orange Free State, in whose midst gold had been discovered. This brought riches to the Republics and also European speculators and settlers or "outlanders," many of them British. The Boer leader, President Kruger, tried to restrict the outlanders' activities. Their mine profits were heavily taxed and they were deprived of influence in local government. Perhaps this did not matter much: many grew rich and departed. But Kruger's stern policy was resented in Britain, where his republics were disliked and his independence scorned. There was bitterness, too, because in British South Africa, and in Rhodesia, no gold had been found. The outlanders hoped that Dr. Jameson's dramatic raid would help reduce Kruger's powers, but it failed. Kruger, sensing danger, imposed further restrictions upon them. Some Boers urged moderation, but Kruger grew more irate. Even nonspeculators were ill-treated if they were not Boers. Kruger's autocratic methods led Britain to take up the cause of the non-Boers in the Republics. Kruger was warned that his highhanded methods could have dire consequences. In 1899 the Boers, fearing an attack, and stimulated by Kruger's aggressive nationalism, took the initiative and invaded British territory. Britain thereupon declared war. The British hoped to defeat the Boer Republics and to reincorporate them into the Empire. It was assumed that victory would come easily and swiftly. This was not so: the two Republics fought back with tenacity and skill. They excelled in rapid dashes on horseback behind the British lines. The war dragged on throughout 1900. Its methods became more violent, its conduct more costly, and loss of life on both sides more severe.

The British, who had seldom troubled about Indian problems, became increasingly anxious about South Africa. How was it possible, men asked, for an uncultured, ill-organized, distant people to resist the mighty arm of the British Empire? Political parties were divided. Many of the ruling Conservatives hoped to thrash the Boers into submission, whatever the cost. At first a majority of the opposition Liberals took the same view. Other Liberals denounced the war as an example of imperialism gone berserk. Their voice was gradually given a sympathetic hearing throughout the Liberal Party. Their criticisms of the war gained respectability as the war progressed.

One such "pro-Boer" was a young Liberal Member of Parliament, David Lloyd George. In the House of Commons on 6 February 1900 Lloyd George made his name as a national figure by challenging the whole idea of the war, which he called "an unnecessary, a damnable, even worse perhaps, a senseless war."

Opposition to the war thus became a part of British politics. But it was difficult at first to distinguish the Boer War from the many imperial wars that had gone before—the Ashanti War of 1896, the fighting along the northwest frontier of India in 1897 or the reconquest of the Sudan in 1898. In these little wars men displayed courage against unlettered peoples. The nations of Europe accepted the slaughter and the sacrifice as part of the inevitable advance of civilization. It was readily argued that barbarians were being driven back into the barren hills or stony desert to make way for European-style progress.

This attitude towards imperial campaigns was aptly expressed by a young British lieutenant who had taken part in the reconquest of the Sudan: "We may consider how strange and varied are the diversions of an Imperial people. Year after year, and stretching back to an indefinite horizon, we see the figures of the odd and bizarre potentates against whom the British arms continually are turned. . . . Perhaps the time will come . . . and there will be no more royal freaks to conquer. In that gloomy period there will be no more of these nice expeditions . . . no more medals for the soldiers, no more peerages for the Generals, no more copy for the journalists. The good old times will have passed away, and the most cynical philosopher will be forced to admit that, though the world may be much more prosperous, it can scarcely be so merry."

The merriment ended much sooner than the lieutenant could have forecast. He himself went to the Boer War, was captured by the Boers, escaped, and became a hero in England. The Boer War taught him a different lesson. On 22 January he wrote in one of his regular despatches to a London newspaper: "Ah, horrible war, amazing medley of the glorious and the squalid, if modern men of light and leading saw your face closer, simple folk would see it hardly ever."

Thenceforward this lieutenant devoted himself to politics, hoping through his own knowledge of war and by his own exertions to avert war among nations. Such is the irony of history that he found himself in positions of power during two European wars. His name was Winston Churchill. He was twenty-five when the Boer War began.

In 1901 the Boer War entered a more violent phase and in Britain criticism became more acute. The British Government decided to intern Boer women and children in the hope that their menfolk would then despair and surrender. While Boer men fought, their wives and children were put into camps, called by an official, unattractive name, "concentration camps." These camps were ill-administered. They had neither water nor food supplies sufficient for their inhabitants. Medical supervision was almost nil. Overcrowding led quickly to disease, and disease to death. The name "concentration" camp soon came to symbolize a place in which suffering was acute.

Lloyd George accused the Secretary of State for the Colonies, Joseph Chamberlain, of deliberately seeking to exterminate the Boers. "Herod of old," he declared, "tried such a thing as this. He sought to crush a little race by killing its young sons and daughters. He was not a success; and I would commend the story to Herod's modern imitator." Joseph Chamberlain was no Herod. He set to work at once to improve conditions in the concentration camps. The death rate fell quickly once the Government's conscience had been roused. But Lloyd George's invective and Joseph Chamberlain's reforms both came too late. The Boer War casualty lists told a terrible tale that gave little encouragement to imperial zealots: 6,000 British soldiers were killed, 16,000 died of wounds and disease; 4,000 Boer soldiers were killed, 9,000 women and children died in the concentration camps. Sickness, not bullets, had caused the greater slaughter.

Such was the cost of crushing two small republics and extending the British Empire in South Africa. Although the British won the war their enthusiasm for imperial conquest disappeared. Not only had there been a higher casualty list than in any war since the Crimean War fifty years earlier, but the hostility of much of Europe had been aroused. In 1900 Kruger was received enthusiastically in Paris and The Hague.

When the Boer War ended in 1902 Britain promised the Boers eventual self-government, which was promptly and fully granted in 1910. A sense of shame and failure filled the nation after its expensive and almost invisible victory. The Archbishop of York proposed a "Day of Humiliation" for the Empire. The war had lasted for three years. It ended and discredited the era of romantic imperial war.

## ☆ 3 ☆

# EUROPE'S UNCERTAIN DOMINION
# IN AFRICA

WHEREAS the British finally achieved imperial dominance in South Africa at a great cost in men, materials, and enthusiasm for empire, the Portuguese failed to obtain a clear military dominance in their African territories before 1914. Yet their losses were almost as great, for it seemed natural to the Portuguese, as it had to the British, to seek to extend their direct political control throughout the areas over which they hoped for power and influence.

The Portuguese had begun to administer Angola in 1576, but had failed to pacify the natives despite 300 years of military activity. In 1897 serious unrest broke out in certain provinces of Angola. The native cattle had been infected with a swiftly spreading disease but the natives refused to allow vaccination. Portuguese officers led native soldiers into the villages, hoping to persuade the villagers to agree to the vaccination of their cattle. The persuasion was unsuccessful and one detachment of soldiers was massacred. The Portuguese mounted a large operation to quell the unrest and reassert Portuguese authority. Over a thousand men were sent on punitive expeditions. Three hundred of them were slaughtered in a single ambush. For some years after this disaster whole regions of Angola were left unvisited and uncontrolled. Only in 1906 was another expedition prepared and 2,000 men sent off to brave the anarchy of the interior. They were only partially successful. It was not until 1915 that any real measure of control was established in the rebellious provinces.

The Portuguese were even less able to control their native populace in Mozambique than in Angola. Not only was insufficient military force available to the colonial administrators but the Portuguese government would not support the men on the spot. Lisbon did not share the enthusiasm of its empire-builders nor would it give them the powers necessary to bring discipline or prosperity to the colonies.

Mousinho de Albuquerque, the Royal Commissioner of Mozambique from 1896 to 1898, continually appealed for greater authority to impose Portugal's will upon the natives, but his powers were reduced by government decree in 1898 and he at once resigned. He had sought an imperial policy that would give Portugal a respected and even a feared place among the nations of Europe. In his book *Mozambique* he expressed his pent-up frustrations:

"The administrative processes by which our colonies have been governed, or, rather, disgraced, may be summed up as conventions and fictions. Vast territories conventionally ours where we exerted absolutely no influence; powerful chiefs tied to the Portuguese crown by fictitious vassalage . . . reserve officers without a reserve; battalions and companies without officers or soldiers; professors without schools, schools without pupils; missions without missionaries; priests without churches, churches without parishioners; even a medical service almost without doctors. . . . And on top of all this, majors and colonels and commanders, endless officers, bulky reports, countless laws, many decrees, a hundred unworkable regulations."

Returning to Portugal Mousinho found few people willing to support his imperial vision. In 1902, despondent and unheeded, he shot himself.

Africa's frontiers were often determined, not by the armies and expeditions of the European powers but by agreements reached between them over areas which they had never visited and whose very location on the map was often dubious. The struggle with the native rulers often began only after the territories had been obtained. The struggle for Africa usually reflected conflicts which originated in Europe. Thus at Berlin in 1885 the European powers defined the frontiers of the Belgian Congo. Yet no white man had cast eyes upon one hundredth of the frontier. Maps were manipulated without any knowledge of the area concerned. Frontier lines, often drawn as straight lines over the map, cut tribes and even villages in half.

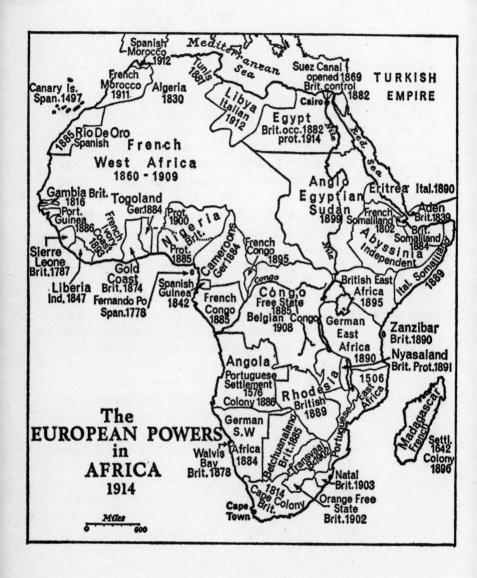

The
EUROPEAN POWERS
in
AFRICA
1914

In 1890 Germany and Britain came to an agreement over their shared African frontiers. In 1891 Portugal and Britain settled the borders of disputed regions, despite Portugal's inability to maintain order on its own side of the boundaries. In 1894 France and Germany reached a settlement along their common African borders.

France's African empire, territorially the largest of all, was not obtained primarily through ambition or avarice. Much of its frontier was drawn by accident. The policymakers in Paris did not initially aim at sovereignty. They envisaged only a loose, commercial control over their African territories. Domestic opinion was often hostile to imperial expansion, and ministers who showed too great a zeal for empire found themselves hissed in the streets of the capital. The French government therefore established spheres of influence where French traders could go about their business unmolested. But there was a great deal of molestation, both from European rivals of France and from the Muslim rulers of the territories involved.

To protect French traders from the British trading companies, in whose train came commercial monopoly and eventual political control from London, the French found themselves obliged to strengthen their own control by continual extensions of French sovereignty. Such maneuvers were seen by the Muslim rulers as attempts to assert total mastery. They therefore took up arms whenever a French trader or missionary penetrated into their territory. The French government again felt obliged to intervene to protect its subjects, since the death of a French trader in some remote African desert could lead to violent anti-Government demonstrations in the French Parliament and shrill calls for the resignation of the Minister who had allowed French blood to be spilt so easily. With each successful extension of territory a new Muslim ruler became France's neighbor or a new British scheme came into conflict with a French-held area.

The German imperialists were particularly unlucky in their African policy. Like the Portuguese, they found little support for their schemes at home. Like the French they were criticized continually by their parliament, which regarded itself as competent to pass judgment over distant colonial problems. Like the British they found themselves confronted by immense natural disasters.

In German East Africa a severe famine caused great mortality among the natives in 1900. The degree of inadequacy of medical facilities was emphasized by the spread of smallpox, plague, and leprosy throughout the coastal districts.

The German Parliament (or Reichstag) constantly interfered in imperial affairs, rooting out much iniquity. Parliaments can create muddle and confusion when legislating for distant lands and unknown people, but the Reichstag was an exception. In 1897 it protested against the tyrannical behavior of Karl Peters, German Imperial Commissioner in East Africa. Peters was brought before a disciplinary court in Germany and eventually dismissed from the imperial service. Among his offenses was the creation of a private harem, the flogging of its inmates, and the murder of a native chief who gave shelter to one of the women after she had escaped.

Peters's dismissal was a credit to the German government. Equally creditable was its interference in the Cameroons. There the Governor had imprisoned native chiefs who protested against the ill-treatment of their people. The Reichstag overruled the Governor's sentences. The chiefs were set free and the Governor was retired. In this way the conscience of Europe came to the assistance of Africa, and the Germans showed themselves capable of wise imperial rule.

But there was one German colony into which Reichstag protests did not penetrate. In German Southwest Africa a policy of deliberate extermination was adopted in 1904 against the Herero tribe, who had rebelled against German rule. Against the instinctive, clumsy protest of a bewildered primitive people was set in motion the terrible vengeance of modern Europe. The Herero tribesmen were driven into the Kalahari desert. Some 80,000 tribesmen entered the desert in 1904. By 1906 only 15,000 were alive.

One explanation of such brutality lay in the small number of Germans who actually lived in the colony. As compensation for their numerical weakness they sought strength through violence. As an ex-governor of one of the colonies explained in 1907: "It was impossible in Africa to get on without cruelty." If so small a group of men really wished to exert control over vast, seminomadic tribes, they would of necessity resort to brute force.[1]

Making war in Africa was dangerous, ambush and disease being severe obstacles. But winning war was not so difficult. Europe's power lay in her technical skill. "Whatever happens we have got the

---

[1] There were under 10,000 German colonists in German Southwest Africa in 1914, and only 15,000 in the whole of Africa.

Maxim gun, and they have not." The English poet Belloc's sarcasm, like the weapon itself, was accurate. Nor was it the Germans alone who made use of it.

The Maxim gun was seen at its most effective during the Matabele War of 1893, when the British South Africa Company, supported by the British government, destroyed the army of King Lobengula. The Company troops totaled 800 or 900; Lobengula had over 5,000 warriors. Yet the African king was utterly defeated. The Maxim gun was the victor. As a British official present wrote: "In spite of a panic flight on the part of our native levies, the column with its machine guns repulsed three furious charges and finally routed the Matabele with great slaughter."

British imperial ambitions were finally settled, however, not by warfare but by agreement with her principal rival, France. In 1898 Britain reconquered the Sudan and pushed the French away from the Upper Nile. In 1904 Britain obtained French recognition of the permanence of the British occupation of Egypt by offering France a free hand in Morocco. British rule in Egypt was profitable and benevolent. But it took the French nearly twenty years to pacify the Moroccan tribes and thus obtain any rapid benefits from their side of the bargain.

Imperial activity outside Africa was more successful, and for Russia more permanent than in Africa. Russia had, over two centuries, extended her frontiers far into Asia until they almost bordered upon the northern boundary of British India. Russian rule over her Muslim and other Asian subjects, like the rule of other Europeans in Africa, was conducted by a small band of dedicated administrators. Government support for territorial expansion was often lacking. Indeed, in 1906 the Russian government vetoed plans for the extension of Russian sovereignty into Persia and accepted instead a Russian sphere of influence in Persia. Britain obtained the other sphere. The two powers signed an Anglo-Russian Convention to this effect in 1907. In this convention they also agreed not to extend their sovereign power into Afghanistan or Tibet.

Both Britain and Russia thus agreed to restrict their respective imperial activity in such a way as to avoid conflict between them. They realized that such conflict might easily spread to Europe, drawing in Russia's ally, France, and Britain's ally, Japan. Imperial interests were not allowed to come into conflict with European interests.

In 1914 Britain and Russia, rivals in Asia, were fighting, together with France, against a European enemy, Germany, over a European quarrel.

As a result of the Spanish-American War of 1898 the Americans conquered the Philippine Islands in the Pacific. Rudyard Kipling was puzzled by America's apparent willingness to become an imperial power. From his own knowledge of British India he was aware of the difficulties and frustrations of empire-building. He therefore addressed his poem *The White Man's Burden* to the new empire-builders of America, expressing in it the frustrations felt by many Englishmen who knew the true implications of imperial rule:

> Take up the White Man's burden –
>   Send forth the best ye breed –
> Go bind your sons to exile
>   To serve your captives' need;
> To wait in heavy harness
>   On fluttered folk and wild –
> Your new-caught, sullen peoples,
>   Half devil and half child.
>
> Take up the White Man's burden –
>   In patience to abide,
> To veil the threat of terror
>   And check the show of pride;
> By open speech and simple,
>   An hundred times made plain,
> To seek another's profit,
>   And work another's gain.
>
> Take up the White Man's burden –
>   The savage wars of peace –
> Fill full the mouth of Famine
>   And bid the sickness cease;
> And when your goal is nearest
>   The end of others sought,
> Watch Sloth and heathen Folly
>   Bring all your hope to nought.
>
> Take up the White Man's burden –
>   No tawdry rule of kings,
> But toil of serf and sweeper –
>   The tale of common things.

> The ports ye shall not enter,
> The roads ye shall not tread,
> Go make them with your living,
> And mark them with your dead!

Not every empire-builder regarded imperial activity as a burden or a trust: Kipling's altruism had no place in the Belgian Congo. The Congo was an invaluable source of rubber and ivory. King Leopold of the Belgians was anxious to exclude private traders from the Congo and to control all development himself. He saw the Congo as the potential source of a vast personal fortune.

In 1890 Leopold quadrupled the export duty for ivory, thus discriminating against his competitors. In answer to criticism he explained bluntly: "You know that I would prefer to harvest my ivory myself." In 1891 he laid claim to all "vacant" land and in 1892 he set up the *Domaine de la Couronne,* an area ten times the size of Belgium, in which he became the personal ruler to whom all profits accrued. And the profits were great.

Within the *Domaine de la Couronne* rubber vines grew wild. Leopold imposed a tax upon the natives which, as they had no money, they had to pay either in services to the state, as porters and woodcutters, or in rubber deliveries. The Negroes would search the forests for rubber. In their anxiety to fulfill the high demand set upon them they would cut down the rubber vines indiscriminately. Failure to deliver sufficient rubber resulted in torture, mutilation, or death, the burning of whole villages and cruel punishment inflicted upon children.

News of the reign of terror in the Congo reached Europe early in the century. A shipping clerk in Liverpool, Edmund Morel, wrote vivid accounts of atrocities which had come to his notice: of women chained to posts as hostages until their menfolk returned with rubber; of punitive expeditions which, on their return to camp, brought baskets of human hands as proof of their ruthlessness. Morel estimated that by such methods Leopold drew £360,000 annually from rubber alone.

In February 1904 Roger Casement, British Consul in the Congo, published a report of Leopold's activities. He had himself seen women and children chained in sheds as hostages and Africans beaten up for failure to produce sufficient rubber at collection points.

He reported that some 10,000 men were kept under arms to police the Congo. He wrote of mass executions and terrible mutilations inflicted on the natives by white officials. He estimated that some three million natives had died of disease, torture, or shooting over fifteen years.

The outcry at Leopold's sanction of and profit from such hideous practices was widespread. President Theodore Roosevelt and King Edward VII among rulers, Mark Twain and Joseph Conrad among writers, joined the chorus of Leopold's critics. The Belgian Parliament began to debate Congo affairs in 1906, spurred on by international protests.

In 1908 Leopold agreed to hand over the *Domaine de la Couronne* to the Belgian Parliament. In return he received a "gift" of £2,000,000 from the Parliamentary exchequer. The abuse had ended, though at a price.

Leopold made a mockery of Europe's "civilizing mission" in Africa. He permitted cruelty on an unprecedented scale. He accumulated a vast fortune. He spent millions of pounds to provide museums, hotels, promenades, and dance halls at Ostend, hoping to make that gray and wind-swept port Europe's foremost resort. He spent over a million pounds beautifying his palaces. At Laeken he installed a royal bed made from malachite. In the gardens he erected a Chinese restaurant and a Japanese pagoda which were illuminated at night by over 2,000 light bulbs. When Albert, the heir to the throne, remarked, "But uncle, it will be a little Versailles!" Leopold growled angrily: "Little . . . ?"

Leopold's political power was broken in 1908: the conscience of his own people and the protests of Europe demanded it. He lived three more years, nervously hiding his enormous beard in a leather bag whenever he felt that it would get damp and give him pneumonia. At the age of eighty-four he married the girl whom he had taken as his mistress in 1902, when she was eighteen and he seventy-seven, and by whom he had had a son. Leopold's death in 1909 ended a discreditable era in Europe's imperial history.[2]

---

[2] There was a strange postscript to the Congo scandal. Roger Casement, who was knighted for his skill in exposing the Congo atrocities, later became active in the struggle to liberate Ireland from British rule. During the Great War he attempted to recruit Irish prisoners of war in Berlin to fight against Britain. He was caught by the British after landing on the coast of Ireland and was tried as a traitor and shot.

# ☆ 4 ☆

# THE CHALLENGE OF
# SOCIALISM

THE SOCIALISTS urged a radical change in the nature of society in order to remedy its many evils. In 1844 Friedrich Engels published a detailed factual study of living conditions in Manchester which catalogued the horrors of an ill-organized, uncared-for industrial city.

According to Engels the remedy for injustice and hardship lay in the complete overthrow of existing society, where, he claimed, the individual becomes rich only by reducing his workers to poverty. Engels urged the handing over of all economic power to the state. He wanted the state to regulate industry, supervise factory conditions, and distribute profits in such a way that every member of the society grew rich as the society itself grew rich.

In 1848 Engels joined with another discontented thinker, Karl Marx, to write the *Communist Manifesto,* which became the handbook of all those who despaired of adequate reforms within the existing state structure. Their theme was that all history was the history of class struggle, and that the final class struggle, between the bourgeoisie and the proletariat, was imminent. According to them the course of this struggle was predetermined: the bourgeoisie would be destroyed and the proletariat would emerge triumphant and omnipotent. With only one class left, society would thus become classless and all oppression by master of servant would come to an end. Marx and Engels considered this process inevitable. But they hoped, by "exposing" its inevitability and by painting the bourgeois in his true colors, to hasten the day of the proletariat's triumph.

The task of raising up the proletariat lay, said Marx and Engels, with the Communists. They were the "elite" of the proletariat and would lead the proletariat to victory:

"The Communists are distinguished from the other working-class parties by this only: (1) In the national struggles of the proletarians of the different countries, they point out and bring to the front the common interests of the entire proletariat, independently of all nationality. (2) In the various stages of development which the struggle of the working class against the bourgeoisie has to pass through, they always and everywhere represent the interests of the movement as a whole . . . they have over the great mass of the proletariat the advantage of clearly understanding the line of march, the conditions, and the ultimate general results of the proletarian movement.

"The immediate aim of the Communists is the same as that of all the other proletarian parties; formation of the proletariat into a class, overthrow of the bourgeois supremacy, conquest of political power by the proletariat."

Marx and Engels called for destruction as a preliminary to construction. They urged violence and revolution, without which, they asserted, no progress towards utopia could be made. Between the world of their vision, where every individual should be free to enjoy the full use of his faculties and abilities, and existing society, they saw a barrier, capitalism, in whose selfish interests contemporary society was defended. The "capitalist," the employer, the laws favoring the employer, the class structure of society, the privilege of education for the few, the manifold advantages of wealth—all these were vigorously attacked by Marx, Engels, and their followers.

The Marxist theory was rudely and prematurely tested in 1871. After Prussia had defeated France the workers of Paris refused to surrender, and took up arms to defend the capital. They established their own government, the Paris Commune. This revolutionary government inside Paris was at once challenged by the French Parliament at Versailles and by Adolphe Thiers, whom the Parliament had selected as Prime Minister. It was Thiers who made peace with the Germans and moved the administration from Paris to Versailles, thus leaving Paris to its own proletarian devices.

The Paris Commune failed, in the two months at its disposal, to establish a working socialist system. It was unlucky in that the leading French revolutionary socialist, Blanqui, was out of Paris, ill, with a price on his head. The lack of his leadership was felt strongly. Only a few of the Commune's ministers attempted to inaugurate a socialist program.

It was almost impossible for them to do so. For the whole of their short existence the prime need was defense against Thiers's forces. They hoped that communes would be set up in other French cities, thus dispersing the army that was pitted against them, but where such communes were set up, as at Lyons and Marseilles, they were quickly crushed by local forces. Paris was alone in the struggle for the revolutionary control of France.

For two months Thiers's artillery pounded the besieged city. Then his forces succeeded in entering the commune's territory and shot a number of communards. Reprisals were immediate: sixty-seven hostages were shot by the communards. Violence increased, and when Paris finally fell to Thiers large numbers of prisoners were tried and shot. The commune, instead of proving an inspiring experiment in socialist government, had become the scene of indiscriminate slaughter and civil war.

The suppression of the commune created a bitter rift between Left and Right in France, a rift that was not healed even during the Great War, when national danger might have created national unity.

The lessons drawn from the commune's failure destroyed socialist unity. Marx asserted that the communards had not been drastic enough in their legislation; that they had merely taken over the existing governmental structure, whereas they ought from the first to have constructed a socialist society. Others claimed that once the socialists had seized power they needed only to add universal suffrage to what existed already, and all the desired reforms would take place. Marx insisted that the bourgeois state was incapable of reform from within and that only a complete revolution involving the destruction of the old society would enable progress to be made.

Marx's theoretical extremism gained few supporters. A Marxist party was founded in England in 1881, but disappeared unnoticed within ten years. The French Marxist Party, founded in 1880, split two years later and part became the Independent Socialist Party, which considered that the best way of improving society was to do so through the existing parliamentary machine.

In Germany the Marxists dominated the socialist movement more effectively than in Britain or France. But in 1899 Eduard Bernstein published a book, *Evolutionary Socialism,* which challenged the Marxist standpoint. Bernstein pleaded with his fellow German socialists to keep socialism nonviolent and make it attractive, not to workers alone, but to people of all classes. Although the German Social Democratic Party rejected Bernstein's plea at their 1900 Congress, the gradualism and parliamentarianism which Bernstein advocated permeated the socialist movement. The German Social Democrats obtained representation in Parliament and accepted the role of a parliamentary pressure group. As in France the revolutionaries were in a minority, and parliamentary socialism flourished.

In Russia the revolutionary parties formed two tiny groups: the Social Revolutionaries, founded in 1901, who were willing to cooperate with less revolutionary groups, and the Social Democrats, who, in 1903, under the leadership of Vladimir Lenin, adopted an entirely Marxist revolutionary program. Lenin dominated the Russian Social Democrats and poured scorn on their rivals. He planned for revolution. Although he had to rally his supporters almost as frequently as he attacked his enemies, his plans were carefully worked out and their aim was clear: the seizure of power and the destruction of the old order. Lenin feared the amateur in politics, the "flabby" theorist, the quibbler and the waverer; "we must have men who will devote themselves exclusively to Social Democrat activities," he wrote. Lenin organized: he gathered around himself a small but dedicated group of men for whom revolution was the essential goal. He believed that the key to success lay in organization. His plans concerned a hundred specific details, factory agitation, the centralization of propaganda, underground newspapers, escape routes, secret codes. But such plans were mere dreams: in Russia the police constantly arrested revolutionaries, some of whom escaped to western Europe, others of whom languished in Siberian exile.

Political activity in Russia centered upon the attempt of the parliamentary parties to obtain the right to legislate. It was not the attempt to overthrow a parliamentary system but the attempt to set one up that appeared revolutionary. Those who advocated actual revolution were seen as insignificant cranks: they might be able to assassinate a minister (and one group devoted itself entirely to assassinations), or even to print occasional revolutionary pamphlets, but their powers were clearly limited to fringe activities. When, in 1905, the Social Democrats helped to rouse antigovernment demonstrations, they were arrested, imprisoned, or exiled. The very fact that Lenin, their leader, had been out of Russia in 1905 seemed to the tsarist authorities to show how feeble and ephemeral they must be. But Lenin did not despair of success. While the tsarist government regarded the suppression of the 1905 revolution as a triumph for order and discipline, Lenin looked at the failure in a different light. For him there were lessons to be learned, new plans to be worked out, alternate methods of revolution to be considered. Perhaps these plans were dreams, but Lenin saw nothing to be ashamed of in that. One of his favorite quotations was from the Russian writer Pisarev:

"My dream may run ahead of the natural march of events or may fly off at a tangent in a direction in which no natural march of events will ever proceed. In the first case my dream will not cause any harm; it may even support and augment the energy of the working men. . . . The rift between dreams and reality causes no harm if only the person dreaming believes seriously in his dream, if he attentively observes life, compares his observations with his castles in the air, and if, generally speaking, he works conscientiously for the achievement of his fantasies. If there is some connection between dreams and life then all is well."

Lenin's movement was busy planning revolution and Lenin, from his place of exile in Switzerland, himself was stimulating the zeal of his followers. But revolutionary socialism did not trouble Europe's governments unduly before 1914. They had loyal police and obedient soldiers to deal with agitators. Their main worry was the ordinary, evolutionary socialist, whose weapon was his tongue and whose platform was parliament.

The very word "socialist" brought many fears into aristocratic and middle-class minds at the turn of the century. It was assumed that all socialists would sooner or later support violence and revolution. The evolutionary socialist, although always willing to work within the parliamentary system, seldom won the trust of his "social superiors." He was always a potential danger. Only in Britain did an uneasy but politically profitable truce exist between the new Labour Party and the ruling Liberals, during the period of social unrest immediately before the Great War. But just as Britain's Liberals tried to lessen the danger of socialist agitation by cooperation with the socialists, so, elsewhere in Europe, the ruling parties tried to outmaneuver and outwit their own working-class movements.

It was Bismarck, the German Chancellor, who discovered that if reforms were inaugurated by the parties of the Right, the parties of the Left would be obliged to accept them and would lose some of their influence over the depressed classes. The skillful conservative learned to destroy as much of the attraction of socialism as he could by inaugurating his own program of social legislation.

Many evolutionary socialists accepted the idea that their role was not so much to initiate reform as to stimulate others into doing so. By exposing injustices in society, by fiery speeches in favor of particular items of progressive legislation, the socialist, from his minority platform in parliament, could often stir up sufficient interest and apprehension in the ruling parties for something to be done.

It was perhaps in France that this side-line socialism was least effective. Trade unions had been legalized in 1884. Different socialist groups competed for their support. The unions did not wish to be political pawns and refused to have anything to do with political parties. This split between unionists and socialists made the socialists seem less dangerous to the other political parties. It was the unions who advocated strikes and mass demonstrations; the socialists wished on the contrary to merge into parliamentary respectability.

The unions had a vigorous independent existence, organizing strikes which were then suppressed by Governments that often contained socialist ministers. There was some danger of the unions quite eclipsing the socialists, but they failed to do so. Union membership was impressive: in 1886 there were 100,000 members, in 1892 400,000 and by 1912 over a million.

As union strength grew, so did the strength of the employers. Some set up mutual insurance funds to pay indemnities to those who were injured fighting strikes; others fined factory managers who hired union officials with their other laborers.

Within the unions the "revolutionary syndicalists" maintained the Marxist belief in class conflict as the basis of political development. In 1906 the French syndicalists produced their manifesto, the Charter of Amiens, in which they outlined a twofold program of agitation for immediate reforms and more long-term planning for the eventual overthrow of capitalism. The syndicalists opposed all political parties, including the socialists, and described parliament as "a sink of jobbery, corruption, and compromise."

The syndicalists advocated a policy of direct action, based on the strike. But the syndicalists were never a majority within the union movement. At their most active, in 1914, they probably numbered only 400,000 (out of over a million union members). Their most dramatic strike, on May Day 1906, a twenty-four-hour strike to obtain an eight-hour working day, was a failure. Most of their members were quite willing to accept whatever benefits the despised parliamentary socialists might obtain for them.

In 1899 Alexandre Millerand became the first European socialist to sit in a "bourgeois" cabinet. Although Millerand's action was defended by Jaurès, France's leading socialist, "Millerandism" became a word of derision and contempt among revolutionary socialists.

But the social legislation of the Government was not impressive, despite a socialist minister and socialist support. In 1900 children's work was restricted to ten hours a day; in 1906 a one day's rest in seven was decreed for all workers. But more important measures— old-age pensions and social insurance—were less successful than in Germany (where they had been inaugurated by Bismarck) or in England (where Lloyd George, who had become a Cabinet minister, was their chief advocate). A serious program of social legislation was not inaugurated in France until the Popular Front Government of 1936, while in Germany and England social legislation was well advanced by 1914.

# ☆ 5 ☆

## THE COMING OF WAR

THE HABSBURG EMPIRE was superficially the most permanent state structure in Europe. It had none of Britain's imperial problems, for its empire was entirely European and geographically self-contained. No frontier was further than five hundred miles from Vienna. It had none of Germany's anxieties, none of the ambitions and frustrations of a nation late in the imperial game. The Habsburg Empire, though cumbersome, appeared complete and satisfied.

Its politicians saw no need for adventurous activities abroad. It had none of France's political isolation, none of the unrest that came from republicanism or radicalism. Austria-Hungary was conservative, massive, and immovable. The Emperor was the center of affairs in every way, much more so than Queen Victoria in England, who was bound by constitutional practice to defer to the wishes of her Prime Minister. In an empire of many races, many languages, and many national antagonisms the Emperor was above the fray. Though German-speaking, he did not necessarily support the aspirations of the German-speaking people in his empire. He supported one group until it grew too powerful; then he supported its rivals.

The very complexity of the Empire gave it a certain strength. With so many conflicting interests, no single interest could obtain political mastery. The Emperor could play off against each other the ambitions of his German-speaking subjects and the aspirations of the Slavs. He could threaten to cause havoc with the Magyar dominance in Hungary. He could also give them his full support when the Slavs in Hungary became troublesome. Everyone appeared to receive his particular status or authority from the Emperor. To an-

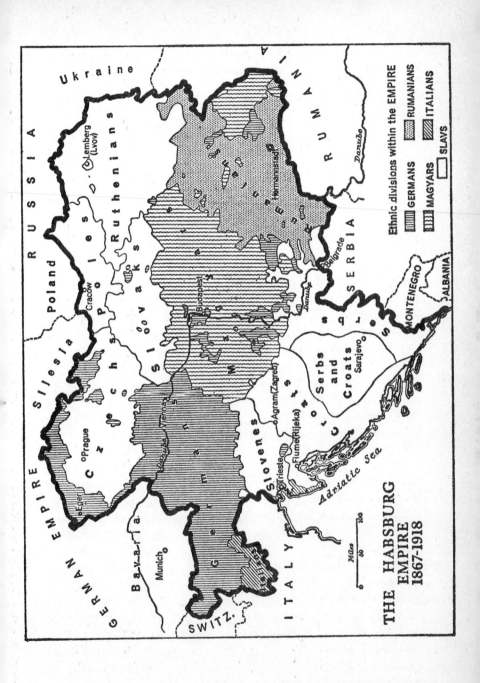

THE HABSBURG
EMPIRE
1867-1918

tagonize the Emperor, or criticize his methods, would only undermine the very source of one's power.

Franz Josef's treatment of his ministers was arbitrary and absolute. From dismissal there was no appeal. One minister is said to
have arrived in his office to be confronted by a letter of resignation,
awaiting only his signature: in this way he discovered that he himself was to be dismissed. The Emperor kept in office those with
whom he could work, those who would obey, and those who were
skillful enough to give their own initiatives the disguise of compliance. No one was tolerated beyond his useful span; obedience was
essential. The Empress Elisabeth summed up her husband's method
and authority when she said that at the very moment when, full of
hope, a minister took up office, the death knell of his authority was
already sounding.

Franz Josef held Austria and Hungary together, willing to bully
either, and using the division between them as a source of strength,
just as, in India, the Hindu-Muslim division gave the British greater
power, and, in Russia, Nicholas II gained by the gulf between the
intellectuals who agitated for reform and the peasants who were to
be its recipients: the universally successful system of "Divide and
Rule."

The Emperor's private life was an unhappy one. His son Rudolf, a
married man and heir to the Habsburg dominions, had fallen in love
with a seventeen-year-old baroness, Mary Vetsera. He had faced his
wife's jealousy and his father's disapproval in order to be with her.
Finally he approached the Pope, hoping to obtain papal support for
a dissolution of his marriage. Franz Josef heard of this and ordered
his son to break off the liaison at once. Rudolf agreed: on the following day, he joined Mary Vetsera at his hunting lodge. For two
days they were together; then on 30 January 1889 Rudolf killed his
mistress and committed suicide.

Franz Josef could not be comforted. He became more reserved
towards the outside world and harsher towards his immediate circle. By 1894 the succession had fallen upon one of his nephews.
The new heir to the throne, the Archduke Franz Ferdinand, hated
the Magyars and favored some form of independence for all the
nationalities of the Empire. Franz Josef had learnt to support Magyar fears of Slav dominance in order to keep the Magyars docile.
Franz Ferdinand wanted principles, not expediency, to govern imperial policy.

On 10 September 1898 Franz Josef's life was again struck by misfortune. The Empress Elisabeth was killed by an anarchist while she was boarding a steamer at Geneva. The man had determined to kill a royal person; which particular person did not concern him. He stabbed the Empress with a dagger and she died at once. Franz Josef was left almost alone. He told one of his generals: "The world does not know how much we loved each other." The world was filled with sympathy at his tragedy, but for the old, isolated man there was tragedy yet in store. Before the century ended Franz Ferdinand, the heir to the throne, fell in love and became engaged. His proposed bride was the Countess Sophie Chotek, daughter of an ancient Bohemian noble family. Unfortunately her family did not come within the strict limits which laid down who was suitable for marriage with princes of the royal blood. Though noble, she belonged to a second order of nobility. Franz Josef refused to allow the laws, as confirmed in 1814, to be altered or infringed. On 28 June 1900 Franz Ferdinand had to swear on oath, in the presence of the Emperor and leading nobles, that his children could not succeed to the Habsburg throne and that his wife could never take the title of empress or queen. Franz Ferdinand accepted these terms and married Sophie Chotek on 1 July 1900. Nevertheless the Emperor and his nephew drew rapidly and irrevocably apart.

Franz Josef was a man of peace: it was clear to his subjects that he would never drag Austria-Hungary into war. But Franz Ferdinand and his friend Conrad von Hötzendorf, Chief of the General Staff, had other ideas. Conrad favored a war against Serbia, the Empire's weakest neighbor, who, by encouraging the Slavs in the Empire to demand nationhood, hoped to disrupt the multinational imperial structure. Conrad wished to strike at this source of unrest. In 1907 he wrote a memorandum for Franz Josef urging: "We must take the first opportunity of settling accounts with our most vulnerable enemy." The Emperor was unimpressed, but Conrad gave his advice to all who would hear it, and many were influenced.

The confidence and calm of the European powers were disturbed by two events originating outside Europe. In 1905 the Japanese defeated Russia and exposed Russia's military weakness to the world. In 1908 the Young Turk revolution broke the power of the Sultan and stimulated anti-Turkish ambitions throughout the Turkish Empire.

Russia's defeat in 1905 encouraged social revolutionaries

throughout Russia to try their hand at overthrowing the government. They failed to do so, but the ease with which they had aroused violent passions in many major cities, and encouraged rebellion in the fleet, persuaded Nicholas II to pursue a less liberal policy. He saw the answer to discontent in a greater exercise of his autocratic powers, and at once destroyed the independence of the Duma, or parliament, whose newly found status was the most important result of his liberalizing tendencies. After 1905, though revolution had been averted, the Russian government was unwilling to sponsor a comprehensive scheme for parliamentary institutions. The gulf between the governing classes and liberal opinion widened. Intellectuals resented being deprived of political influence. Revolutionaries advocated extreme solutions with increasing vigor.

The Japanese victory ended Russia's dream of becoming a Far Eastern power. It revealed her military weakness so clearly that she had also to abandon her ambitions in Central Asia, recognizing Chinese control over Tibet, agreeing with Britain not to penetrate into Afghanistan, and giving up plans for a railway through Persia to the Indian Ocean.

Only one corner of the world remained open for Russian activity. Since 1897 Russia and Austria had agreed to put the Balkans "on ice." Russia, denied an Asian policy after 1905, turned her interest back to the Balkans. The Balkan Slavs welcomed the reappearance of the Russian bear. The Serbs, in particular, hoped to enlist Russian support for their own nationalist ambitions. Serbia wanted to expand at the expense of Turkey, either westwards to the Adriatic or southwards to the Aegean. She wanted a port, and more territory; she hoped to become the leading Balkan power, able to resist Austrian encroachments and to dominate Balkan politics.

Serb ambitions were agitated by the Young Turk revolution. There seemed a danger that the Turks might reform themselves from within, and, as a result, become more efficient imperialists. The Young Turks, though challenging the corrupt system of government directed from Constantinople, were in all things patriots, and had no desire to reduce the size of the Ottoman Empire. Yet, in humiliating the Sultan, they had shown how easy it would be to challenge Turkish sovereignty.

It was not the Serbs, however, who took the first advantage of Turkish weakness. Austria had occupied the Turkish provinces of

Bosnia and Herzegovina since 1878. This area was coveted by Serbia. Inside Austria the Serb minority was beginning to agitate for greater autonomy. Austria, to humiliate the agitators, and to show the Serbs in Belgrade that Austrian power should not be derided, annexed Bosnia and Herzegovina in May 1908.

Austria had taken the initiative in the Balkans. Russia at once protested against the extension of Austrian sovereignty, and announced her support for Serbia. War suddenly seemed a possibility, with Russia trying to oust Austria from the Balkans. Germany, Austria's ally, threatened to support Austria against Russia. The Russians therefore appealed to their own ally, France. But France did not relish a war on behalf of Russian ambitions.

The crisis passed; Serbia even put out friendly suggestions to Austria for a general agreement between them, but Austria ignored them. The Austrians feared the growing strength of their Serb minority. They wished to crush minority agitation and at the same time to reduce Serbia's power. Both these aims were partially successful. The leaders of the Serb minority in Austria were accused of treason and brought to trial. They were found guilty, but the trial was so obviously unfair that Franz Josef pardoned them. Yet the initial injustice of the trial angered the Serbs and weakened Habsburg prestige throughout Europe.

The Turkish revolution resulted in many internal reforms. To ensure effective defense against the growing number of enemies, the Army was put under intensive German instruction, the Navy was put in the charge of a British admiral, and a French expert was brought in to reform the Financial Department. But these vigorous and sensible measures came too late.

In 1908 Bulgaria declared its full independence, and the Turks were unable to prevent this challenge to their sovereignty. In 1911 Italy, having obtained the neutrality of the European powers, invaded Tripoli and, in May 1912, occupied Rhodes. Five months later Montenegro, Greece, Serbia, and Bulgaria joined in alliance, defeated the Turks, and drove them almost entirely out of the Balkans. Discontent over the division of the spoils led to a second Balkan war in 1913, in which the Turks were able to recapture Adrianople, but Turkey in Europe was all but destroyed.

The Balkan wars destroyed Turkey-in-Europe. But for Serbia the results of the Balkan wars were disappointing. Austria had forestalled a Serbian outlet on the Adriatic by persuading the European powers to set up an independent Albania, and Greece and Bulgaria had themselves occupied the formerly Turkish coastline along the northern Aegean. The Serbs, who had hoped to reach either Salonika or Dures, reached neither. Victory brought bitterness, not elation.

Serbian discontent was matched by Austrian anger. The Austrians had been shocked by the defeat of Turkey and the great increase in Serbia's size. They feared a revival of Serb nationalist and separatist activity inside Austria itself. They saw their Balkan influence crumble still further when, in June 1914, Rumania renounced its Austro-German alliance and went over to friendship with Russia.

Austria was afraid that her growing weakness would alienate Germany, and convince the Germans that Austria's friendship was of little value. When, on 28 June 1914, the Austrian heir to the throne, Archduke Franz Ferdinand, was assassinated by a Serb living in Bosnia, many Austrians suddenly saw their opportunity to win a quadruple success. They could use the excuse of a Serb assassin to crush Serbia and teach that ambitious nation once and for all time the folly of seeking to oust Austrian influence from the Balkans; by humiliating Serbia, they could show the Serb minority in Austria how little reliance they should place on Serbian help; by defeating Serbia they could show Germany that an Austro-German alliance was a virile, worthwhile affair; and by occupying Belgrade they could show Russia that despite the defection of Rumania, Austria remained the leading European influence in Balkan affairs. All these benefits would accrue once Serbia was defeated. And Franz Ferdinand's murder provided an obvious if unexpected opportunity for going to war.

However much Austria might wish to chastise Serbia, she could do nothing without a powerful ally, willing to support her whatever the consequences. In 1908 Germany had been so vigorous in her support of Austria's annexation of Bosnia that Russia had remained inactive. Whether Germany could again force Russia to ignore Austrian activity in the Balkans was uncertain. But Austria knew that she could rely on German military support if Russia attacked Austria.

Germany under Wilhelm II was prepared to encourage Austria to move southwards, and was indeed willing to face a war, not only against Russia, but against Russia's ally, France. This willingness to risk a European war sprang, not from German brashness, but from a morbid sense of insecurity. Alone of the European Powers, Germany had failed to build up an impressive empire. She possessed large tracts of African territory, but most of it was desert and the natives hostile. German imperial aspirations had been encouraged by disagreements between other European powers. In 1899 Britain and France had been on the brink of war when a small French military force appeared on the Upper Nile and claimed Fashoda for France. Britain and Russia also appeared on the verge of conflict as Russian sovereignty pressed through Central Asia, towards British India. But these quarrels, which Germany welcomed, and from which she even hoped to gain, were ended by 1907. Germany saw the colonial market closed to her. Britain and Russia specifically agreed, for example, in 1907, not to allow the Germans to build railways in Persia. The only German outlet in Asia was the Berlin-Bagdad railway, but this could hardly make Germany powerful in the East while Russia controlled the Black Sea, Britain the Mediterranean and the Persian Gulf. Thus, by 1910, Germany was faced, not only with a bleak prospect for imperial expansion, but also with growing friendship between the three former rivals Britain, France, and Russia, who were joined together in a loose but enigmatic series of agreements. Germany was afraid that the Anglo-French Entente of 1904 and the Anglo-Russian Agreement of 1907 were more than colonial settlements; she saw behind every "agreement" the hint of a military alliance. No such alliances existed between Britain and either France or Russia. But their shadow hung over German policy, and encouraged extremism.

In 1905 Germany had tried to revive the old antagonism between Britain and France. She failed to do so, but did succeed in procuring the dismissal of the pro-British Foreign Secretary, Delcassé. In 1911 a second German attempt to frighten France had more serious repercussions. A German warship, the *Panther,* was sent to the Moroccan port of Agadir to support a claim against France. France resisted; the Germans demanded the French Congo in return for giving up their Moroccan claims; France continued to resist and enlisted British support. Against the violent protests of the Reichstag, Bethmann-Hollweg, the Chancellor, withdrew the *Panther* and settled for a mere fragment of the Congo. The Agadir crisis revealed the belli-

cose mood of the German press and parliament; it showed France
and Britain the sort of bullying tactics to which Germany could resort; it convinced the British that it was in their interest to support
France; and it subjected Germany to a humiliation she could not
forget.

Bethmann-Hollweg tried to lessen European tensions. He was
prepared to reach an agreement with Britain over their respective
naval strength. But Admiral Tirpitz refused to restrict the size of his
navy, and the Kaiser was equally anxious to press forward with
naval construction. The mood of Germany was not entirely for war,
yet there was a deep desire to break out from the supposed "encirclement" by Russia, France, and Britain. Germany was industrially and
militarily strong, yet it seemed to her Kaiser, her soldiers, and her
people that she was still despised by the rest of Europe. The German
dream was to be respected, feared, admired: isolation was hateful and
humiliation unbearable. Yet how could the ring of seemingly hostile
powers be broken? How could Europe be shown that Germany was
a great power, and capable of achieving the mastery of Europe? The
question was urgent, the answer unknown.

The murder of Archduke Franz Ferdinand surprised the Germans
as much as the Serbs. Yet here was an issue on which all German
aspirations could build. Germany could support Austria, and be prepared to challenge Russia if the Tsar offered help to Serbia; she
could teach Russia the danger of interference even if France came in
on Russia's side. To this end the Schlieffen Plan had been devised in
1905: a plan to defeat first France, then Russia, and to avert the difficulties of a two-front war. The German calculations had certain un-
written but essential premises: that Britain would remain neutral;
that France would be defeated within six months; that Austria would
crush Serbia at the outset of the war; that Italy would support Austria; and that within a year victory would be assured, honor re-
deemed, and little blood spilt. None of these premises was correct.
Yet they propelled Europe into war. "Ah! foolish-diligent Germans," wrote Churchill when the war was over and Germany defeated, "working so hard, thinking so deeply, marching and counter-
marching on the parade grounds of the Fatherland, poring over long
calculations, fuming in new-found prosperity, discontented amid the
splendour of mundane success, how many bulwarks to your peace and
glory did you not, with your own hands, successively tear down?"

Franz Joseph's reaction to the murder of his nephew was resignation rather than resentment. Indeed the Emperor appears to have regarded it as a not altogether unfortunate incident. He told his aide-de-camp: "A higher power has restored the order that I was unhappily unable to maintain." For him it was as if God had cleansed the sin of his nephew's marriage and thus made it impossible for Franz Ferdinand to go back on his oath after the Emperor's death. The assassination took place on 28 June, the exact day on which, fourteen years earlier, Franz Ferdinand had taken the oath barring any children he might have from the throne and denying to his wife the dignity of empress. In Bosnia Franz Ferdinand had persuaded the Austrian Army to treat Sophie Chotek, for the first time in fourteen years, with royal favor; in Bosnia they had both been struck down.

# ☆ 6 ☆

## JULY 1914

FRANZ FERDINAND was buried. He was interred next to his wife, a decision made by the Lord High Steward in order to make full court honors impossible: there could be no magnificent official ceremony if Sophie Chotek had to be included. Many nobles saw this maneuver as an insult to the dead Archduke and resented it. The Emperor was not offended. He even wrote to the Lord High Steward, in his own hand, expressing his confidence in him.

Austria-Hungary was shocked by the murder and wanted Serbia to suffer for this deed. The young man who had shot the Archduke lived in Bosnia, under Austrian rule. His crime had clearly been plotted with other Serb malcontents; but it was in no way certain that the Serbian government had encouraged him.

Berchtold, the Austrian Foreign Minister, and Conrad von Hötzendorf, the Chief of the Austrian General Staff, had both been seeking an opportunity to attack Serbia, which the murder of Franz Ferdinand provided. They had no clear plans, only a clear objective: to humiliate Serbia. They had not even asked themselves whether this should be done by annexing all or a part of Serbia, or by defeating her and then only demanding a large indemnity.

Franz Josef was at first unwilling to contemplate any war against Serbia. He was reported to have said that he did not see why the death of one man should lead to war, even if that man *was* heir to a throne. What Franz Josef feared most of all was that a general European war might follow an Austrian attack on Serbia. When Berchtold convinced him that Austria could chastise Serbia without any other powers taking Serbia's side, the Emperor reluctantly agreed to an ultimatum. Almost a month had passed since the Archduke's assassination. The indecision in Austria's policy was reflected in equal uncertainty elsewhere. Sir Arthur Nicolson, a former British Ambassador to Russia, and in 1914 Permanent Under-Secretary of State at the Foreign Office, wrote on 9 July: "I have my doubts as to whether Austria will take any action of a serious character and I expect the storm will blow over." This expert opinion, typical of many all over Europe in early July, was written in answer to a less optimistic suggestion by an assistant clerk in the Foreign Office who had dared to suggest to his superiors that "the unwisdom of a blindly anti-Serbian policy is not at all appreciated in Austria, and that is the real point in a rather threatening situation." The assistant clerk was right.[1]

It was indeed not appreciated, either by Franz Josef or by his people, that war against Serbia might involve other powers, and above all Russia. The Austrian ultimatum to Serbia appeared quite unacceptable to the Serbian Government: among the Austrian demands was that the Serbs should punish anyone circulating anti-Austrian propaganda, either in schools or in the various nationalist societies that existed in Serbia, and that Austria-Hungary should be allowed to take part in any judicial decision that was reached thereby. Churchill, then Britain's First Lord of the Admiralty, wrote in retrospect: "It was an ultimatum such as had never been penned in modern times . . . it seemed absolutely impossible that any state in the world could accept it, or that any acceptance, however abject, would satisfy the aggressor." Most Europeans, including friends of Austria, thought the terms an intolerable interference in Serbian sovereignty.

Serbia, to everyone's surprise, virtually accepted the ultimatum. Her main reservation was that she would allow only such Austrian collaboration in suppressing subversive movements as was consistent with international law. She could not allow representatives of a foreign power to take part in her judicial affairs. But she agreed to suppress the subversive movements and bring anybody connected with the Archduke's murder to justice. The Serbian reply to Austria's ultimatum was sent on 25 July and ended by stating that Ser-

---

[1] Later he became Permanent Under-Secretary at the Foreign Office himself. His name was Robert Vansittart. He was a leading critic of Britain's attempt to reach agreement with Nazi Germany in 1938.

bia was willing to submit the whole question either to the International Tribunal at The Hague or to the Great Powers. This was submission indeed. The Kaiser's reaction was: "A great moral victory for Vienna; but with it every reason for war disappears." So it seemed, but the Kaiser added that, "as a visible *satisfaction d'honneur* for Austria the Austrian Army should temporarily occupy Belgrade as a pledge." The German High Command now encouraged Austria to take the risk of war, regarding war with Russia as a possible means of increasing German power. On the same day, 28 July, the Austrian Ambassador in Berlin telegraphed to Berchtold: "We are urgently advised to act at once and present the world a *fait accompli.*" Sir Edward Grey, British Foreign Secretary, advised to the contrary, urging Austria to submit her quarrel with Serbia to a conference of the European Powers. But Grey's ambassador in Vienna made the Austrian attitude clear: "postponement or prevention of war with Serbia would undoubtedly be a great disappointment in this country, which has gone wild with joy at the prospect of war." On 28 July Austria-Hungary declared war on Serbia, and prepared to march on Belgrade.

Russia was in a difficult position. Morally she seemed committed to defend Serbia. On Russia's broad shoulders appeared to fall the burden of Slav solidarity. Strategically the Russian government was unwilling to see the buffer of Balkan states between themselves and Austria fall under Austrian dominance. Rumors circulated in St. Petersburg on 29 July to the effect that the "designs of Austria may extend considerably beyond . . . a punitive occupation of Serbian territory." Russia took alarm. On 29 July she ordered partial mobilization on the Austro-German frontier and, on 30 July, full mobilization. The Russian government hoped, by a show of strength, to deter Austria from attacking Serbia. Germany did not relish the prospect of a fully mobilized army on her eastern front, and felt obliged to threaten Russia both in German and Austrian interests. Furthermore the idea of a Russo-German war appealed to many politicians and strategists in Berlin. On 30 July the Germans therefore demanded that Russia demobilize within twelve hours. This was the second European ultimatum in two days. Russia paid no attention, and on 1 August Germany declared war on her. The German High Command thus showed itself prepared to exploit Russia's willingness to defend Serbia in order to further its own military ambitions.

France was Russia's ally. The Franco-Russian alliance, negotiated in 1892, was the rock upon which French security was known to rest. On 31 July Germany wanted France to state categorically that she would remain neutral in the event of a Russo-German war. France could not desert her ally. Germany had long known that she would have to face a war on two fronts if she attacked Russia. She was prepared to do this, and had indeed long planned for such an eventuality. To ensure a swift victory over France, which would then enable her to concentrate on defeating Russia, German troops entered Luxembourg on 1 August, and on 3 August Germany declared war on France. Then the Germans demanded from Belgium free passage for their troops. Only by such passage could German victory over France be swift and easy. The Belgians refused with the words: "Were the Belgian Government to accept the propositions conveyed to it, it would be sacrificing the nation's honor and betraying its engagements to Europe." Belgium was pledged to neutrality and among the guarantors of her neutrality was Britain. The Belgians appealed to Britain for support. On 4 August the British Government, which had taken no action against Germany after her declaration of war on France, demanded that Germany respect Belgian neutrality. The British had no treaty of alliance with France; they did have a treaty binding them to defend Belgian neutrality. But, as Sir Edward Grey told the American Ambassador immediately after the British ultimatum had been sent to Germany, it was not only Belgian neutrality that activated Britain: "The issue for us is that, if Germany wins, she will dominate France; the independence of Belgium, Holland, Denmark, and perhaps of Norway and Sweden, will be a mere shadow; their separate existence as nations will really be a fiction; all their harbours will be at Germany's disposal; she will dominate the whole of Western Europe, and this will make our position quite impossible. We could not exist as a first-class state under such circumstances."

Germany ignored Britain's ultimatum, merely expressing surprise that Britain took the independence of Belgium so seriously. On 4 August, seven hours before the ultimatum was due to expire, the Germans took the initiative and invaded Belgium. The British Cabinet decided to wait until their ultimatum expired in the desperate hope that there was still time for Germany to reverse her decision, and that, confronted by Britain's determination, she might even then call a halt. Lloyd George has described the Cabinet's wait: "As the hour approached a deep and tense solemnity fell on the room. No one spoke. It was like awaiting the signal for the pulling of a lever which might hurl millions to their doom—with just the chance that a reprieve might arrive in time. Our eyes wandered anxiously from the clock to the door. . . . 'Boom!' The deep notes of Big Ben rang out into the night the first strokes in Britain's most fateful hour since she arose out of the deep."

So Britain declared war. Shortly after eleven o'clock the telegrams were sent out on Churchill's orders from the British Admiralty, and received within the hour by the commanders of Britain's mighty fleet: "ADMIRALTY TO ALL SHIPS     COMMENCE HOSTILITIES AT ONCE AGAINST GERMANY     ACKNOWLEDGE." As the acknowledgments were telegraphed back to the Admiralty during the night, Germany knew that she must face the combined strength of Britain, Russia, France, and Belgium. Austria, who had only declared war on Serbia, was pushed by Germany into war with Russia on 6 August. Italy, bound by alliance to support both Germany and Austria, but the only Great Power to realize that she might not be invincible, at once declared her neutrality.

Austria and Britain had no cause to fight. "Balkan quarrels," Churchill had written on 1 August 1914, "are no concern of ours." But the drift to war spared no one. Britain declared war on Austria on 12 August on the grounds that Austrian troops on the German frontier "were a direct menace to France." The Austrians were saddened by the British ultimatum but could do nothing to avert it. Their policy was now too closely bound up with Germany's to enable them to take an independent line. The British Ambassador, on leaving Vienna, could not believe that an era was drawing to a close and asked Berchtold "to present my profound regrets to the Emperor Francis Joseph, together with an expression of my hope that His Majesty would pass through these sad times with unimpaired health and strength." The Austrian Ambassador in London, Mensdorff, was distraught and angry. The American Ambassador to whom he handed over the charge of Austrian interests in England recalled: "Mensdorff denounced Germany and the Kaiser; he paraded up and down the room wringing his hands." Thus war came to Europe, unexpectedly and bewilderingly. To those few who welcomed it certain things seemed clear: it would be a short war, it would be a war confined to the battlefields, and it would be a war of skill, courage, and glory. The Germans hoped swiftly to humiliate France and Russia, thus asserting the German right to dominate European politics, as "befitted" a nation of such size and industrial power. The Austrians hoped swiftly to humiliate Serbia, and then to sit back satisfied, and untroubled by small Balkan nations. The third partner, Italy, deemed it prudent to keep out of the war, either to avoid war altogether, or to enter it only when it became clear who would win, or at a price.

Against Germany and Austria (the "Central Powers") were ranged the "Entente Powers" Russia, Serbia, France, and Britain. Both Russia and France wished to put a stop, as swiftly and as cheaply as possible, to German ambitions. They feared a powerful Germany and hoped by a quick victory to maintain the existing frontiers in Europe. Britain, who cared less for Europe, hesitated to fight for a French quarrel, or against German rashness. But the invasion of Belgium by Germany brought Britain in: once in, she aimed only to teach Germany not to commit such uncalled-for aggression again.

As August progressed, few of the belligerents could guess that the war would be neither short nor glorious, or that it would destroy empires and dynasties with callous abandon.

## ☆ 7 ☆

---

# THE WAR IN THE WEST

### 1914

THE WAR IN THE WEST began with the German attack on Belgium. The Germans hoped to drive rapidly through Belgium and on to Paris. They planned on a single blow to knock France out of the war and thus enable them to concentrate on the war with Russia. German strategists had long contemplated the means whereby they could destroy France at the outset of a European war. Their "Schlieffen Plan" was designed to sweep the German Army across Belgium and to approach Paris from the north.

The drive through Belgium, by-passing the great French fortresses of Verdun, Toul, and Epinal, was begun on 4 August. But within twenty-four hours the Germans had been forced to a halt at Liège. So fierce was the Belgian defense that some German units retreated. It seemed that the invincible army would be unable to proceed. In the words of the song about the Kaiser that delighted the Music Halls of England:

> With his luggage labelled "England,"
> And his programme nicely set,
> He shouted, "First Stop Paris,"
> But he hasn't got there yet;
> For Belgium put the kibosh on the Kaiser,
> Europe took a stick and made him sore,
> On his throne it hurts to sit,
> And when John Bull starts to hit
> He will never sit upon it any more.

But the arms factories of Austria came to Germany's aid. A 17-inch howitzer, the heaviest artillery piece yet used in war, was able to bombard the fortifications of Liège from such a distance that it lay outside the range of the Liège guns. At the same time the German General Ludendorff advanced a small number of men during the night, who slipped, virtually unnoticed, between two of the fortified positions, making the task of their defenders more difficult. The forts still held; but one by one they were destroyed by the long-range howitzers. On 16 August Liège fell. It had delayed the German advance for twelve days, a delay totally unforeseen in German plans.

Further south the French advanced. On 14 August they crossed into the "lost" provinces of Alsace-Lorraine, which had been ceded to Germany after France's defeat in 1870, and captured Morhange in Lorraine and Mulhouse in Alsace. Neither town was held long. The Germans counterattacked and halted the French advance. The French then fell back, surprised at the strength of the German blow. This southern frontier remained throughout the war almost as it had been in peace. The French drew back a little behind the Lorraine border, the Germans behind that of Alsace.

Further to the north the German advance continued. On 21 August the German Army reached the outskirts of Mons, almost half-way between Aachen and Paris on the planned line of advance. It was here that the results of the delay at Liège made themselves felt to the Germans' disadvantage. While Liège was resisting, the British Expeditionary Force crossed the Channel. It had left England on 9 August, and by 21 August it was at Mons. The Germans had not expected such a sudden confrontation. As at Liège, their advance was halted. Although the British were driven from Mons on 23 August, the two days during which they stood firm enabled the French to retreat in good order. The British followed, pursued by the Germans. On 26 August the British turned to face their pursuers at Le Cateau, thirty miles southeast of Mons, on the route to Paris. Carrying out a brilliant delaying action, they withdrew once more. But although the Germans were advancing across France, they were not without worries of their own. Bad news from the Russian front resulted in two army corps being despatched eastwards, while a strong Belgian resistance in Antwerp forced them to send a further two corps northwards. Antwerp was defended by British as well as by

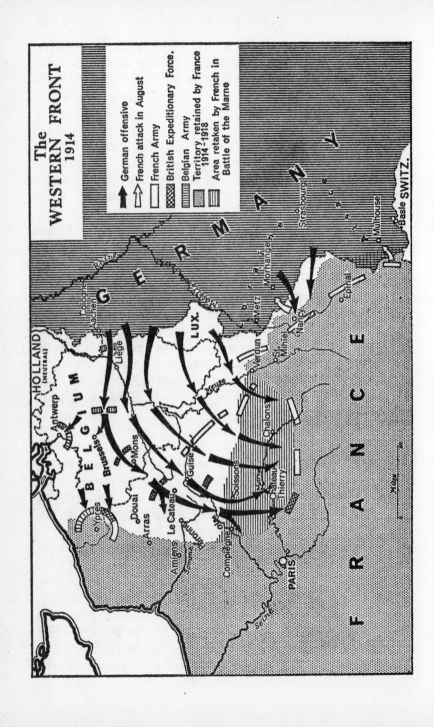

Belgian troops, another surprise for the Germans. The city did not fall until 9 October. With such delays it was clear that Paris would not be encircled easily. The Germans therefore turned south towards the River Marne, which, if they could reach it in good order, would lead them into Paris from the east. But on their southward march the Germans again encountered the British and realized that, despite two retreats, British morale was untarnished. The same was true of the French. The "knockout" blow had failed to depress or to panic its recipients. For two days the British held up the German advance at Guise. Then the Germans swept forward, crossing the Marne on 4 September. Their advance was spotted by a French airplane, and French troops were rushed from Paris by taxi. For four days the battle raged. The British, having regrouped, joined it on 7 September. German enthusiasm waned; despite the extent of their advance and the almost constant retreat of the French and British, the expected victory had not been achieved. The Allied army was still intact, standing between the Germans and Paris. The whole point of the Schlieffen Plan had been lost; a surprise attack on Paris from the north had become impossible. First the Belgians, whose neutrality had been violated in the interests of the Schlieffen Plan, then the British, whose participation in the war was thereby ensured, had deflected the machine from its prearranged course.

The German advance was halted on the Marne. The Allied victory was not sufficient to destroy German morale, but it saved Paris. The Germans retreated; the British hurried to the sea to defend the Channel ports. A separate German army tried to drive through the French defenses at Nancy, but failed. The German army in the north made one last effort to break through to the Coast. It captured Antwerp on 9 October and reached Ypres on 18 October. The Battle of Ypres lasted for a month. The British, Belgians, and French withstood a series of violent attacks by superior numbers. Ypres was the grave of the "knockout" blow. The Schlieffen Plan had finally to be discarded. There could be no more swift advances across large tracts of land, no more sudden encirclement, no more skillful flank attacks: in November 1914 the two armies faced each other across a long line from the Channel to Switzerland. Dramatic war had ended; trench war had begun.

## 1915

In 1915 the western front was conducted with great ferocity and hardly any advantage to either side. The French hoped to push the Germans back from Compiègne, and thus from threatening Paris. General Joffre planned a threefold attack, from Compiègne itself, from north of Chalons, and, when the Germans began to weaken, a final assault from Verdun to cut them off from Germany. Such strategy was bold and deserved success. But strategy is concerned with the grand plan: the strategist is the theorist of war. Behind him, awaiting orders, is the tactician, the organizer of the actual fighting. In 1915 the strategist was at the mercy of the tactician. Unless a means could be found to destroy the effectiveness of the machine gun and of barbed wire the most imaginative plan of attack had no chance of success.

The trench was a world to itself; an endless, twisting burrow from which the war was waged and to which the weary troops could re-

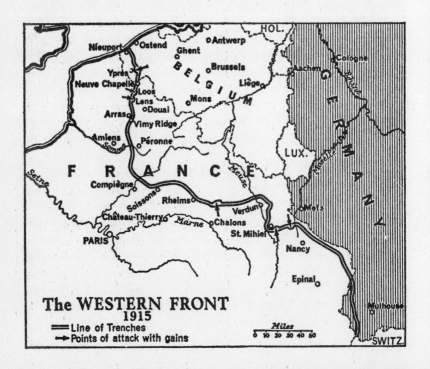

The WESTERN FRONT
1915
Line of Trenches
Points of attack with gains

tire. It was the only haven in a desolate landscape, guarded by the
wire, protected by the gun, and threatened by gas. It possessed its
own specialized equipment: tram railways bringing supplies from
the rear, pipes carrying water, telephone cable buried in the mud,
shellproof shelters, dugouts and, facing forward, the firestep, standing on which enabled the soldier to poke his gun forward, over the
lip of the trench into no-man's-land, searching for the enemy. And
from the firestep the attack would be launched and the men go "over
the top," out, with their rifles and bayonets across no-man's-land, to
the line of enemy wire and trenches beyond. The enemy could deci-
mate the advancing line by machine-gun fire, or shoot the attackers
when, having reached the trenches, they found the wire intact and
had no means of crossing it. Retreat being almost impossible,
amounting to disobedience and even to treason, the attackers would
grapple with the wire with their bare hands or try to push at it with
their boots. Such tactics could not succeed. Only if the wire had been
breached previously by their own artillery could the attackers penetrate to the trenches beyond. And there, awaiting them, were the
machine guns and bayonets of the defenders.

A French officer described the psychological impact of the machine gun's rattle: "I know of nothing more depressing in the midst
of battle—when there is nothing but noise and tumult, confusion
and disharmony around us—than the steady tac-tac-tac of that
deadly weapon. It spreads suffering in a precise and methodic fashion. The emotions of the gunner behind it never hinder its evil
effects. There appears to be nothing material to its working. It seems
to be dominated and directed by some powerful, scheming spirit of
destruction."

The other horror was barbed wire. The same French officer wrote
of its effect upon the infantryman: "The barbed wire terrified and
obsessed the infantryman. All his daring and courage came to
naught when he ran against an incompletely destroyed network. He
knew that he would get caught and lacerated in its entangled mass
of snares and meshes. His would be a slow, agonizing death. The
horror which such a network caused in the minds of the assailants
was probably equaled by the satisfaction it gave to the defenders.
Our commander, who was a battle-seasoned officer, kept sending us
coils and coils of barbed wire."

With such obstacles it is not surprising that Joffre's attack failed or that it resulted in some 90,000 men killed, wounded, or taken prisoner on either side. With such a toll further attacks might well have been discouraged. But the strategists of both armies were convinced that a breakthrough was ultimately possible. They realized that it could be achieved only with great loss of life, but argued that once it had succeeded the fortunes of the war would flow rapidly in their favor. The persistence of this belief in every army accounted for the seemingly senseless continuance of the war.

On 10 March the British, under General Haig, attacked at Neuve Chapelle. The Germans were surprised and their positions overrun. But there were so many minor delays and misunderstandings that the British troops failed to take full advantage of their success. The Germans were able to bring up reinforcements. After three days of battle the British were the victors. They had won a strip of land only a mile and a quarter long and less than three-quarters of a mile deep.

The Germans were the next to attack, on 22 April. They decided to attack Ypres, where they had been checked in November. They improved their tactical advantage by adding a third weapon to the machine gun and the barbed wire. This weapon had not been seen before in war. A Belgian grenadier described its first appearance: "We saw a thick cloud rising from the German trenches opposite ours. Surprise and curiosity riveted us to the ground. None of us knew what was going on. The smoke cloud grew thicker, which made us believe that the German trenches were on fire! Slowly, the cloud began moving toward our lines, but the north wind carried it toward our right flank, over the French lines. . . . French soldiers running toward our trenches cried: 'An attack! The Boches are coming!' Some of them fell. To our corporal, who asked them what was the matter, they replied: 'We have been poisoned!' . . ."

It was poison gas, whose use had been condemned by international law. Its first victims were the French. As far as the Germans were concerned this gas attack was only experimental. But seeing the havoc they had created the Germans advanced. Then they reached the very gas they had discharged and could advance no further. The gas had gathered in the trenches and made it impossible for the Germans to enter them.

But the new weapon did not entirely disappoint those who used it. On 8 May the Germans attacked Ypres again and the battle continued for six days. The British were slowly driven back and on 24 May the Germans mounted a second gas attack, on a much bigger scale than the first. They gained an area five miles wide at its widest and seven miles long. Over 100,000 men were killed or wounded.

While "Second Ypres" was wreaking havoc among the English, the French launched an attack against Vimy Ridge. The French troops, under General Pétain, drove two and a half miles through the German lines, almost to the crest of the ridge. Then, as happened to the British at Neuve Chapelle, reserves were held back too long, the Germans brought up fresh men and the attackers were driven back. For six days men were slaughtered on both sides with no visible gains. When Vimy Ridge fell finally to the French their casualties were over 100,000; German casualties 75,000. As a result of this battle the French General Staff concluded that victory would eventually be won if the Germans were so harassed that they could no longer call up sufficient reserves. It seemed that what was required was to kill so many Germans that their manpower would eventually be exhausted. This concept was called the "war of attrition." It led the Allies to retaliate with equally lethal gas attacks.

During the summer of 1915 there was a lull in the fighting. A new volunteer army was recruited in England, drawn in by the dramatic poster "Your country needs you" and by the popular song:

> We don't want to lose you,
> But we think you ought to go,
> For your king and your country
> Both need you so.

Those affected by war fever turned their eyes away from the casualty lists and saw no sense in discussing the futility of mutual slaughter. The causes of the war were forgotten in the endless orgy of killing; even justifying the war appeared superfluous to all but a few politicians. The holocaust seemed self-justificatory and self-perpetuating.

In the autumn of 1915 the Germans shot an English nurse, Edith Cavell, who worked in German-occupied Brussels and had helped British and French soldiers to escape. The shock of her death gave rise to a sudden awareness of the senselessness of the war. Shortly before being shot she had said: "I realize that patriotism is not enough. I must have no hatred or bitterness towards any one."

But Edith Cavell's message did not last. Although it was carved on the base of her statue in London after the war, its sentiments vanished almost as soon as they were uttered. Asquith, the British Prime Minister, was typical in misinterpreting them:

"If there be moments such as come to all of us when we are tempted to be faint-hearted, let us ask ourselves what year in our history has done more to justify our faith in the manhood and the womanhood of our people? It has brought us, as we cannot at this moment forget, the imperishable story of the last hours of Edith Cavell, facing a terrible ordeal worse than that of the battlefield. She has taught the bravest men amongst us the supreme lesson of courage. Yes, and in this United Kingdom and throughout the Dominions of the Crown there are thousands of such women. A year ago we did not know it. We have great traditions, but a nation cannot exist by traditions alone. Thank God, we have living examples of all the qualities which have built up and sustained our Empire. Let us be worthy of them, and endure to the end."

The endurance for which Asquith called was indeed necessary. On the day on which Edith Cavell was shot, and in the weeks during which the shock of her death pulsated through Britain and France, the new British volunteer army was attacking at Loos. Two of the divisions had never seen fighting before. They reached the front after three night marches and were made to move up into their positions during the fourth night to avoid being seen. They attacked on 26 October and were smashed.

The British losses for the autumn were 60,000, the French 190,000, the German 210,000. No goals were reached and no territory gained. Equally, no breach had been made in the line. For such negative but "essential" aims were the lives of men expended.

## 1916

The battles of 1916 on the western front favored neither side. The war had begun with mostly professional troops, regular soldiers, some of whom had been in the army for as long as thirty years. By mid-1916 it was the youth of each nation which faced the wire and the guns; young men who, but for the demands of that muddy, trench-scarred strip of death, would be in the factories, the fields and universities of their homelands.

In February 1916 the Germans, weary of the endless war of attrition in the trenches, decided to capture Verdun, a French fortress so

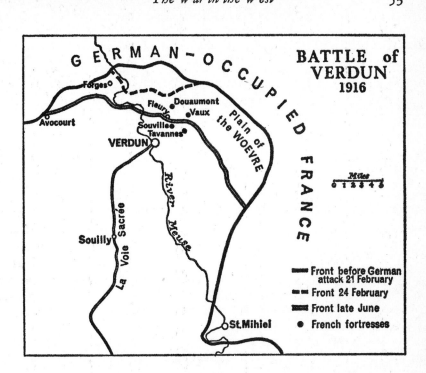

strong that the Schlieffen Plan had been devised to make its capture unnecessary. The western front ran around Verdun, three miles beyond the outer ring of its fortresses. The Germans brought up six divisions for the attack; the French had two in defense.

The Germans began to bombard Verdun on 21 February 1916. So powerful was their artillery fire, aided by gas shells, that one French regiment was virtually annihilated [1] and a foothold obtained in the French trenches. By 24 February the Germans had advanced three and a half miles. The French decided to abandon the Plain of the Woevre, which had not been attacked, a decision hastened by the indiscipline and panic that had begun to break out in the French lines. Far worse, psychologically, was the loss of one of the outer forts, Fort Douaumont, which by an oversight had been left ill-garrisoned and was seized by a single German company. The news of its capture thrilled Germany and depressed France.

[1] The regiment consisted of 2,000 men. Of these 1,800 were killed.

Disaster threatened; at midnight on 25 February General Pétain
was given command of the defenses. His enthusiasm and his powers
of organization were formidable assets for France. He saw at once the
need to improve communications between Verdun and the rest of
France and ordered intensive work to widen the rough, secondary
road that was Verdun's vital artery. Pétain was successful; the road,
known as the *"Voie Sacrée,"* was able to carry an endless stream of
lorries. Pétain also ensured that French artillery pounded the Germans on every sector of the front, driving them into their trenches
and making all open ground impassable.

The Germans, faced with deadlock on 28 February, looked elsewhere. On 6 March they attacked west of the Meuse, at Forges.
Within two days they had advanced almost two miles along the west
bank of the Meuse and extended their advance some five miles westward to Avocourt. Again the fighting reverted to trench fighting; the
element of surprise and the chance of rapid advance being both lost.
The "Hell of Verdun" affected attacker and defender alike. Pétain
watched his troops moving up to Verdun from his headquarters at
Souilly:

"It was with a heavy heart that I watched our twenty-year-old
boys go into battle at Verdun, for I realized that in their very youth-
fulness they might all too easily fall from the enthusiasm of their
first combat into the weariness caused by suffering or even become
despondent over the enormous task ahead of them. . . . What a
pitiful sight they presented when they returned from battle, either
individually, limping or injured, or in the thinned-out ranks of their
companies! In their unsteady look one sensed visions of horror,
while their step and bearing revealed their utter despondency. They
were crushed by horrifying memories and hardly answered my questions."

Only remnants of units survived at Verdun. The survivors were
shattered, broken men. In June the Germans captured the Fort de
Vaux, which they had bombarded so effectively that the latrines
were separated from the men by fallen masonry and the water
supply also cut off. The commander of the fort surrendered: there
could be nothing ignominious in that. He was congratulated on his
fortitude by the Kaiser's son. The Germans had little to be proud of
at Verdun. In an attempt to seize the inner forts of Souville and
Tavannes they used, for the first time, a new gas—phosgene. Its

effect was terrible; the French batteries were silenced and thousands of Frenchmen lay writhing in their trenches or reeling backwards, crying and blinded. The town of Fleury fell to the Germans, but Souville held out. Excess of horror only served to draw out a stubborn courage.

Verdun served no military purpose. Although the Germans gained as much territory there as in the attacks of 1915 further north, Verdun itself did not fall. French dead were estimated at 350,000, German dead at 300,000. General von Hindenburg, the German supreme commander on the Russian front, commented: "As time went on Verdun was spoken of in yet another tone. Doubts gradually began to prevail, though they were but seldom expressed. They could be summarized shortly in the following question: Why should we persevere with an offensive which exacted such frightful sacrifices and, as was already obvious, had no prospects of success?"

At Verdun both sides rested. But on the Somme a new Allied offensive was planned for which, as the French were so exhausted, the British were allotted the main tasks. The Germans had two initial advantages, one physical, one psychological. Their trenches were dug deeply and firmly in chalk (as opposed to earth), proof against all but the most accurate artillery. And on 21 May German morale was lifted by the capture of Vimy Ridge, which the French had handed over to the British after its capture from the Germans at fantastic cost in 1915. The loss of the Ridge did not improve Anglo-French relations, already much strained after long arguments about which sector of the front each one should hold. The Germans did not suffer from such dissension.

The auguries for the Battle of the Somme were unfavorable. Its actual course was disastrous. Britain's volunteer army was destroyed as it advanced. Sir Douglas Haig, who had become Commander-in-Chief of the British forces in France, hoped to break the military stalemate of the war by rapid and deep penetration of the German lines. But the German machine gunners were accurate and relentless and by nightfall of the first attack on 1 July 20,000 British were dead, 30,000 wounded. For that price the British obtained the villages of Mametz and Longueval. The French reached Biaches, across the Somme from Péronne.

Haig, learning of his losses, decided to justify them by success. On 14 July a second attack, made in darkness and so risky that the

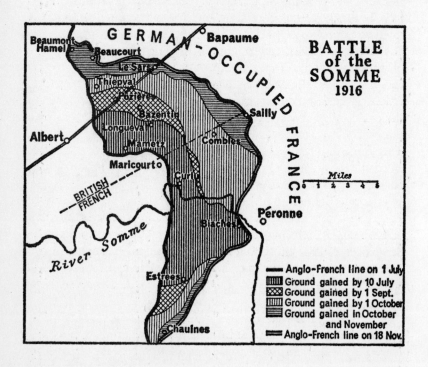

French refused to take part in it, succeeded. Bazentin fell to the British. It looked as if attrition was ending, and that a swift, unchecked advance might be possible. It was three miles from the old front line to Bazentin; a further seven would bring Haig to Bapaume. Thus would the fortunes of war be reversed. The Germans would be driven back, by such means, to the frontiers of Germany. On 23 July the British attacked again. Pozières was captured by two Australian divisions. But advance was slow, death rapid, and conditions foul. Men sank so deeply in the mud that they had to be dug out; artillery pieces became immovable. Thiepval was captured in September. The French entered Combles. On 13 November a further burst of energy advanced the line over half a mile and saw the capture of Beaumont Hamel, one of the most brilliant actions of the war. During the next five days, encouraged by what would at the beginning of the war have been laughed at as an unimportant gain at absurd cost, but was now indeed a triumph, the soldiers continued the attack. Le Sars and Beaucourt fell; Chaulnes was captured south of the river, the British pressed forward to within two and a half miles of Bapaume; the French moved up to Sailly. Then, on 18 November, a blizzard and continual rain brought the Battle of the Somme to an end. It had been the most notable Allied victory of the war, clearly visible on large-scale maps, just noticeable on a small one. The Allies could count 125 square miles of German-held territory in their possession after three and a half months of concentrated attack. They could also count, if they had a mind to, the casualties: 418,654 British; 194,451 French; 650,000 German, a total of 1,263,105.[2] So ended 1916 on the western front.

A certain light relief had been provided by the appearance in the Allied lines of a cumbersome, incomprehensible machine that rolled across fields by some magic means: the tank. It was first used on 15 September, to little effect. Ten days later it played an important part in the capture of Thiepval. But it seemed something of a joke to the soldiers who watched it trundle forward so uneasily and it was not until 1918 that its influence was decisive.

The Battle of the Somme showed the impossibility of a breakthrough by force of fire and arms. It disappointed Haig, who lived to bear much odium and misdirected criticism on account of his plans and ambitions. Yet he only strove, as a commander must, to break the deadlock and to bring the war to a rapid and successful conclusion. To many of the soldiers of the volunteer army the battlefield was a graveyard. New men were brought to take their place who were not volunteers, but conscripts. The conscript army did not have the enthusiasm of the volunteers. Nor, with so many dead before them, could they be as hopeful either of victory or of survival.

Churchill wrote of the soldiers of the Somme: "No attack however forlorn, however fatal, found them without ardour. No slaughter however desolating prevented them from returning to the charge. No physical conditions however severe deprived their commanders of their obedience and loyalty. . . . Unconquerable except by death, which they had conquered, they have set up a monument

---

[2] Care has to be taken with all such figures, which are, by their very nature, approximations. A further difficulty arises because German figures for casualties involved only those men seriously wounded; the British included minor injuries in their totals.

of native virtue which will command the wonder, the reverence and
the gratitude of our island people as long as we endure as a nation
among men."

## 1917

Throughout 1917 the Allies were confronted by a new enemy, demoralization. In direct contrast to Haig's belief that a decisive attack
could be made through the German trenches was the growing weariness and dissatisfaction of the troops.

Joffre, the French Commander-in-Chief, sensed the growing defeatism of his men and wanted the British to take more of the burden. Haig agreed to this, hoping that from greater responsibility
greater rewards would come—the recognition of British abilities,
and of his own genius.

But Joffre's powers were resented in Paris. The French Parliament, which sought greater control over the war, hoped to obtain it
by removing Joffre. He was appointed to an ancient and disused
title, that of "Marshal of France," and his services were dispensed
with altogether. In his place was put General Nivelle, a younger
man who had distinguished himself at Verdun. Nivelle did not wish
to unload French worries on British shoulders. He hoped to be responsible for a great French victory, for which French troops with
himself at their head would receive the laurels. Nivelle's plans were
looked upon askance by Haig. But Nivelle made contact with the
new British Prime Minister, Lloyd George, who saw in Nivelle a
man of courage and vision, and wished to make Haig subordinate to
the Frenchman. In part he was successful. Although Haig was able
to refuse total submission, Nivelle obtained overall command during the course of the proposed offensive. Discussions about the new
attack were continually interrupted by arguments about seniority.
Haig and Nivelle disagreed as to when the major thrusts should be
made. Nivelle, as a result of the position which Lloyd George had
given him, overruled his ally. In the strict world of military hierar-
chies it is not surprising that the sight of a French general giving
orders to a British field-marshal created annoyance, bickering, and
mistrust.

An unexpected German withdrawal along a wide front meant
that areas for whose capture the French had made elaborate plans

were no longer in enemy hands. The German withdrawal was prompted by prior knowledge of the proposed offensive. After criticism, Nivelle threatened to resign. But the French Government feared a wartime scandal that would weaken morale and Nivelle remained. His offensive, with its objectives changed and its surprise element lost, was still to take place.

On 9 April, Easter Monday, the British launched the preliminary phase of the April breakthrough. From Arras the army advanced, striking towards Douai. Tanks were again in use, but suffered heavily from mechanical breakdowns. An initial Allied advance was met by a spirited German counterattack. Then the British began to drive the Germans back and captured five miles in depth of enemy held land. Orders were needed as to "what next" but were not forthcoming. The success, though hoped for, was unexpected. The staff officers, on being asked for orders, fussed and debated. They were not ready to exploit success. The Germans re-formed in new positions and the battle ended. The battle of Arras was certainly a British victory, but like earlier engagements it was in no way decisive for the war.

Nivelle sought the final honor, the attack against which no German resistance could stand. On 16 April his offensive was launched along a broad front from Condé to Courcy, to the words of his confident message: *"L'heure est venue! Confiance! Courage! Vive la France!"* The troops advanced, supported by tanks and drilled to the need for speed. But facing them was the ubiquitous machine gun.

Nivelle's offensive failed to break the German line. But even while he might have retrieved its fortunes he was recalled to Paris to face angry politicians. Before the battle was ended he was relieved of his command and replaced by Pétain. Nivelle was treated as if he had suffered a catastrophic defeat. Actually he had been successful, according to the pattern of battles over three years. But France wanted a miracle and this Nivelle could not achieve.

Criticism of the war spread from Paris to the trenches. Upon this muddy soil defeatism arose. Between 25 May and 9 June there were eighty acts of "collective indiscipline," or mutiny, at the front. Men on leave fought with police and railwaymen in attempts to prevent trains from returning to the front. Twenty-three thousand verdicts of guilty were passed by courts-martial on mutinous troops. At least fifty-five men were shot. The French defenses were weaker than they had ever been; parts of the line were virtually unguarded. But when the Germans were told of gaps in the line, by escaped German prisoners and even by French deserters, they did not believe them. For the first time since they were checked in August 1914, the Germans could have taken the road to Paris with confidence. They failed to do so.

The Nivelle offensive came to a halt on 20 May. Haig decided to counter its failure by a British success. His plan was to drive through Messines Ridge and force the Germans off the Flemish coast. The ridge was captured but the greater objective lost. Beyond Messines lay Ypres, scene of two earlier battles, now destined for a third. The assault against Ypres was launched on 31 July 1917. The battle lasted into November.

"Third Ypres" was the worst slaughter of the war since the Somme. British losses numbered some 400,000, German over 250,-000. Among the many phases of the battle the capture of Passchendaele on 6 November was the most terrible. So great were the losses that the offensive was halted on 10 November. In England the heroism of the troops was widely applauded. But Lloyd George was bitter in his criticism of Haig and the Headquarters staff, which, he wrote: ". . . never witnessed, not even through a telescope, the attacks it ordained, except on carefully prepared charts where the advancing battalions were represented by the pencil which marched with ease across swamps and marked lines of triumphant progress without the loss of a single point. As for the mud, it never incommoded the movements of this irresistible pencil."

For the first time in the war British soldiers lost confidence in their leaders and were able to muster nothing but bitterness in their songs:

> If you want to find your sweetheart,
>   I know where he is,
> I know where he is, I know where he is,
> If you want to find your sweetheart,
>   I know where he is,
> Hanging on the front line wire.

And Siegfried Sassoon, an officer who became a pacifist after his experiences in the trenches, wrote for those who did not go to war:

You smug-faced crowd with kindling eye
Who cheer when soldier lads march by,
Sneak home and pray you'll never know
The hell where youth and laughter go.

## 1918

In 1917 two events took place which altered the course of the war in 1918. First, the Bolshevik revolution in Russia resulted in Russia's withdrawal from the war. The vast German army that had been tied down in the east was thus released to fight in the west.

The second event was the entry of the United States of America into the war. As American troops began to reach Europe early in 1918 it was clear that the Germans would quickly lose the advantages which they had gained because of the Russian revolution. To survive the arrival of America's unsullied troops they needed a swift victory. Once the Americans arrived the chance of victory would be lessened and the danger of defeat increased.

On 21 March 1918 General Ludendorff, who had brought America into the war by his insistence upon German submarines sinking American ships, launched his attack over every section of the western front. This was the plan's weakness. Although the German advances of March and April outdistanced anything that had been seen since trench warfare began, the Germans outran their artillery and to a large extent their transport. Although French demoralization enabled them to drive some thirty miles towards Paris, through Péronne to Montdidier, a strong British line at Arras and at Armentières denied them an open road to the sea.

German losses were so heavy that once the offensive came to a halt it was clear to both sides that it could be renewed only with difficulty. Ludendorff had inflicted a loss of 240,000 men on the British and French, but his own losses were just as great.

On 27 May the Ludendorff offensive resorted to its last stratagem, a concentrated drive towards Paris from the Chemins des Dames. Within two days the Germans were at Soissons and on 2 June had reached the outskirts of Château-Thierry. Once again, as in 1914, the Germans were within forty miles of Paris. Ludendorff was surprised; he later wrote that he had never expected to push be-

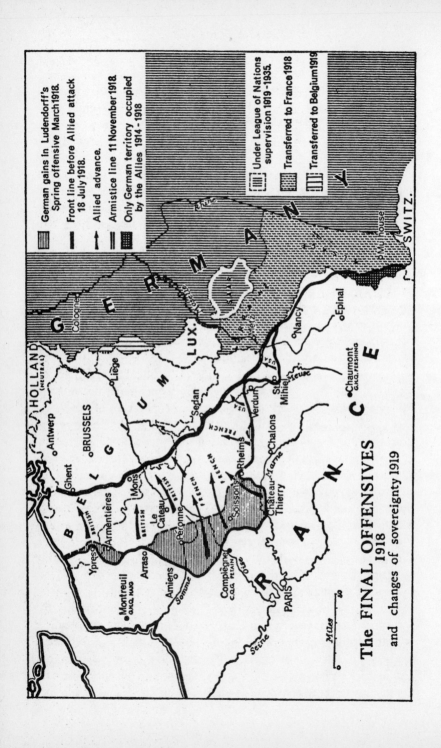

The FINAL OFFENSIVES 1918
and changes of sovereignty 1919

German gains in Ludendorff's
Spring offensive March1918.

Front line before Allied attack
18 July 1918.

Allied advance.

Armistice line 11 November 1918.

Only German territory occupied
by the Allies 1914 - 1918

Under League of Nations
supervision 1919-1935.

Transferred to France 1918

Transferred to Belgium 1919

yond Soissons. Yet within two days his men had penetrated to the Marne.

An unexpected hazard slowed the German advance and lowered morale. Beyond Soissons, especially at Fismes, were the great wine cellars of the Champagne country. No sooner was a town captured than the cellars were looted. Within hours the victorious troops were in a drunken daze. Lorry drivers joined in and transport was disrupted. After discipline was restored a further hazard remained. Though no longer incapable of marching, many of the men suffered hangovers which gave them little enthusiasm for the coming attack.

If the wine cellars of Fismes had been the only obstacle to advance the Germans might well have reached Paris within a week. But as the Germans moved into position around Château-Thierry they were aware of a new enemy facing them, the Americans.

The American troops did more than halt the German advance. Within four days they launched a counteroffensive. Their enthusiasm, their training, and their expectation of victory revitalized the despondent Allies. The Americans had not been conditioned to trench warfare. But of its unpleasantness they had been well informed by German propagandists in a leaflet circulated in America in 1916: "Dig a trench shoulder high in your garden, fill it half full of water and get into it. Remain there for two or three days on an empty stomach. Furthermore, hire a lunatic to shoot at you with revolvers and machine guns at close range. This arrangement is quite equal to a war and will cost your country very much less."

The Americans had no intention of succumbing to such absurdities. Their very enthusiasm was infectious: the British and French troops sensed a new hope and prepared with some optimism to take the offensive again. When, after nineteen days of stubborn fighting, the Americans captured Belleau Wood, the fortunes of the war had turned.

The final Allied offensive began in August. The British, based on Amiens, drove the Germans back to Péronne. By 9 September nearly all the territorial gains of Ludendorff's offensive were lost. Large numbers of Germans began to surrender. Demoralization, similar to that which had affected the French in 1917, spread through the German ranks. On 11 September the Americans attacked the St. Mihiel salient, which had been in German hands since

1914, and which guarded the most vulnerable sector of the German frontier. Within four days the Americans drove the Germans back halfway from St. Mihiel to Metz.

On 26 September "The Grand Assault" began; a combined British, French, and American advance. The Germans were unable to resist the tanks, the numbers of men, or the sudden outburst of energy with which they were faced.

Germany's collapse in the west was hastened by misfortunes elsewhere. Germany's allies were weary of war. Austria had sued independently for peace, the Bulgarians were being chased from Macedonia, and the Turks had been beaten in Palestine after the Arab revolt against Turkey, organized and directed by Lawrence of Arabia, a British officer and enthusiastic supporter of Arab nationalism. On 29 September Ludendorff told the German Council of War that an immediate armistice was needed to prevent the Allies from reaching the German frontier in the west. But the hypnosis of war delayed the various answers, conditions, and deliberations. By the time the armistice terms were finally agreed upon, the Allies had driven forward to Ghent, Mons, and Sedan. The armistice was signed in the forest of Compiègne on 11 November 1918. While the discussions progressed Germany had been proclaimed a republic, and a socialist had become Chancellor. The Kaiser went silently into exile in Holland. The terms of the armistice were, in outline, as follows:

Cessation of hostilities at 11 A.M. that day.
Evacuation of Alsace-Lorraine.
Repatriation of citizens of Allied nations.
Surrender of vast stocks of war material (including 5,000 guns and 25,000 machine guns).
Evacuation of the left bank of the Rhine and bridgeheads behind it, to be held by the Allies.
Repatriation of Allied prisoners of war, without immediate reciprocity.
Surrender of all submarines.
Internment of surface vessels as designated by the Allies.

The war was over; the arduous task of peacemaking and the complexities of national recovery had yet to be faced. Dangers loomed up outside the western front: revolutions threatened in many countries, social unrest in all of them. New frontiers had to be drawn, new forms of government consolidated and the gains of victory digested. The moment of victory was one of grandeur and magnificence, but it could not escape the shadow of impending misfortunes. As one French officer wrote:

"One can easily imagine the joy of our brave soldiers. . . . Yet, they did not show their joy outwardly by shouts or songs, as one could have expected. . . . Without doubt, they were deeply happy to know that the terrible storm which had swept their country was definitely over. They kept talking about it among themselves, but remained remarkably composed and dignified. Actually, peace had come so suddenly that we were all rather stunned, asking ourselves whether it was possible, or whether we were dreaming. When walking along the trenches several hours after the armistice, I was surprised to see all our soldiers at their listening posts, or in their shelters, as if the war was still on. . . . On November 13 a German officer quite earnestly and naively came to inquire whether it was true, as rumors had it, that a revolution had broken out in Paris, that Clemenceau had been assassinated, that Foch had committed suicide, that the British Fleet had mutinied, and that a republic had been proclaimed in England! He was utterly surprised to learn that absolutely none of this nonsense was true."

# ☆ 8 ☆

## THE WAR IN THE EAST

### 1914

THE WAR IN THE EAST began, on 12 August 1914, with the Austrian attack on Serbia. Austria's desire to punish Serbia had stirred the world into war. That tiny state, threatened by a sprawling empire, could hardly be expected to survive the onslaught. But the Serbs had not driven the Turks out of the Balkans in 1912 in order to allow Austria to enter two years later.

While Austria looked nervously in the direction of Russia and Serbia feared an attack in the rear from Bulgaria, battle was joined. The Austrians marched from Bosnia towards Belgrade. General Potiorek, the Governor of Bosnia who had failed to protect Franz Ferdinand from the assassin's bullet, led the Austrian army in revenge for his, and Austria's, humiliation. But the Serbs did not melt away as was expected. The Serbian commander-in-chief, General Putnik, drove Potiorek back across the Bosnian frontier. A rash Serbian attack into Bosnia was itself repulsed by 25 October.

Potiorek attacked again, and defeated the Serbian army in a fierce battle. On 2 December the Austrians entered Belgrade, the Serbian capital. Victory seemed assured, but Putnik rallied his men and within two weeks the Austrians were driven back across the Danube and beyond the Sava. Serbia was saved. The cost had been terrible to both sides. Austrian losses were 227,000, Serbian losses 170,000. For Serbia it was salvation, despite the cost. For Austria it was humiliation. The Germans ridiculed their ally, against whom Serbia had displayed such courage: "Allies?" they mocked. "Why, we're shackled to a corpse."

Russia had mobilized with greater ease than was expected. Her cumbersome armies advanced with zest and on 17 August the northern army, commanded by General Rennenkampf, and the southern army under General Samsonov, both crossed into East Prussia. On 20 August Rennenkampf's army met the Germans at Gumbinnen. The Germans fled in panic, leaving 6,000 of their soldiers prisoners. The German commander was at once dismissed. His successor was a retired general of sixty-seven, not perhaps an auspicious choice. This retired general, Paul von Hindenburg by name, was given as his staff officer the man who had just distinguished himself at the capture of Liège in the west, General Ludendorff. These two were on their way to the front by train when a plan, devised for the emergency of defeat, was put into operation on the initiative of Lieutenant Colonel Max Hoffman. Hindenburg and Ludendorff duly approved this plan. The Germans retreated in two directions, west by rail and southwest on foot. The rail movement turned south at Elbing, and at the nearest point to the Russian southern army the troops detrained. The spot at which it was decided to meet Samsonov's army was a hill called Tannenberg.

At first the Germans were at a strong disadvantage. The troops

who had been moving southeast on foot had only reached Bischofstein. For two days Samsonov held the advantage. But what he
might have gained by military skill was lost by technical folly. The
Russians, not planning for the possibility of their own rapid advance, had neglected their communications system. Their telegraph
facilities were inadequate and messages passed from front to rear
with dignified sloth. At the same time they neglected to use code.
Their messages passed undisguised. The German wireless station at
Königsberg listened to the discussions of the Russian plan of campaign. What they heard was comforting. It appeared that Rennenkampf could not reach Gerdauen until 26 August, and was thus
quite unable to come to Samsonov's assistance. At the same time the
Russian wireless messages revealed that Samsonov himself did not
regard the presence of German troops at Tannenberg as part of a
concerted plan of attack. He thought that the army was an army in
retreat. He thought that he had only to strike hard, follow closely,
and thus drive the Germans to Danzig.

Samsonov was told of troops coming from Bischofstein but did
not take alarm. Here, he argued, were more men in retreat, doubtless
in hopeless disorder, flying from Rennenkampf's advance. He therefore despatched a small force northwards to break the advancing
rabble. But the troops with whom they were faced were marching
*towards* battle, not away from it. They were determined to reach
Tannenberg as quickly as possible and far outnumbered the men
whom Samsonov had sent to crush them. Thus Samsonov's right
flank was pierced. But such was the inadequacy of Russian communications that he did not learn of this in time to regroup his forces.
The Germans drove in from the north, passing Ortelsburg on 27
August.

General François, commander of one of the German armies, ignored instructions from Ludendorff to turn north when he reached
Neidenburg. François decided on a more subtle tactic. He moved on
to Willenberg. It was precisely across the Neidenburg-Willenberg
line that the Russians could retreat. Now that line was denied them,
thanks to the virtual disobedience of Ludendorff's subordinate. As
the German Army from the north pressed beyond Ortelsburg and
swung west Samsonov was surrounded. The Germans took 122,000
prisoners, of whom François obtained over a half. Samsonov walked
alone into the woods and shot himself.

The Russian attack was at an end. The Germans had a victory which was to remain a symbol of national revival for many generations. At Tannenberg the invading armies had been checked; at Tannenberg German honor had been saved. To whom did the laurels of this triumph go? A study of the battle shows that Max Hoffman devised the plan and that François enabled it to be carried out to maximum effect. In the heat of war other conclusions were reached, chief among them that Ludendorff was the victor of Tannenberg and that in combination with Hindenburg, his aging superior, he had marshaled the forces of Germany against the foe. For François and Hoffman there was to be no such immediate fame.

The Austrians were denied a Tannenberg. Their armies, deployed at the foot of the Carpathians, were spread across a front 175 miles long. Conrad von Hötzendorff, Chief of the General Staff, was in charge of their deployment. Fighting began on 23 August 1914. Along the vast front the Austrians advanced. The first clash occurred at Krasnik and for three days the opposing armies battled. Then the Russians retreated to Lublin. "This," as Conrad wrote, "was a joyful and welcome beginning."

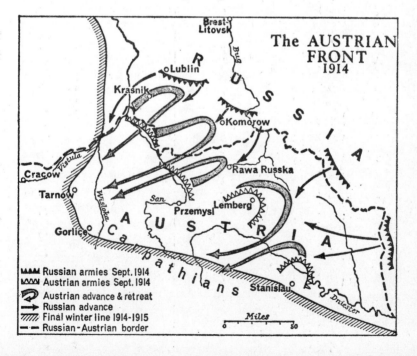

A similar Austrian success, costly in men but visible on the map, was won at Komorow. After a week of constant fighting it appeared as if the Russians were to be enveloped as completely as at Tannenberg. But at the moment of crisis the Austrians further south appealed for help: they were being pressed back to Lemberg by the Russians under General Brusilov. The encirclement at Komorow was thus abandoned. On 30 August, a black day for Russia at Tannenberg, a Russian victory outside Lemberg destroyed any chance of Austria joining Germany in a knockout blow. The prudent Austrians withdrew.

The Russians saw a chance to break the Austrians entirely. The Austrian Army was concentrated between Rawa-Russka and the Wereszyka River. The Russians planned to let them hold this line, while rapidly surrounding them by a cavalry movement launched from Krasnik and Terespol. The Russian plan was bold and potentially decisive. But it failed. Once more the Russians sent details of the plan to the various commanders without coding them. These open messages were soon picked up by Austrian intelligence. The Russian surprise was planned for 12 September. On 11 September Conrad ordered a general withdrawal of the whole Austrian force. Back they went, orderly and unharassed, for sixty miles, to the San River. The Russians prepared a counterstroke: a rapid cavalry movement from Lublin that would swing round the San from the north. Again the plan was sent to commanders unciphered. Again Conrad considered it prudent to withdraw. On 3 October the Austrian armies came to rest west of the Wisloka River, 140 miles west of Lemberg.

In the west the Germans had been turned back from the Marne, their dreams of a swift entry into Paris shattered. On both fronts the Central Powers were thus frustrated in their hopes of winning the war by Christmas 1914.

The Germans were unable to exploit their Tannenberg success. They were needed to support the northern wing of the Austrian army and to prevent a Russian breakthrough into Silesia. In terms of offensives, they also had an opportunity to move into Russia's exposed Polish province, and to capture Warsaw. The Russians forestalled this by a magnificent infantry march to the Vistula. During this march road conditions were bad, speed essential, and supplies appalling. One Russian division is said to have gone without bread for six days. But they reached the Vistula and Warsaw was saved.

The Russians now planned to strike at Germany through Silesia. Hindenburg, learning of this, at once withdrew, avoiding contact with the Russian armies but incurring the scorn of his subordinates. The man of iron was shown to be of wood; Ludendorff also panicked, afraid to risk an encounter. Only Max Hoffman was willing to attempt a second Tannenberg. But he was not allowed to do so. Forbidden to deploy his guns, he took up his pen and filled his diary with a bitter account of how his superiors had lost their nerve. The Germans withdrew, leaving a gap in the armor of the Central Powers. Ironically it was left to Conrad, the despised "corpse," to rush Austrian troops northwards to fill the dangerous gap. The Germans retreated from outside Warsaw to beyond Lodz. The Russians cast avaricious eyes upon Posen and Breslau.

But the spirit of Tannenberg was not dead. On 10 November the Germans launched a counteroffensive towards Lodz. The Russian advance was violently checked. The Germans took 12,000 prisoners in three days. The Russians retreated to Lodz. By 18 November Lodz was encircled. But the Russians moved their other armies with great speed. By 21 November the German armies surrounding Lodz were themselves surrounded. The Russians sensed a spectacular victory with myriad prisoners. In their enthusiasm they ordered trains to be sent from Russia to carry back their prisoners. Such enthusiasm was premature.

The Germans east of Lodz broke through the Russian ring on 24 November. Not only did they escape with their wounded and their guns, but, while fighting through the trap, they captured and took with them 10,000 prisoners. It was the most magnificent escape story of the war. The Russians were driven from Lodz on 6 December and the invasion of Silesia abandoned. The Germans claimed 135,000 prisoners. But the Lodz offensive was Germany's only success at the close of 1914. Northwards the Russians advanced again into East Prussia, with the Germans too exhausted to plan a second Tannenberg. In the south the Austrians fared no better. Conrad was forced to remain in the Carpathians. The Russians even set foot upon the Dukla Pass, gateway to Austria from the east, but failed to penetrate beyond the crest.

## 1915

The Russians, though winning no great victories in 1914, and despite the defeats of Tannenberg and Lodz, had extended their front
most remarkably by the beginning of 1915. Their armies had penetrated far into Austrian territory and were lodged in East Prussia.
But the cost of this success was formidable. Nor was it certain that it
could be sustained.

The Central Powers decided upon a winter offensive. This, con-
sidering the Carpathian snows, was a grave risk. But it succeeded,
and the Russians were driven down the Carpathian passes. In the
north the Germans attacked on 7 February and drove the Russians
from East Prussia. Within two weeks the Germans advanced seventy
miles, crossing into Russia at Suvalki on 14 February, and capturing
30,000 Russians at Augustov on 18 February.

The Russians feared total defeat, and while the Central Powers
mustered their forces for a further advance, the Russians appealed to
Britain to make a diversion elsewhere. It was difficult to find any
German weakness in the west, where the trenches had imposed their
own inexorable rigidity upon the line of battle. But Germany's forgotten ally, Turkey, was less well equipped to defeat an attack by the
Entente Powers. Britain, after much hesitation, decided upon a naval
assault through the Dardanelles. British ships would enter the Sea of
Marmara, bombard Constantinople, and force Turkey to its knees.
Such a result would be exceedingly dangerous to the Central Powers,
exposing their Balkan front to an offensive from the south, enabling
Serbia to plunge into Austria, and perhaps encouraging three neutrals, Italy, Greece and Rumania, to take arms against Austria.

The Englishman responsible for this bold plan was Winston
Churchill. The navy was to accomplish the breakthrough which armies had failed to effect. On 19 February, the day after the Russians
found themselves surrounded at Augustov, British and French ships
bombarded the outer forts at the Dardanelles. Though they destroyed many of the Turkish guns they failed to pass through the
Narrows. The Turks had sown an effective barrier of mines. A more
determined assault was planned, assisted by minesweepers. On 18
March the British and French ships attacked again, moving forward
towards the Narrows. The Turkish batteries along the Narrows were
silenced. Then came the dreaded hazard: one French and two British

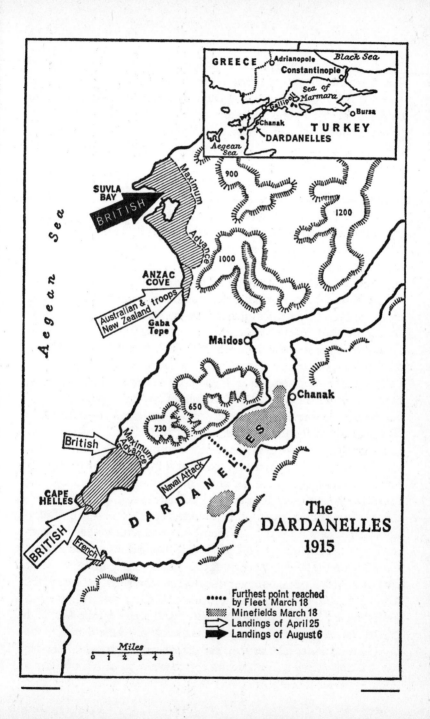

The
DARDANELLES
1915

GREECE

Black Sea

Adrianople

Constantinople

Sea of Marmara

Gallipoli

Chanak

DARDANELLES

TURKEY

Bursa

Aegean Sea

SUVLA BAY

BRITISH

Maximum Advance

900

1200

1000

ANZAC COVE

Australian & New Zealand troops

Gaba Tepe

Maidos

Chanak

650

730

Maximum Advance

British

Naval Attack

D A R D A N E L L E S

CAPE HELLES

BRITISH

French

····· Furthest point reached
by Fleet March 18
▒▒ Minefields March 18
▭ Landings of April 25
◆ Landings of August 6

Miles
0 1 2 3 4 5

battleships were sunk by mines, others severely damaged. The British admiral was not prepared to continue the assault if it meant the loss of more ships. One of his subordinates, Roger Keyes, insisted that if the Narrows could be passed it did not matter if more ships were sunk. No matter how few ships sailed beyond Maidos, he argued, victory was assured. Keyes hoped that, if the attack were continued, Churchill's plan would proceed with ease. But the admiral was not moved by arguments of grand strategy. Having lost a third of his force, and not sharing Keyes's optimism, he called off the attack.

The British naval diversion had failed. The Turks were alerted and their position in Gallipoli reinforced. The Russians continued to be pressed back upon the eastern front. Churchill was determined to do all in his power to hasten the Allied victory in which he had such faith. He wished to press forward with plans for a further naval attack. But the senior officers at the Dardanelles doubted whether such an attack could succeed. They planned a different stroke: a military landing on the Gallipoli shore, troops advancing from Cape Helles, the Turks at Maidos caught in the rear, Maidos in British hands, the Hellespont opened for a triumphant naval entry into the Sea of Marmara.

The landings were made on 25 April. The expected advances did not take place: the terrain was too rough and the Turks too tenacious in their defense. The soldiers, Australians, fought towards the hills. A Turkish officer, Mustafa Kemal, forestalled them. His superiors did not wish to commit too many men to any one section of the peninsula. Mustafa Kemal saw the vital importance of holding the high ground, and, with his division, drove the Australians back to the coast. Their final position was a desperate one, a beach two miles long and rugged country to a depth of under a mile. Instead of driving the Turks in panic before them, they were confronted with an unforeseen energy. Mustafa Kemal fought tenaciously. The Australians responded with extraordinary courage. Gallipoli became the scene of the same stagnant trench warfare as on the western front. The Turks held their position. A second Allied landing at Suvla Bay on 6 August failed to dislodge them. The slaughter at Gallipoli mounted. In one morning 5,000 Turks were killed and 5,000 wounded in the space between the trenches. The stench of bodies was so nauseating and the groans of the wounded so terrible that a day's truce was arranged. Australians and Turks worked together, attending to the wounded and burying the dead. A strange camaraderie developed as a result of this brief contact. The slaughter continued, but was accompanied by courtesies unknown on the western front. One old Turk who regularly left his trench to hang out the socks and shirts of his platoon on a washing line, was allowed to go about his business unmolested. The historian Alan Moorehead has recorded: "There was a constant traffic of gifts in the trenches, the Turks throwing over grapes and sweets, the Allied soldiers responding with tinned food and cigarettes. The Turks had no great love for British beef. A note came over one day: 'Bully beef—non. Envoyez milk.' "

On 27 April a British submarine slipped under the minefields of the Narrows and, after six hours of perilous surfacing, being bombarded, and plunging down again, surfaced unscathed in the Sea of Marmara. For three weeks the submarine was mistress of the Marmara, sinking a Turkish ship with 6,000 troops on board, all of whom were drowned. On 18 May a second submarine reached the Marmara. Its captain, M. E. Nasmith, formed a bolder plan than random sinking. He reached Constantinople and methodically torpedoed ship after ship just off the city. The Turks imagined that half a dozen submarines were attacking the capital. Crowds ran panic-stricken through the streets. Activity in the docks came to a standstill. Troops embarking for Gallipoli were sent back to their barracks. For his exploit Nasmith won the Victoria Cross. His example was followed in May by others. One man swam from a submarine to the shore, blew up a railway viaduct, and gave the impression of being a magic army. Nasmith, on his second mission, demoralized the Turks further. A cargo of coal had reached Constantinople from the Black Sea. The coal shortage, affecting as it did the city's supply of water, electricity, and rail transport, gave the coal-carrying ship an air of grandeur. Delighted municipal officials stood on the quayside to welcome it. Hardly had it berthed when it was blown up before their eyes.

These exploits off Constantinople could not compensate for the failure at Gallipoli. The Germans were justly proud of the success of their Turkish ally in repulsing such a dangerous attack. Their own armies could concentrate on the war against Russia.

Conrad persuaded the Germans to launch a joint Austro-German offensive from the Carpathians along a thirty-mile front from Gor-

The
EASTERN FRONT
1915

- ▦ Area gained by Germany and Austria Jan.–July
- ▥ Area gained by Germany and Austria Aug.–Sept.
- ➤ October offensive
- ▦ Serbian Army–November
- ⇨ Final Serbian withdrawal
- ⧠ French Expeditionary Force
- ⇨ British landings April & August

lice to Tarnow. The offensive began on 2 May. The Russians were unable to stand up to the intensive artillery bombardment. As the Germans recorded: "Here and there lone gray figures jumped up and ran back weaponless in gray fur caps and fluttering, unbuttoned greatcoats, until there was not one remaining. Like a flock of sheep they fled in wild confusion." The German advance was relentless. Only in the south did General Brusilov hold his line after the initial retreat. But he was forced to give up Przemysl on 3 June and Lemberg on 22 June.

The German advance continued until the end of September. As a result of the disaster the Tsar took over the personal command of his armies. Over a million Russians had been killed or wounded; three-quarters of a million had been taken prisoner.

With Russia exhausted, the Austrians and Germans turned on Serbia, whose ability to resist invasion had so humiliated Austria in 1914. Not only were they secure against a Russian diversion in their rear; they also obtained Bulgaria as an ally, willing to attack Serbia in the flank. On 7 October the Central Powers launched their attack: the Bulgarians struck on 11 October.

The Serbs were unable to resist such an overwhelming force. Belgrade fell on 9 October. The Bulgarians cut the single railway track that joined north and south Serbia. The Serbs appealed to Britain and France for help. The British were unwilling to throw men into a new caldron. The French sent a regiment which reached Nish. But further French troops were thrown back to the Greek frontier by the Bulgarians. Churchill urged the British to attack Turkey at Chanak, using ships and troops from the Dardanelles. But Churchill's opinions were discredited as a result of the Dardanelles failure. In November 1915 he left the Cabinet and crossed over to France to join in the battle on the western front. His Chanak scheme was dismissed. As he wrote in retrospect: "The fleet continued idle at the Dardanelles. The armies shattered themselves against the German defence in France. The Bulgarians carried an army of 300,000 men to join our enemies; and Serbia as a factor in the war was obliterated. I found it unendurable to remain participant in such crimes against truth and reason."

The Serbs were defeated. The remnant of their army crossed into Albania and eventually reached the shelter of Corfu. They managed to take with them on their strenuous journey 24,000 Austrian pris-

oners who had been captured by General Putnik in 1914. But they
left behind them over 100,000 Serbs killed or wounded, a ravaged
countryside and a wilderness inhabited by widows and orphans. Before the year ended, even the existing desolation was made more
terrible when a typhus epidemic killed over 250,000 Serbs. On 18
January 1916 King Ferdinand of Bulgaria entertained the German
Emperor in Nish. The Emperor was greeted with a Latin invocation
of dubious veracity:

> *Ave Imperator, Caesar et Rex. Victor et gloriosus es. Nissa antiqua*
> *omnis Orientis populi te salutant redemptorem, ferentem oppressis*
> *prosperitatem atque salutem.*

> Hail Emperor, Caesar and King. Thou art victor and glorious. In
> ancient Nish all the peoples of the East salute thee, the redeemer,
> bringing to the oppressed prosperity and well-being.

## 1916

One new combatant, Italy, entered the war in 1915 on the side of
the Entente Powers. She was promised a series of territorial acquisi-
tions if she would take up arms against the Central Powers. Repeated Italian offensives in the summer and autumn of 1915 resulted in great losses for both the Italian and Austrian armies but in
little territorial advantage to either. Austrian commitments on the
Italian front did not help Serbia. The Italians could hardly be said to
possess even a nuisance value.

In May 1916 the Austrians took the offensive on the Italian front.
The Italians appealed to Russia to create a diversion in the Austrian
rear. General Brusilov, who in April 1916 was appointed commander of the Russian armies south of the Pripet Marshes, took the
offensive. This diversion prevented the total defeat of Italy, although
any chance of an Italian victory was shattered when the Austrians
defeated the Italian Army at Caporetto. Brusilov began his eastern
offensive on 4 June; two days later the Austrians were in retreat and
by 9 June Brusilov had taken over 70,000 prisoners.

Brusilov was not well supported by the Russian generals to the
north. Attacking rather unwillingly on 13 June, another general
was driven back without penetrating the enemy lines. Brusilov realized that he must act alone. Another effort by the troops in the north
on 4 July was an equal fiasco. The front remained unbroken. But

The WAR in the EAST
1916

*Baltic Sea*

Danzig
Tannenberg

GERMANY

Vilna

Under GERMAN Occupation

R U S S I A

Pripet Marshes

Warsaw

Pinsk

Lublin

Cracow

Lemberg

AUSTRIA –

Budapest

HUNGARY

MOLDAVIA

Jassy

Odessa

TRANSYLVANIA

Hermannstadt

Kronstadt

Miles
0        100

BANAT

R U M A N I A

DOBRUDJA

Belgrade

Bucharest
Occ.
6 Dec.1916

Black Sea

SERBIA

Sofia
BULGARIA

1914 Frontiers

Russian gains
June 1916.
(Brusilov offensive)

Rumania: occupied by
Austria, Germany & Bulgaria,
December 1916.

Rumania: protected by
Russia,1916-1917.

Initial Rumanian Gains,1916.

Front line, Dec.1916.

Constantinople

TURKEY

GREECE

Gallipoli

Dardanelles

Brusilov's advance continued. Austrian regiments disintegrated and fled. Rumania was so impressed by Russia's success that she declared war on Germany and Austria on 27 August. But Brusilov's offensive came to a halt in September. Although it had cast confusion among the Austrians it had failed to capture Lemberg or Lublin. The verdict of the German victories of 1915 could not be reversed. Brusilov took 400,000 prisoners. But his own armies were exhausted.

The Rumanians had joined the war hoping for easy victories. They would take part, so their leaders argued, in the final victorious offensive against the Central Powers. They would annex Transylvania and the Banat. But the Germans did not encourage such bold dreams at the expense of their Austrian and Bulgarian allies. They did not relish another enemy at so trying a time. Speed was the essence of the German answer to the treachery of their former friend. On 30 September the Rumanians were driven from Hermannstadt, on 8 October from Kronstadt. The Carpathians were crossed on 26 November and Bucharest, the Rumanian capital, occupied on 6 December. The Rumanians suffered terribly for their decision to enter the war. One hundred and fifty thousand men killed, an equal number taken prisoner, all territory lost except the northern province of Moldavia, the government removed to the provincial town of Jassy: such were the fruits of ill-considered adventure and uncritical avarice.

The eastern front came to a standstill. The Germans were elated by their success in Rumania; the Austrians were depressed by Brusilov's advance. On 20 November 1916 Franz Josef died. It had long been rumored in Vienna that he was already dead, that he was being preserved as a symbol. Such rumors were themselves a sign of discontent. With his death all Austria seemed to shudder. Could there be an Austria without Franz Josef? Could an allegiance ever be found as powerful as the loyalty which the aged monarch had personally inspired? Could Nicholas II, the Autocrat of All Russia, take advantage of his fellow emperor's demise?

## 1917

The Entente Powers met in Petrograd in January 1917 to discuss new offensives. They had cause for optimism. If a successful Anglo-French attack could be launched in the west, carefully combined with another Russian offensive, if Italy could put pressure on Austria and if France could drive the enemy troops from Macedonia, the war might end in 1917.

In Russia itself the murder of the monk Rasputin on 30 December 1916 suggested that the pernicious influence at court of this shadowy figure was to be followed by a more attractive court life. But social discontent in Russia went deeper than dislike of court intrigues. Factory conditions were bad and wages were low. Strikes involving half a million workers broke out in 1915. Over a million workers struck in 1916. There was no improvement in the new year: strikes in January and February 1917 were widespread and violence rose to the surface when the government arrested the factory representatives who sat on the Central War Industries Committee.

Soldiers coming home on leave swelled the ranks of the discontented. One general wrote in his diary on 10 March: "I am firmly convinced that the common soldier today wants only one thing—food and peace, because he is tired of war." Two days earlier Nicholas II returned to his headquarters at Moghilev and wrote to his wife: "I greatly miss my half-hourly game of patience every evening. I shall take up dominoes again in my spare time."

These domestic thoughts were disturbed by news of street demonstrations in Petrograd. Extreme socialists and parliamentary liberals were cooperating to demand reform. Soldiers, called out to halt the demonstrations, had first fired on the crowds, killing indiscriminately, then fraternized with the marchers. Imperial authority could not be exerted; Petrograd was in the hands of revolutionaries.

The aim of the demonstrators was to end the autocratic rule of the Tsar. The Duma, or Russian parliament, had for many years sought greater control over the administration. At times Nicholas had heeded its liberal recommendations; at times he had ignored them. Once the war began the Duma was deprived of its control of financial affairs. But it continued to sit and to criticize the conduct of the war. When revolution came to Petrograd the Duma sought to lead it. When dissolved by the Tsar it refused to disperse. It urged Nicholas to abdicate but he decided to return to Petrograd and reassert his authority. At midnight on 11 March he entered his train. For six hours no movement was possible as the line was blocked. The line was cleared by morning and the train moved on, but in the afternoon it stopped again. It was said that a bridge was damaged. Nicholas suggested an alternative route. But the "authorities" refused to allow him to proceed. Nicholas had ceased to be the sole and undisputed source of power. Others were exercising authority. Others were saying where or where not the autocrat could go.

A deputation from the Duma reached Nicholas and demanded his abdication. On 15 March he agreed. Tsardom was dead; the Provisional Government ruled. At its side the socialist Council of Workers' and Soldiers' Deputies, a "parliament" of left-wing parties known as the "Soviet," made it clear that the wishes of the masses must be taken into account in all governmental decisions. The Soviet set up its own committees, passed its own resolutions, and even took up rooms in the Duma building.

The War Minister of the Provisional Government was Alexander Kerensky. He believed that Russia could still play its part in the defeat of the Central Powers. He was convinced that he could revive the shaken morale of the army and re-create the discipline which had been lost during the excitement of revolution. He looked forward to the day when the Provisional Government would become permanent, liberal, and respected.

On 4 June Kerensky appointed Brusilov as commander-in-chief of the Russian armies. The more conservative officers looked askance at their colleague's acceptance of command under a republican regime. Kerensky himself toured the front, endeavoring to create enthusiasm for the continuance of the war. Appealing to the radical sentiments of the troops, he said: "Our army under the monarchy accomplished heroic deeds; will it be a flock of sheep under a republic?" His speeches created some enthusiasm on the spot. The appearance of a Minister was a rare occurrence. But once he returned to Petrograd the men lapsed into lethargy.

Britain and France were delighted that the new Russia was to continue to fight. Many of Britain's liberals and France's republicans had felt uneasy with an autocrat as an ally. They welcomed the support of a democratic Russia. They were not particularly worried by the arrival in Petrograd of Vladimir Lenin, the Social Democrat leader who had spent most of the war in Switzerland. Lenin rallied the Bolshevik element in the Soviet to his policy of "No support for the Provisional Government." He spoke of the day when the Soviet would come to power, unfettered by a liberal regime. But the Bolsheviks were only a minority in the Soviet. There was no evidence that they could succeed in dominating that body and no chance that the other parties in the Soviet might agree to overthrow the Provisional Government. When, at the April Congress of the Soviet, Lenin demanded a further revolution, the overthrow of the Provisional Government, and the ending of the war, he was treated as a crank by the other socialists. At the Soviet's April Congress only 105 of the 1,090 delegates were Bolshevik supporters of this strange extremist.

On 1 July Kerensky launched his summer offensive. By a successful advance he hoped to raise enthusiasm for the Provisional Government at home and support for it abroad. But on Hoffman's insistence Ludendorff transferred four divisions by train from the western front. At one point the Russians advanced sixty miles, only to be met by the reserves hurried from the west. The Kerensky offensive was forced back, becoming first a defensive action, then a rout. On 1 September the Germans entered Riga. The Russians fled at their approach. Nine thousand, finding the Germans close behind them, surrendered. Russian morale was destroyed. Kerensky dismissed Brusilov, but it was not enough. The war had lost its appeal. No new commander could rally the disrupted, weary troops.

On 29 July Kerensky had convened an emergency Council of War. General Denikin, commander of the western front, explained why the offensive had collapsed: "The officers are in a terrible position. They are insulted, beaten, murdered." Discipline had entirely collapsed. The Soviet had asserted the rights of the common soldier and encouraged disobedience. The death penalty for disobedience and desertion (abolished during the March revolution) was revived. But few could be found to accuse, to condemn, or to inflict punishment upon disobedient soldiers. On 8 September over 19,000 deserters were captured. How could they be tried? How could they be shot? It was almost impossible to find enough troops to guard them; punishment was out of the question.

The Kerensky offensive destroyed what faith was left in Russia in the usefulness of further war. Lenin's Bolsheviks gained innumerable adherents with a program of "immediate peace." On 7 November, after careful planning and with brilliant leadership, the Bolsheviks seized power. Kerensky fled the capital flying an American flag on his car to avoid capture.

Lenin fulfilled his promise to bring the war to an end on coming to power. Certainly any prolongation of the war was politically impossible. On 8 November Lenin issued his "Declaration of Peace," demanding "A just and democratic peace for which the great majority of wearied, tormented, and war-exhausted toilers and laboring classes of all belligerent countries are thirsting, a peace which the Russian workers and peasants have so loudly and insistently demanded since the overthrow of the Tsar's monarchy, such a peace the Government considers to be an immediate peace without annexations (i.e., without the seizure of foreign territory and the forcible annexation of foreign nationalities) and without indemnities.

"The Russian Government proposes to all warring peoples that this kind of peace be concluded at once."

On 16 December the Germans agreed to an armistice. Britain and France were powerless to reverse Lenin's decision. In vain they referred to a Tsarist pledge that none of the Entente Powers would make a separate peace. In vain they encouraged the anti-Bolshevik Russians to overthrow Lenin and his peace party. In vain they themselves intervened, in an attempt to create an Entente force in the east

Treaty of
BREST-LITOVSK
1917

=== Front line at Armistice 1917
▨ Ceded by Russia to Germany 1917
▨ Occupied by Germany 1918
▨ Occupied by Austria
▨ Occupied by Rumania

that would continue to harass the Germans. But they could not force Russia to go back to war.

The Bolsheviks negotiated peace with Germany. The Treaty of Brest-Litovsk was signed on 3 March 1918. The Russians conceded vast territories to the Germans and released the German armies in the east for further battles in the west. In return they were themselves freed from the need to pay indemnities to the Germans. Prisoners of war were exchanged. The treaty fell harshly on Russia but left Lenin free to consolidate his new government. It fell more harshly on Britain and France, in the form of a sudden and successful German offensive in the west. But the Great War in the east was ended.

## ☆ 9 ☆

# THE AFTERMATH OF WAR

RUSSIA LEFT THE WAR in March 1918 and Germany felt the joy of victory. Eight months later all cause for joy disappeared. Germany was defeated in the west. In terms of power politics Britain, France, America, and Italy were the principal victors; Germany, Austria-Hungary and Turkey the vanquished. In the peace treaties this concept was preserved, the victors styling themselves "Allied and Associated" Powers and describing the defeated states as "Enemy" Powers. But this was the language of diplomacy; the realities were different.

All Europe was exhausted by the war. None of the great Powers had been able to avoid fantastic expenditure on armaments; none had been able to spare their youth from the holocaust of front-line fighting. Politically the structure of both liberal and autocratic regimes underwent profound changes. In order to mobilize their countries for war, liberal governments had been forced to resort to strong measures of state control and organization. In England, which had prided itself on never needing a conscript army, volunteers proved insufficient for the purpose of the new-style war. The machine gun needed more targets than a volunteer army could supply and in 1916 the Government was forced to institute conscription.

In Germany, where industrialists had represented the most independent section of the community, proud, exclusive, and rich, the dictates of war economy led to increasing state control of industry. It was not enough for profit-searching individuals to fix quotas, prices, and markets. The state's needs were such that industrial independence had to be pushed aside. In every country the severity and length of the war led to the abandonment of old traditions and treasured patterns of political behavior.

Socialists learned a bitter lesson about the brotherhood of man. In 1900 they swore at rallies and conferences never to go to war against their working-class brothers in other countries. They denounced all war as a capitalist plot. But in 1914 a war fever gripped socialists everywhere. Lone figures stood out, notable because they were so rare. In Rumania the Balkan socialist leader Christian Rakovsky had, by a narrow majority, persuaded his Social Democrat followers to oppose war. In 1916, when Rumania declared war on Germany, Rakovsky was fervent in his denunciation of war. He was imprisoned for his pains.

In France only one socialist leader, Jean Jaurès, spoke against war in 1914. He was assassinated before war broke out. His fellow socialists abandoned their pacific doctrine and ignored his teaching. In Paris, as in Berlin, London, and Vienna, war fever clutched at peoples' throats. The cry of the French general: *"Tout le monde à la bataille"* was echoed in every coffeehouse, every beer cellar, and every public square. By revealing its basic national allegiance, socialism showed that it had come to join and not to destroy the state structures of which it was so critical.

Those who opposed war were reviled in every country. A conscience was not regarded as the equipment of a good citizen. Conscientious objectors were imprisoned and no pity was spared for those who refused to join the carnage at the front line. If one man's objections were seen as valid, might not the whole careful apparatus of death be regarded as absurd? And if death in war had no meaning, how could governments justify prolonging the war? Even sober statesmen were ridiculed when they suggested negotiating for peace in 1915, 1916, or 1917. The word "negotiation" came to be regarded as impertinent, treacherous, and immoral. Diplomacy, once considered honorable, was discredited.

Before the war statesmen of all nations had met in unity to discuss difficult problems. Educated men pondered long on how to eliminate national quarrels. But in 1914 the bayonet replaced the despatch box. The least educated and least well-born citizens of every nation were considered able enough to argue the national cause from the firestep of their trench. The salons and debating chambers of diplo-

matic intrigue and conference were forgotten. Men met only in no-
man's-land, at the point of some weapon of death.

The Europe of 1900 considered itself the center, not only of
world political power but of intellectual and technical advancement.
The development of the steam engine, the internal combustion engine, the telephone, the wireless and, by 1914, the airplane, suggested that within a few decades there would be no material benefit
beyond man's reach. At the same time, through their great empires,
each European nation could impart its wisdom and its skills to back-
ward peoples. The light would shine in the jungle, carried, not by
priests, but by engineers and teachers.

The confidence of Europe was also a source of blindness. No one
asked what would be the outcome of this pulsating progress. Education was geared to a faith in upward movements. Just as railway
trains would go faster, motor cars go further and airplanes higher, so
too human happiness would always expand. The newly promoted
clerk would become happier, the toiling worker learn to smile, the
black man and the yellow man would appreciate the benefits of belonging to the Western world.

A few pessimists argued that national exuberance would turn
sour, producing national rivalry; a few cynics predicted that the existence of great armies would inevitably lead to war.

One man, wiser than most, went further. He agreed that war
would come and that victors would emerge at the end of it. But he
emphasized that the cost of war would be such that even the victors
would be poorer. War, he argued, would only increase human misery, whatever its cause and whoever its arbiters. This bold prophecy
came from Norman Angell, an Englishman who had lived on a desert ranch in California and edited an English newspaper in Paris.
His predictions of the futility of war were published in 1910. Naturally, they were ridiculed; ironically, they were true.

Before 1914 it was impossible to alert people to the dangers of
war. It was generally assumed that the hardship would be confined
to the fighting zones alone. War was something distant, rapid, and
noble. The heroism of individual soldiers would become part of the
national saga: the victors would add a further glorious page to the
delight of their historians, novelists, and teachers. The empires that
went to war expected either the easy glory of a swift victory or the
passing humiliation of sudden defeat. They saw the war as providing

an opportunity for further expansion and the consolidation of power. It was for this reason that war had been embarked upon with such levity.

Only Britain succeeded in both keeping her monarch and acquiring imperial property. The German colonies in Africa went to Britain, in the form of "mandates." The word "mandate" indicated an awareness of responsibility. It was intended to suggest benevolence in imperial activity and the eventual granting of self-government. The British did not doubt that their imperial rule was already responsible, progressive, and benevolent. They therefore accepted mandates from the peace treaties with a good grace.

Other empires were not so fortunate. The British gains were not paralleled elsewhere. France gained Alsace-Lorraine, but had long claimed it, regarding its annexation by Germany in 1871 as a crime. The return of Alsace-Lorraine was the settlement of an old grievance, not the acquisition of a new glory. In the Near East France also gained, as did Britain, from the defeat of the Turkish Empire. But the Near Eastern mandates were never as secure as the African ones. France found herself with troublesome subjects. She could ill afford the new responsibility. She was weary of ownership and control. Her old African empire provided enough problems and drained off enough manpower: Morocco, acquired in 1905, was not yet pacified.

The British maintained a vast army in India that could be sent to any spot where trouble might arise; an army that had long borne the burden of imperial control, and had even been used in the European war. France had no such reserve of manpower. The war had cut down the flower of French youth. The defense of Verdun and the Nivelle offensive had drained the lifeblood of France into the ground. Her energetic, excitable, emotional manhood had been severely reduced in both numbers and ability. The remnant were listless and purposeless. Too many brothers and too many sons had been lost in the mass slaughter for France to feel pride or optimism. A mood of lethargy and hopelessness spread over a noble people. Fear of Germany was the only emotion capable of arousing passion. To this fear were sacrificed leadership and conciliation in postwar Europe. France looked only to her frontiers; her soul languished and her initiative was lost.

In Britain the same problem was reflected in a different way. The losses had themselves been terrible, but added to the numbers of

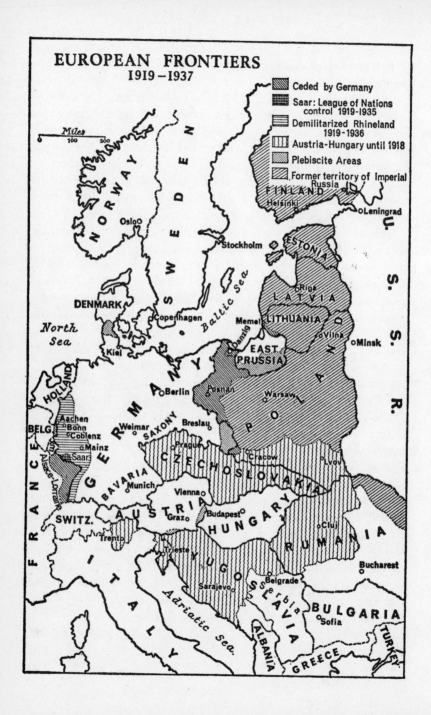

dead was the fact that for the first two years of the war military service had been voluntary. It was usual for the volunteers to be the bravest, most courageous, and most ambitious men, the potential politicians and civil servants, colonial administrators, and men of literature and learning. The volunteers flocked from the universities and private schools which up to 1914 had provided the leaders in all branches of English life. Men whose main talent was to write a sonnet or whose only experience of life had been in their school or college football team marched off to the trenches. The dead were the potential leaders of the nation. The survivors determined that never again should Britain be deprived of its "gilded youth."

The lesson of all this was a simple one: ignore Europe and leave the Continental nations to settle their problems among themselves. Some men argued that France had helped provoke war by her alliance with Russia, thus threatening Germany with "encirclement." Others argued that Germany, having been last in the race for colonies, had only sought to redress the unfavorable position of "inferiority" in which she languished.

Some Englishmen began to write as if Germany's attack on France and Belgium was only an accident; only a part of a more complicated movement in which guilt and innocence were merged and ill-defined. Had not Britain's great navy, built up with such fervor and diligence by Winston Churchill, been a direct threat to German power, a direct insult to German pride? Was it not right that Germany armed herself? Was it not right that Austria resented Russian patronage in the Balkans? Was it not right that Turkey sought to maintain the integrity and unity of her ramshackle empire? Had not Britain herself gone to war in 1854 in order to preserve Turkey against Russian ambitions? Had the Crimean War been an absurdity, that sixty years later the British should seek to destroy their old Turkish ally, at such desperate cost?

If the Crimean War could appear in retrospect as unnecessary, who dare say the "Great War" might not one day appear ridiculous and inexplicable? If particular wars seemed senseless, why should war itself not be rejected as a method of settling problems between civilized states? Had technical progress been effected solely to make war more terrible, with poison gas, the machine gun, the torpedo, and the bomb? Could not Britain harness her martial skills for peaceful improvements?

As a result of such questionings, which began while the Peace Conference was still in session in Paris, and continued with little abatement for twenty years, Englishmen began to draw away from Europe. They wished to avoid any future entanglement in causes which were not directly their own. They wished to avoid being tied to France and finding themselves once more at war with Germany in order to defend France. More urgently, after an outburst of anti-Germanism, they wished to avoid imposing a severe peace on Germany. They wished to see a Europe without strife: a dull, lethargic, contented Europe which they could then ignore.

If, however, Europe became excited; if, among its many states, particular problems were to arise threatening further war, Britain's role was clear. She would mediate, arbitrate, seek to calm the hot tempers and try to satisfy particular grievances as they arose. By the skill of her argument and the moral force of her neutrality she would bring peace. By her mature example she would modify even the harsh aspects of the peace treaties. As the English historian and politician H. A. L. Fisher, who was at Paris during the months of treaty-making, wrote: "The moral atmosphere in Paris isn't encouraging. All the small States out for more territory and France is not unnaturally in fear of a revived and vengeful Germany. My own view is that passion still runs too high to get a really enduring settlement now, but that if a Treaty *tel quel* is signed there will be an appeasement and by degrees readjustments and modifications can be introduced which will give Europe a prospect of stability."

Here we have the first mention of appeasement in its diplomatic sense: the introduction of fair-dealing among nations once tempers have cooled. In its origins it is among the noblest concepts of international relations. If properly pursued it could lead only to the spread of peace. But the nations of Europe neglected appeasement after 1918. They failed to see the need for it. They mistook it for weakness. But in reality it was strength.

At the Paris Peace Conference the French hoped to achieve security for all time against Germany. Yet they were convinced that Germany, with her much larger population, and with the stigma of so severe a defeat, would one day seek to reassert German dominance in Europe. The only solution France could see was severity. The French wished to set up an independent Rhineland state, to impose a heavy financial burden on Germany by demanding payment for all damage done in the war, and to obtain specific promises of support from Britain and America in the event of a German attack.

In all these aspirations France was foiled. Englishmen opposed the total crushing and humiliation of Germany, already so battered, already so reduced in power. France's fears appeared exaggerated; unworthy, said France's friends, of a great and magnanimous nation. But the French could not afford to listen to these cautionary words. The war had inflicted a wound upon their cheek that was still raw. They could not see the logic or need to distinguish between "security" and "revenge."

Being in this bellicose frame of mind, France considered America's idealism and Britain's moderation as stupidity. President Wilson hoped to make use of the disruption of Europe to build a more equable structure upon the ruins of the old. His "Four Principles," published before the end of the war, struck directly at the French hope of making an anti-German peace. The principles were as follows:

> *First,* that each part of the final settlement must be based upon the essential justice of that particular case and upon such adjustments as are most likely to bring a peace that will be permanent.
>
> *Second,* that peoples and provinces are not to be bartered about from sovereignty to sovereignty as if they were mere chattels and pawns in a game, even the great game, now forever discredited, of the balance of power; but that
>
> *Third,* every territorial settlement involved in this war must be made in the interest and for the benefit of the populations concerned, and not as a part of any mere adjustment of compromise of claims amongst rival States; and
>
> *Fourth,* that all well-defined national aspirations shall be accorded the utmost satisfaction that can be accorded them without introducing new or perpetuating old elements of discord and antagonism that would be likely in time to break the peace of Europe and consequently of the world.

Wilson stood for idealism; Lloyd George was more pragmatic. He argued that if Germany were treated as severely as France desired she would soon seek, and soon be able to obtain, revenge.

The Conference at Paris did not resolve the conflict of interests satisfactorily. It was conducted in an atmosphere of haste and rivalry which resulted in a raising of tempers and an unwillingness to listen too carefully to one another's arguments. The Allies began to bicker. The French were made to abandon their independent Rhineland state and accept instead a temporarily demilitarized Rhineland. They agreed also to an international reduction of armaments, even though they wanted the security which would be theirs with Germany totally disarmed and their own armies intact.

At almost every point France found her proposals blocked by her former allies. Her only achievement was the acceptance of reparations. Even then the amount was not fixed at the Paris Conference, but left to some future agreement. Thus France could not know if her demands, criticized by Britain as absurdly high, would ever be accepted. In the end they were not. One French achievement, later to cause much trouble, was the insertion of Article 231 into the Treaty of Versailles, intended as an explanation of why Germany must pay reparations. The article read:

> The Allied and Associated Governments affirm and Germany accepts the responsibility of Germany and her allies for causing all the loss and damage to which the Allied and Associated Governments and their nationals have been subjected as a consequence of the war imposed upon them by the aggression of Germany and her allies.

The Germans interpreted this article as implying that they alone were responsible for the war. Brockdorff-Rantzau, leader of the German delegation, refused to admit German guilt in this crude way. "Such an admission on my lips," he said, "would be a lie." Although the Germans signed the treaty, this particular imputation they resented and denied. Many Englishmen shared Germany's resentment and felt bitter that France had been allowed to go so far.

At the Paris Peace Conference Britain tried to act as a mediator. She had seen the reasons for French demands but denied that those demands would be effective. Britain regarded an irridentist Germany as the worst possible legacy the war could bestow and sought to forestall any German desire for revenge by making the treaty notable for its moderation and reasonableness. The Germans never fully recognized the efforts which Britain had made—often successfully—on their behalf.

Britain's political dominance had been sufficiently unharmed by the war for her to think in these terms. She was, perhaps, the only

European Power whose confidence in her own international status had not been tarnished. She could therefore look at Europe with a somewhat patronizing gaze and see herself as an impartial arbiter of European fortunes.

Germany, Russia, and Austria-Hungary felt no such confidence. These three empires had entered the war believing that war would enhance their power. Germany had wished to show France that she could tilt the balance of power away from the republic and towards the empire; Russia to show Germany that the eastern autocrat possessed all the dynamism and capabilities of his German cousin, the Kaiser; Austria-Hungary to show her German ally that she was an equal partner, not a cipher, and that she could exert her authority in the Balkans with effortless ease. With such thoughts drumming through their brains the three emperors sent their armies into battle. But when battle had ended the emperors were no more. Three dynasties had been destroyed. Three systems of government had been broken into irreparable fragments. The three European empires had vanished into the cordite-embittered air.

The war helped to weaken the power of privilege: the common man became the chief instrument of the progress or regress of the former empires. In Russia Vladimir Lenin showed that neither noble birth nor wealth was needed to succeed to the powers formerly wielded by an emperor. He and his fellow revolutionaries were sustained by the dynamism of their ideals, not by their origins. But enthusiasm could be perverted. By exploiting revolutionary zeal Lenin's successor, Stalin, tyrannized over those who did not see the benefits of the changes he proposed.

The common man began his rise to power as an orator, a pamphleteer, or a journalist. But he could use his success to create the very same armies, the very same police forces, and the very same spy systems with which his imperial predecessors had maintained their power at home and asserted their greatness abroad.

Thus, in Russia the serf's son, Stalin, in Italy the journalist Mussolini, in Germany the unsuccessful artist Hitler, became leaders of nations. These men grew like weeds upon the compost heaps of defeated Europe; like weeds they were parasites, rising to prominence only by destroying the goodness that was around them. In 1923 Corporal Hitler revealed some of the common man's respect for authorities and titles when he plotted to overthrow the state in company with Field-Marshal Erich von Ludendorff, former power behind the wartime imperial throne. But within ten years Hitler came into his own. By the time he was invited to become Chancellor of Germany in 1933 he had learned the lesson of self-reliance: the common man did not need high-titled supporters if he could command the applause of his fellow commoners. One generation trusted in emperors and aristocrats and gave its best blood on the battlefield: the next generation, in desperation or in the hope of something better, trusted in the "man of the people," the low-born demagogue, and found itself plunged into a second war in 1939.

In 1945 Europe was eclipsed. Other nations and other continents took upon themselves the business of world mastery and influence. The America which Europe had consistently and deliberately ignored; the China which she had sought to dominate; the Africa which she had partitioned and exploited; the Russia which had been cast out like a germ when it became Communist in 1917: these giants walked the world's path. Europe's pigmies were pushed aside.

The war of 1914-18 inaugurated the process of Europe's demise. The Peace Treaties of 1919 showed that the national antagonisms of imperial Europe could survive intact in the Europe of republics. These antagonisms shaped Europe's history for twenty years. If Britain's noble concept of appeasement had succeeded, it might have lessened the areas of conflict. But the British were slow to see the need for direct action on their part. They preferred to stand apart. When, in 1937 under Neville Chamberlain, they made an effort to mediate in Europe, it was too late. The dictators had turned aside from mediation; the grievances which they exploited had lain unsatisfied for too long.

# ☆ 10 ☆

## REPUBLICANISM AND REVOLT
## IN GERMANY

BEFORE 1914 Wilhelm II had ruled supreme. His Chancellors accepted the policies which he suggested and the Reichstag voted the financial credits which were needed for efficient government. The army was his personal instrument. It played no part in politics, except to encourage an adventurous foreign policy, or to come in, at the request of the Chancellor, as a strikebreaker.

In 1909 Bethmann-Hollweg became Chancellor. He was a civil servant and held few independent views. He allowed Wilhelm to pursue an adventurous and provocative foreign policy. When war broke out he was distressed, but remained in office. For the first two years of the war the Army was too busy seeking victory in the field to interfere in politics. The Kaiser took less and less interest in the conduct of domestic affairs. Bethmann-Hollweg ruled without interference, devising many schemes to please many people.

He sought to open an avenue of peace with Britain and France by offering to make peace on the basis of a German withdrawal from Belgium and northern France. But at the same time he promised German industrialists that he would support their claim for the annexation of industrially valuable territory in the west. He promised the Social Democrats that he would consider the possibility of Polish independence, but he also agreed with Prussian landowners that Germany's Polish provinces should not be given up. In this way Bethmann-Hollweg combined personal popularity with political inertia.

Bethmann-Hollweg was opposed to war with Britain and, being an honest man, told the Reichstag that he was unhappy about German violation of Belgian independence. In private he told a Berlin newspaper editor: "When one comes to the question of the responsibility for this war we must candidly admit that we have our share of it. To say that I am oppressed by this thought would be to say too little. The thought never leaves me. I live in it."

War cannot easily be conducted efficiently by those who doubt its moral correctness. Yet Wilhelm saw no need to remove Bethmann-Hollweg. In 1916 von Tirpitz, the Secretary of State for the Navy, obtained the support of the Chief of the General Staff for his proposal to begin unrestricted submarine warfare. Bethmann-Hollweg opposed this, partly because it would alienate the Americans, partly because he thought it immoral. Wilhelm supported Bethmann-Hollweg and Tirpitz resigned. Bethmann-Hollweg's position seemed unchallengeable. Though no "iron" Chancellor like Bismarck, he was conscientious and cautious. The fact that he was Chancellor when Germany went to war has made him seem, in retrospect, a wicked, unprincipled villain. This he never was. His only fault was docility.

In 1916 Germany's armies in both east and west were subjected to severe strain. Defeatists in Berlin spoke openly of a German collapse by the end of the year. Then, on 29 August 1916, Erich von Ludendorff, the hero of Tannenberg, became military dictator of Germany with Hindenburg as his nominal superior. It was a swift and bloodless revolution. Wilhelm accepted Ludendorff's argument that the war could only be won if a Hindenburg-Ludendorff coalition were in charge. Hindenburg was made Chief of Staff, Ludendorff General Quartermaster. Bethmann-Hollweg's authority was rapidly undermined. Sheltering easily beneath Hindenburg's respectability, Ludendorff took charge of policy-making. Wilhelm became a shadow, accepting the advice which Ludendorff offered.

Much of Ludendorff's activity benefited the war effort. On 5 December 1916 the so-called "Hindenburg Program" brought military leaders and trade unionists together and inaugurated a policy of forced labor for essential industrial enterprises. Every male between the ages of sixteen and sixty not in military service came under the direct control of the military authorities. He could be sent to whatever factory the supreme command desired to send him. Ludendorff insisted upon efficiency: Germany must put herself in a position to win the war.

The Hindenburg Program was put under the control of General Gröner, who for the first two years of the war had been in charge of the transport of troops by rail, an operation whose brilliant success had been instrumental in making possible many of the German victories.

Ludendorff did not rest at administrative reform. He wanted to alter the political structure in his favor. There was one obvious obstacle to his supremacy—the Chancellor with a conscience, Bethmann-Hollweg.

In July 1917 Ludendorff persuaded Wilhelm to dismiss Bethmann-Hollweg. Wilhelm asked Hindenburg, and thus Ludendorff, whom they would like to suggest for the Chancellorship. Although Wilhelm admitted that he did not know the man whose name was given him, the suggestion was naturally accepted. Throughout Germany men asked: "Who is Michaelis?" The answer was that on Monday he had been Food Controller of Prussia and that on Tuesday he became Imperial Chancellor. The appointment was made without the Reichstag party leaders being consulted. Thus Ludendorff ruled Germany. His political intrigues ensured control of domestic policies. His military plans ensured, or appeared to ensure, eventual victory and public acclamation.

An indication of the antiwar feeling against which Ludendorff fought was given on 6 July 1917. Matthias Erzberger, a Reichstag deputy and a leading member of the Catholic center party, made a speech in the Reichstag of great fervor and brilliance. He urged the Reichstag to denounce annexations and inaugurate immediate negotiations for peace. He gave a vivid portrayal of Germany's military weakness. Two weeks later, on 19 July, he proposed a "Peace Resolution" which was passed in the Reichstag by 212 to 126 votes. The resolution embodied his peace proposals of 6 July. The Chancellor, Michaelis, supported the resolution. But he was not Ludendorff's nominee for nothing. He gave his support to the resolution, but added a short proviso—"*as I interpret it.*" This was a severe blow to Erzberger's efforts. Michaelis wrote to the Kaiser's son in triumph: "The hateful resolution has been passed. . . . I have deprived it of its greatest danger by my 'interpretation.' One can, in fact, make any peace one likes, and still be in accord with the Resolution."

On paper this was plausible: by his qualification Michaelis certainly nullified the political force of the resolution. But the feeling which produced the resolution could not be destroyed so easily. In the summer of 1917 the International Socialist Congress, meeting in Stockholm, urged an immediate peace. On the last day of July, under the influence of the Congress, 400 sailors on the German battleship *König Albert* signed a Peace Proclamation which included the sentence, "we wish it to be known that we are in favor of a peace without annexations and reparations, and that we are therefore anxious for a conclusion of hostilities." Throughout 1918 the sailors organized antiwar groups. Throughout 1918 there were hunger strikes and mass walkouts in the fleet. Such revolutionary activity, though it resulted in neither bloodshed nor political repercussions, was symptomatic of a deep malaise in Germany.

The Russian withdrawal from the war, the Treaty of Brest-Litovsk in March 1918, and the Ludendorff offensive of May were the high points of German enthusiasm for the war and of Ludendorff's personal supremacy. Yet even amid these potential preludes to victory the rumblings of popular discontent were heard. On 28 January 1918 nearly half a million workers in Berlin went on strike, opposing the Hindenburg Program and demanding an early peace. On the following day the strike spread to every major German city. On 31 January, at Ludendorff's command, Berlin was declared in a state of siege. Strikers' meetings were dispersed by the police. Hundreds of strikers were arrested. Strikers who were members of the army reserve received their mobilization papers and were then ordered, as soldiers, to resume work. For a soldier to disobey was mutiny: the penalty for mutiny was death. The strikers resumed work.

These repressions were the actions of a victorious government; by September a German victory was no longer certain. The Ludendorff offensive was driven back. The arrival of American troops tilted the balance of men in favor of Britain and France. At the same time Germany's allies, Turkey, Bulgaria, and Austria-Hungary, were beaten to their knees.

On 29 September 1918 Wilhelm held a conference at Spa. Hindenburg and Ludendorff were present. So was Chancellor Hertling, who had replaced Michaelis at the end of 1917. Hindenburg announced categorically that the military situation was so bad that negotiations for an armistice should be begun at once. Hertling was so disgusted at this suggestion that he resigned. Ludendorff then handed back the executive power to the Reichstag. His political strength depended upon his military success. Only military setbacks could be expected now. Ludendorff drew aside. The new Chancellor, Prince Max von Baden, was told to request an armistice.

Prince Max opposed this, pointing out to Hindenburg that if Germany asked for an armistice it would be obvious that she recognized defeat, and this being so, the peace terms were bound to be severe. But Hindenburg and Ludendorff saw no sense in delaying the public announcement. On 3 October 1918 Hindenburg wrote to Prince Max von Baden: "The Supreme Command continues to hold to its demand expressed on September 29 of this year that a request for an armistice should be sent to our enemies immediately. As a result of the collapse on the Macedonian front, the consequent weakening of the reserves on our western front, and of the impossibility of making good the very severe losses which we have suffered in the last few days, there is, as far as it is humanly possible to judge, no further chance of forcing a peace on the enemy. Our adversaries are continually bringing up fresh reserves. The German army still stands firm and is successfully resisting all attacks. Nevertheless, the situation becomes daily more critical, and the Supreme Command may be forced to take very grave decisions. The circumstances call for a cessation of hostilities in order to spare the German nation and its allies needless sacrifices. Each day that is lost costs the lives of thousands of brave soldiers."

Prince Max was satisfied with such definite authorization. A higher authority, the highest in Germany, had ordered the same solution that many lower beings had long desired. The order was obeyed. Prince Max got in touch with President Wilson. Hindenburg and Ludendorff abdicated all control and with it all responsibility. On 26 October Prince Max, officially and with Wilhelm's approval, relieved Ludendorff of his post. Hindenburg remained as a cipher. President Wilson announced that he did not wish to negotiate an armistice while Wilhelm was still Emperor. With a curious unanimity the Reichstag deputies agreed that, if Wilson wanted Wilhelm's dismissal, Wilhelm must go. While Prince Max pondered on how to achieve this object a revolution broke out in the fleet. The admirals had planned a last attack on the English coast, unknown to the Emperor, Hindenburg, or the Reichstag. By such an attack they would have roused British anger and destroyed any chance of immediate peace negotiations. But the sailors rebelled against such plans. On 29 October the crews of two ships refused to obey orders. Six hundred sailors were arrested and imprisoned on shore. The mutiny spread. When an officer asked the sailors what they wanted they replied: "We want Erzberger." "Erzberger" was synonymous with "peace." By 4 November over 100,000 sailors had mutinied. They seized control of all the ships. The revolution spread to the shore: the sailors occupied Kiel.

On 7 November revolution broke out in Munich. Under the leadership of Kurt Eisner, a socialist, Bavaria was proclaimed a republic. On 9 November revolution broke out in Berlin. Socialists marched through the streets, demanding the setting up of a republic. Prince Max was alarmed. He could not consult the Emperor, who was at his military headquarters at Spa. He therefore took the initiative, as befits a liberal-minded prince in troubled times. He announced the Emperor's abdication. The Social Democrats then withdrew from Prince Max's Government. They demanded his resignation. The prince, wiser than many of his aristocratic colleagues, promptly accepted. He handed the Chancellorship to the Social Democrat leader, Ebert. Wilhelm's resignation, announced on speculation by the prince, was not confirmed by the Emperor himself for eleven days, by which time Wilhelm was an exile in Holland. But lack of confirmation could not deter the new rulers of Germany. And, with the Allied armies outside the gates and revolutions within them, there was much to be done.

Prince Max's last act as Chancellor before announcing Wilhelm's abdication was to send Erzberger to negotiate an armistice with the Allies. Prince Max feared that if a military man were sent the Allies might reject him. A Catholic civilian, he thought, would be more acceptable to them than a Prussian officer. Prince Max was right, but his prudence had bad results. It was put about that the civilians had stabbed the soldiers in the back by signing the armistice while the army was still prepared to fight. Erzberger's signature on the armistice document became "Exhibit No. 1" in the stab-in-the-back legend.

Erzberger left Germany on 7 November. Negotiations with the French and British began on the following day. Erzberger was able to obtain a number of important modifications in the Allied demands. But when, on 9 November, he asked whether he ought to hold out for further changes in Germany's favor Hindenburg telegraphed: "The armistice must be signed, even if these modifications cannot be obtained." It was the soldier, not the civilian, who wished to call a halt to the fighting, whatever the terms.

That same day, 9 November, Prince Max was succeeded by Ebert as Chancellor. Erzberger, isolated in the forest of Compiègne, did not know whether the new Chancellor would want him to sign the armistice. Ebert telegraphed late in the evening of 10 November, authorizing Erzberger to sign. His telegram was sent openly, not in code. It ended *"Reichskanzler Schluss."* Erzberger recorded the alarm which resulted: "The French interpreter asked if Schluss was the name of the new Chancellor and who this gentleman might be; he was completely unknown to both the French Supreme Command and the Government in Paris."

The French had been busy, before handing the telegram on to Erzberger, with enquiries about the mysterious Herr Schluss. Not knowing him, they feared that the worst had happened in Berlin. They were dealing with nonentities, possibly even with Bolsheviks. Fortunately Erzberger was finally asked his opinion, which he gave readily enough: "I enlightened him that *'Schluss'* at the end of a telegram meant 'Stop.'" After a further day of negotiations, in which Erzberger was successful in obtaining further modifications in the Allied terms, the armistice was signed on 11 November.

Before leaving Compiègne, Erzberger made a short speech of protest at the severity of the terms, ending with the words: "The German people, who stood steadfast against a world of enemies for fifty months, will preserve their freedom and unity no matter how great the external pressure. A nation of seventy millions can suffer, but it cannot die." To this Marshal Foch, the senior Allied negotiator, replied impassively, *"Très bien."*

In Berlin Ebert was obtaining support for his socialist government. Erzberger agreed to take office as Chairman of the Armistice Commission. To him fell the difficult, humiliating task of ensuring that the terms were carried out.

Ebert's Government was tolerated by all but the most extreme socialists. Riots in Berlin were constantly aimed at overthrowing the regime in favor of a communist one. Ebert took one precaution on becoming Chancellor which ensured the survival of his government. The military command, controlled since Ludendorff's withdrawal by

Gröner, enquired whether Ebert was willing to protect Germany from anarchy and to restore order. Yes, said Ebert, he was. Then, replied Gröner, Ebert would have the support of the Army. The Ebert-Gröner alliance was lasting and effective. As Gröner later put it: "The aim of our alliance was to combat the revolution without reservation, to reestablish lawful government, to lend this Government armed support."

Ebert needed the armed support which Gröner could offer. On 11 December the army returned to Berlin with standards flying and bands playing, as if victorious. Ebert addressed the soldiers from the Brandenburg Gate: "I salute you, who return unvanquished from the field of battle." With these majestic but inappropriate words the socialist Ebert cemented his military alliance.

On 23 December Ebert and his Cabinet found themselves besieged. The insurgents were a division of marines who demanded an increase of pay. The Spartacists, a revolutionary communist party led by Rosa Luxemburg and Karl Liebknecht, persuaded the marines to take direct action. They forced their way into the Chancellery and cut the telephone lines. But one line remained, a secret line which had connected the Chancellor with the Emperor. Ebert telephoned for rescue. At the other end the call was taken by Gröner's assistant installed in the Emperor's office. The Army promised immediate help. Actually the marines were persuaded to withdraw before the troops arrived. But Ebert had been given clear evidence that his pact with Gröner was effective. In return Ebert reconstructed his Government and excluded the extreme socialists. He also gave the Ministry of Defense to Gustav Noske, a right-wing Social Democrat who had been appointed by Prince Max to quell the Kiel mutiny. This he had done without bloodshed. Ebert gave Noske full powers to suppress any revolutionary activity. Gröner gave him a fully equipped, well-disciplined force of 4,000 men, the "Free Corps."

Ebert's socialist republican government was bitterly attacked by Rosa Luxemburg's Spartacists. "Socialism," she declared on 16 December, "does not mean getting together in a parliament and deciding on laws. For us socialism means the smashing of the ruling classes with all the brutality that the proletariat is able to develop." She resented the calm which Ebert and Gröner had achieved. For her the class struggle had yet to reach its final stage: civil war and the emergence of a victorious proletariat. She turned the Spartacists away from the idea of participating in the elections for the National Assembly, due to be held on 19 January 1919. She advocated instead a policy of strikes, street fighting, and eventual armed insurrection.

On 6 January 1919 the citizens of Berlin, walking through the center of the city, were bombarded with leaflets announcing that Ebert's Government had been overthrown and a revolutionary government of the proletariat established in the city. A number of public buildings had indeed been occupied by the Spartacists early that morning. A monster demonstration took place that afternoon. It was intended to be a peaceful one, indicative of the pacifist tradition of German left-wing socialism, but strangely out of keeping with the obligatory violence of Rosa Luxemburg's revolution. It marched with slogans chanted loudly, "Down with Ebert! Long live world revolution!" In the opposite direction came the Social Democrats, equally outspoken: "Down with Spartacus! Long live democracy!" The two demonstrations clashed. There was violence and confusion. The proletariat were divided.

For four days the Spartacists held control in central Berlin. Ebert entrusted Noske with the task of rooting them out. "Someone must become the bloodhound," said Noske. "I cannot evade the responsibility." He became Governor-General of Berlin and set up his headquarters in the suburb. For three days he drilled his troops. Then, on 10 January, he marched into Berlin. For three days there was bitter fighting and indiscriminate slaughter. The revolution was wiped out. Karl Liebknecht was shot. Rosa Luxemburg was arrested and beaten to death. Spasmodic fighting continued throughout February and March, when the remnant of the Spartacists were finally crushed. Ebert was horrified by Rosa Luxemburg's murder, describing it as "a disgrace to the German people." But further disgrace was yet in store.

The socialist Kurt Eisner, who had seized power in Bavaria in November 1918, was defeated in the local elections of 2 February 1919. Unlike most dictators he accepted the logic of his electoral defeat. On 20 February he told his Cabinet that he would announce his and his government's resignation on the following day. On his way to the Parliament building to do so Eisner was assassinated. His murderer was an aristocratic student who resented Eisner's republican socialism. As a result of Eisner's death fighting broke out in the streets of Munich. Every political party tried to seize power. Success went to the communists who, on 7 April, proclaimed the Soviet Republic of Bavaria. The aim of the communists was to act as a spearhead for world revolution. On 30 April Noske's Free Corps entered the city. For a week there was terrible slaughter, accompanied by all the abnormalities of civil war: the shooting of hostages, the ill-treatment of prisoners, and executions without trial. The Soviet Republic of Bavaria was destroyed. Its leaders were shot or imprisoned. Brutality had become the hallmark of peacetime Germany.

The elections of January 1919 did not favor Ebert's socialists. It was the middle-class and Catholic parties that received a majority of the votes. There was a strong right-wing bloc. As Berlin was still the scene of sporadic violence, Ebert decided to avoid the risk of meeting within sight of the revolutionary mob. The National Assembly therefore met (on 6 February) in Weimar, guarded by Noske's troops.

The Weimar Assembly elected Ebert President of Germany. A system of coalition governments came into being, the first three Chancellors being Social Democrats. The number of other parties represented in their cabinets increased with each administration. By June 1920 the Social Democrats' ability to form governments was lost. The only other government led by a Social Democrat was in office from 1928 to 1930. During the period of socialist governments peace was signed at Versailles. It was a bitter moment for Germany. Right-wing newspapers appeared with black bands of mourning on their front page. Socialist editorials were equally outspoken. Many people swore never to fulfill the terms of the treaty.

The Weimar Assembly proceeded to more acceptable activities. On 14 August 1919 it agreed to a Constitution, which ended the uneasy relationship between Berlin and the German states by increasing the powers of the central government. It vested control over the army in the central government. It introduced votes for women before either Britain or France. It declared boldly: "The German Reich is a republic. Political authority is derived from the people."

Article 61 of the final draft of the Constitution foreshadowed the swift union of Germany and Austria. It gave representatives from Austria a voice in all discussions before union was finalized. Once united with Germany, Austrians were to have seats in equal proportion to Germans. But the Allies had stated at Versailles that Germany and Austria were not to be united and the Germans had signed the Versailles Treaty. They were therefore made to strike Article 61 from their Constitution. Otherwise there was no outside interference. The Constitution provided for many generations of democratic rule. Unfortunately one Article, 48, granted dictatorial powers to the President and Chancellor in emergency. By using these powers Hindenburg, who succeeded Ebert as President in 1925, was able to give absolute power to three chancellors from 1931 to 1933. The last of those privileged chancellors was Adolf Hitler.

The early years of the Weimar Republic were marred by many tragedies. There was an attempt by a military group to seize power in Berlin in March 1920. Fortunately the *Putsch* was ill-organized. While Berlin was in the hands of the insurgents all the pessimists forecast the immediate collapse of Weimar. But the *Putsch* petered out and the troops which had taken part in it were allowed to leave Berlin unmolested. As they passed the Brandenburg Gate the last few files turned back and fired into the crowd which thronged behind them, hooting and laughing. Many of the crowd were killed. The troops then marched away singing.

In 1919 Erzberger became Minister of Finance. As the man whose pen had signed the armistice he was treated with contempt by the right-wing parties. His financial reforms were successful. He reduced the financial independence of states. He gave Germany a unified, efficient railway system which by 1923 was making a profit and by 1924 playing a significant part in the payment of reparations. He introduced a series of drastic taxes, on war profits, inheritance, land transfer, and tobacco. He brought into operation the first centralized income tax and abolished all provincial and local taxes. Although the actual value of Erzberger's taxes was reduced almost to nothing by the inflation of 1921 and the subsequent collapse of the value of the mark, the centralization of taxes which he introduced remained a permanent and beneficial feature of the economy. The confusion of each state having its own tax scales, its own leniencies, and its own methods of collection was ended. Erzberger brought financial discipline to Germany.

But economic achievements could not spare Erzberger from the odium of the supposed "stab in the back." On 26 August 1921, while on holiday in Bavaria, he was assassinated. His murderers were two young officers. Their crime was condoned by the right-

wing press. "Erzberger," wrote one paper, "has suffered the fate
which the vast majority of patriotic Germans have desired for him.
. . . He was alone responsible for the humiliating armistice." The
news of Erzberger's murder was met with glee and applause, as if
the humiliation of the armistice could be wiped out by the death of
the man who had signed it. Yet five years later the Germans elected
Hindenburg President. It was he who had urged Erzberger to sign,
whatever the conditions. This the public did not know, but the public is rarely in a position to know its own immediate history. For this
reason its judgment is often awry.

The major problem confronting the Weimar Government abroad
was the payment of reparations. Initially the German attitude had
been extremely truculent. It was considered patriotic not to pay
taxes, since a portion of those taxes would go towards reparation
payments.

Germany had two good friends in postwar Europe: Lloyd George
and Aristide Briand. When, in January 1922, the Germans announced that they would be unable to meet their reparation payments for January and February, Lloyd George and Briand agreed to
a conference at Cannes to work out some new method of reparation
payments. The German delegation was led by Walther Rathenau,
who during the war had been responsible for introducing cohesion
and discipline into Germany's economic planning.

Rathenau believed that the Treaty of Versailles should be
fulfilled. He also believed that the Allies could be persuaded to modify the reparations clauses if they could be given evidence of the
absurdity of severe reparations. By his own skill at argument
Rathenau set about trying to persuade Lloyd George and Briand that
reparations should be modified. Lloyd George was impressed by
Rathenau and listened sympathetically to his views.

The French, who saw their security threatened every time modifications in the treaty were suggested, were afraid that Briand would
be outargued by Rathenau and outmaneuvered by Lloyd George.
During the Cannes conference Briand was therefore turned out of
office, and the burden of preventing changes beneficial to Germany
fell upon the shoulders of the new Premier, Raymond Poincaré. As
soon as Briand left Cannes, Poincaré made it clear that he regarded
compromise as weakness. If America had not dissociated herself
from Europe in 1919 and if she had been willing to sit on the Repa-

rations Commission to mediate between Britain's leniency and France's harshness, German claims might well have been met. The absence of America from the councils of Europe in 1922 prevented justice being done to the German point of view. No one felt this more keenly than Lloyd George. As a result of America's withdrawal from the Reparations Commission, he wrote, "the most interested party is in the chair, with a casting vote. That was not the treaty signed by Germany." Lloyd George wished to help Germany. He regarded Briand as a worthy partner in a policy of leniency and moderation. But with Poincaré he sensed an inflexible opponent. "Arguments," he wrote, "reinforced by irrefutable facts and figures were as fruitless with M. Poincaré as a shower on the Sahara." So Lloyd George returned to London and Rathenau to Berlin unsatisfied.

On his return from Cannes Rathenau was made Minister of Foreign Affairs. He was persuaded by his colleagues to accept the Rapallo Treaty with the Soviet Union in April 1922, in which both countries renounced reparation claims. This treaty, though sparing Germany a further reparations claim and opening up trade relations with a nation that could provide Germany with much that was denied her by the West, alienated Poincaré entirely.

Rathenau still urged a policy of full reparations payments. He wanted to avoid the danger of independent French action, which Poincaré threatened, by proving Germany's sincerity. As he told the Reichstag: "We Germans are obliged by our signature, by the honor of our name that we have affixed to the treaties. We will fulfill and we will go to the limits of our ability in order to preserve the honor of our name. . . . We recognize the binding character of the treaties even if they do not express our wishes."

Rathenau was certainly a patriot. But he was also a Jew. For the nationalists the Jew was the lowest form of life, responsible for all that was evil, the enemy of all that was good. Rathenau was attacked in the Reichstag as if he were an alien. And in the streets men sang:

> Knock off Walther Rathenau,
> The dirty, god-damned Jewish sow.

On 24 June 1922, while driving to the Foreign Ministry, Rathenau was assassinated. His murderers had overtaken his car. One shot at him with a machine gun, the other threw a grenade onto the seat. Rathenau was killed instantly. His murderers were eventually found and committed suicide. The Nazis later erected a monument on their grave.

Rathenau's cruel death did not silence his critics or lessen the popularity of anti-Semitism. As one general wrote in retrospect: "The nomination of this ethnic alien," had constituted "a sharp challenge to those Germans mindful of their race."

The foreign policy of fulfillment did not die with Rathenau. It was carried on by Gustav Stresemann, who, as Chancellor in 1923 and Foreign Secretary from 1923 to 1929, negotiated the admission of Germany to the League of Nations and the Locarno Pact, by which France and Germany guaranteed to each other the permanence of their common frontiers. Stresemann's task was a difficult one. He had to face French hostility abroad and nationalist abuse at home. He came to power when France had occupied the Ruhr in protest against nonpayment of reparations. He persuaded the Germans to accept the payments and the French to withdraw. He then negotiated two agreements under which France agreed to lower the scale of payments. Stresemann was fortunate that Poincaré had gone and Briand returned to power. At the same time a Labour government in England, with Ramsay MacDonald as both Prime Minister and Foreign Secretary, carried on the work which Lloyd George had initiated of treating Germany fairly. Even the Conservative Foreign Secretary, Austen Chamberlain, under whose guidance Locarno was concluded, took a sympathetic view of German aspirations which many of his more bellicose supporters regarded with alarm. The friendship of Briand, MacDonald, and Austen Chamberlain towards the enemy of five years earlier is a tribute to European statesmanship. To Europe's detriment, men with such vision and wisdom were lacking in the decade after 1933. Nor did the Germans find other men of the quality of Erzberger, Rathenau, and Stresemann. Their minds were swayed by lesser men and the example of the postwar leaders was forgotten.

The postwar violence in Germany lasted too long. The assassination of prominent figures, followed by a chorus of approval, made murder respectable. It became commonplace for street demonstrations to be accompanied by bloodshed. It became normal to abuse the Jews. These grotesque aspects of German life were accentuated by the French occupation of the Ruhr in January 1923: a clumsy attempt by France to enforce reparations payments. At the Krupp works in Essen, French troops turned a machine gun on the protesting crowd, killing thirteen. Nine people were killed when a bomb exploded in a train. As a reprisal the French sentenced seven "conspirators" to death. The Germans responded by a campaign of passive resistance: workers left the factories, shops closed, transport was brought to a standstill. Resistance continued for eight months. Germany's economic existence was threatened by the paralyzed Ruhr. Stresemann, on becoming Chancellor in September 1923, called an end to passive resistance. The French withdrew from the Ruhr. But Germany had a grievance which Stresemann's *rapprochement* with France at Locarno could not obliterate. Diplomatic compromises brought calm to the foreign ministries of Europe, but in the minds of men the storm still raged.

Immediate repercussions in Germany to this French humiliation were a semi-communist rebellion in Saxony and a military coup in Bavaria. The Saxon communist ministers were persuaded to resign by the appearance of government troops with fixed bayonets outside all government offices. But Stresemann was less certain of how to suppress the military insurrection in Bavaria. He waited, and his task was done for him by a "counterrevolutionary" plot.

The leader of the military coup called a meeting in Munich on 8 November 1923. The meeting was interrupted by a small man in a gray raincoat jumping on a chair, firing a pistol and crying out "The national revolution has begun." This little man was the leader of an extremist group with strong anti-Semitic tendencies. He had won the support of Germany's wartime dictator, Ludendorff, for his "counter-revolution." He planned to seize Munich and march on Berlin. On 9 November he and Ludendorff set out at the head of their supporters to the center of Munich. They were met by a line of well-disciplined police. They were ordered to halt but refused to do so. The police opened fire and the little man fell to the ground. Fourteen of the insurgents were killed. Ludendorff, oblivious of the noise and bloodshed around him, marched on into the square. He and the little man were arrested. Their rebellion came to nothing. The little man was sent to prison, given by sympathetic judges a lenient punishment for his treason: six months' detention. His name was Adolf Hitler. He was not the last man of violence to attempt to seize power in 1923 —separatists proclaimed governments in Aachen, Bonn, Coblenz, and Mainz in October. But these absurdities were suppressed forever by Stresemann. Hitler's absurdity was not so easily obliterated.

# ☆ 11 ☆

## THE TRIUMPH OF
## COMMUNISM IN RUSSIA

LENIN and the Bolsheviks seized power in Petrograd in October 1917. They at once withdrew Russia from the European war. They announced the victory of the Russian proletariat and urged the workers of the whole world to rise up in arms and seize power from their capitalist overlords. This appeal failed, despite brief revolutionary outbreaks in Austria and Germany, and a more serious if ultimately unsuccessful revolution in Hungary.[1] The world's workers continued to serve in their national armies or to work in munition factories at home. There was much disaffection, war weariness, industrial unrest, and even mutiny. But there was no revolution.[2] Only in Russia, through Lenin's opportunism and Trotsky's superb organization, did revolutionaries come to power. But it was one thing to seize power in Petrograd, quite another to assert authority throughout Russia.

Kerensky's troops were marching on Petrograd and Trotsky found it difficult to raise enough soldiers to stop him. It seemed as if it would be just as easy for Kerensky to return to power as it had been to remove him. Trotsky's soldiers were unwilling to risk their lives. They had supported the revolution in order to end war, not

[1] The Hungarian communists, led by Bela Kun, were in power in Hungary for just under a year. Their own butchery was answered with equal ferocity by their right-wing opponents, who drove them from power. Bela Kun went to Moscow, where he was finally murdered during Stalin's purges.

[2] Trotsky was so certain that every European country would soon have its communist revolution that, on accepting the post of Foreign Minister in October 1917, he said: "I shall publish a few revolutionary proclamations and then close shop."

prolong it. Trotsky sought a leader who could rouse them to action. No Bolsheviks had the experience of leading troops. Trotsky therefore accepted an offer of help from a tsarist officer, who was known only by the zeal with which he had suppressed the Bolsheviks during Kerensky's rule. This was hardly a good recommendation for a revolutionary leader, but Colonel Walden bore a grudge against Kerensky. He thus served the revolution well. Kerensky's troops were defeated on the outskirts of Petrograd.

In Moscow the Bolsheviks seized power after much bloodshed. Elsewhere in Russia Bolshevik groups took over local government. They were watched uneasily by the old order. If the Bolsheviks in Petrograd could consolidate power, the Bolsheviks elsewhere might be accepted. If the Bolsheviks failed at the center, those in the provinces would be swept away. The old tsarist autocracy survived on obedience—to an individual, the tsar, the Father of Holy Russia, the great benefactor and protector of his people. Now the tsar had abdicated and that particular loyalty had snapped. The other aspect of obedience was not personal but institutional. Obedience went to whoever held power. If the Bolsheviks could show that their power was real, then the obedience due to autocratic institutions could fall, as by inheritance, to them.

The most serious threat to Bolshevik dominance came from a rival revolutionary party, the Social Revolutionaries, who held the allegiance of the peasantry. The Social Revolutionaries had dominated the Petrograd Soviet, the "parliament" of left-wing parties, which, before the revolution, existed as a radical pressure group alongside the Provisional Government. After coming to power Lenin paid lip service to the Social Revolutionaries and to the summoning of the proposed Constituent Assembly on which they were insisting. He went so far as to say: "Even if the peasants should return a Social Revolutionary majority to the Constituent Assembly we shall say, so be it."

There was a chance that the Social Revolutionaries really would receive a majority. They gained support in the towns by attacking various unpopular Bolshevik policies, including the complete press censorship which Lenin had instituted. The peasants, by tradition, voted for the Social Revolutionaries, knowing their politics and personalities better than they knew those of the Bolsheviks.

The election for the Constituent Assembly took place at the end of November 1917. Enthusiasm for Bolshevik rule was waning. At the same time the Bolsheviks were not powerful enough to browbeat the electorate or to imprison their opponents for the duration of the election. The result was that the Bolsheviks, who won under a third of the votes, could only form a majority if they united with the Social Revolutionaries. This was compromise, not revolution. Lenin finally acted by accusing one of the small anti-Bolshevik parties of plotting counterrevolution. Their delegates were arrested. Reelections were held, but gave little extra strength to the Bolsheviks.

The Constituent Assembly opened on 18 January 1918. The Bolsheviks proposed a motion limiting the legislative powers of the Assembly. The motion was angrily rejected by a vote of 237 to 136. The Bolsheviks were outvoted; the moment of crisis had come.

Lenin called a meeting of his stalwart supporters. There was some reluctance to resort to force. But Lenin overcame the scruples of his more idealistic followers. One of them, who spoke of the danger of "socialist banners reddened with proletarian blood" was shouted down. Lenin proceeded with his plan. As the delegates arrived at the Assembly on the second morning they found the building surrounded by soldiers. The delegates were not allowed to enter; the Assembly was at an end. A mass demonstration of workers marched through the streets, demanding the reopening of the Assembly. The demonstration was broken up by the soldiers with some casualties. Both the Assembly and its supporters were dispersed by the threat of force.

Bolshevism now ruled by the strength of its fist. The very reassertion of its authority in closing the Assembly rallied to its side many who earlier doubted its strength. But with the burial of the last slim hope for constitutional government in Russia it is well to remind ourselves of the distribution of votes in the Assembly, Russia's last elected body not overshadowed by coercion or fraud. The Bolsheviks had 10,000,000 votes, their opponents 31,000,000.

Trotsky conducted Bolshevik foreign policy with skill and vigor. It soon became clear that, contrary to Allied suspicions, the Bolsheviks were not mere German agents sabotaging the Allied war effort by withdrawing Russia from the war. They had policies and ideas of their own. By the end of November Trotsky had published, for the world to see, Russia's secret wartime treaties and the tsarist plans to occupy Constantinople and dominate the Balkans. Within a month of becoming Foreign Minister he spoke scornfully of "the routine-ridden mind of bourgeois Europe." This hardly improved matters with the Allied ambassadors in Petrograd. Yet they sensed the justice of Russia's antiwar position. When the British arrested Russians in England for making antiwar propaganda, Trotsky at once retaliated by arresting those Englishmen who were urging Russia to remain in the war. The British Ambassador noted in his diary: "There is, after all, something in Trotsky's argument that, if we claim the right to arrest Russians for making pacifist propaganda in a country bent on continuing the war, he has an equal right to arrest British subjects who are conducting war propaganda in a country bent on peace." Such was the logic of a diplomat on the spot. But when Russia withdrew from the war Britain and France were in a dangerously exposed position. They had lost their eastern ally. The whole weight of Germany's army could be turned against them. The Germans could take advantage of Russian weakness to seize vital materials: vast quantities of Allied military aid which had been sent to Russia during the days of the alliance. This valuable material was now lost to the Allied effort. There seemed only one hope for the anti-German nations—the defeat of the Bolsheviks and their replacement by a prowar regime. To this end Allied diplomacy began to work.

The first intervention on Russian soil was hardly aggressive. But it brought foreign troops to Russia and provided a focal point for anti-Bolshevik activity. Allied troops landed at Vladivostok, Murmansk, and Archangel, in order to guard the large military supplies. At the same time a large body of Czech soldiers, who had come to Russia during the war as prisoners, and decided to join in the fight against Austria, were ordered by the Bolsheviks to demobilize. Austria and Germany had ordered the Bolsheviks to disarm them at Brest-Litovsk fearing that they would attack Germany from the east. The Czechs refused to give themselves up. They feared that they would be extradited to Germany if they did so. Being militarily strong they took the initiative and seized Samara on the Volga; they then joined forces with General Kolchak, leader of a Russian anti-Bolshevik army. This well-armed coalition moved rapidly towards Ekaterinberg, where the Tsar and his family were imprisoned. The Bolsheviks, fearful lest the Tsar should gain his freedom and lead an

# The CIVIL WAR
## in RUSSIA

Advance of the anti-Bolshevik armies 1918-1920

Annexed by Turkey

Annexed by Rumania

Pre revolutionary Russia Independent from 1918

Miles
0   100   200   300

SWEDEN

Murmansk

FINLAND

Kronstadt

Archangel

R U S S I A

Gulf of Bothnia

Baltic Sea

ESTONIA

Riga

LATVIA

LITH.

Petrograd

Ekaterinburg

Volga

Moscow

Kazan

POLAND

Warsaw

Minsk

WHITE RUSSIA

Orel

Samara

Volga

Kiev

U K R A I N E

Don

Tsaritsin

RUMANIA

BESSARABIA

Odessa

CRIMEA

Rostov

Novorossisk

Astrakhan

BULG.

Black  Sea

Caucacus Mts

Tiflis

Constantinople

Batum

GEORGIA

AZERBAIJAN

oil fields

Baku

Kars

ARMENIA

T U R K E Y

PERSIA

1. Norman Angell. Before 1914 he insisted war would not pay, even for the victors. The world was skeptical. In 1933 he won the Nobel Prize for peace.

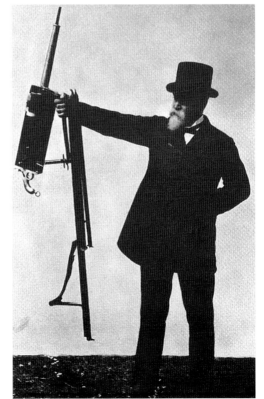

2. Hiram Maxim. His quick-firing, automatic gun was originally intended for use against natives, not against Europeans.

3. Winston Churchill (*far right*), Kruger's prisoner in 1899. His spectacular escape made him a hero in England, and in 1900 he was elected to Parliament.

4. Paul Kruger, Boer President who, in 1899, challenged the British to a war he could not win.

5. Leopold of the Belgians. His Congo atrocities provoked European anger, and he was forced to give up his vast and lucrative empire.

6. King Leopold's private life intrigued cartoonists. No European monarch was so frequently or so savagely cartooned.

7. David Lloyd George and Winston Churchill in 1910. Lloyd George became Prime Minister in the First, Churchill in the Second, World War. Yet both spent long and lonely years in the political wilderness.

8. Ignace Paderewski, famous pianist who became President of the new Poland in 1918.

9. (*below*) Georges Clemenceau, Woodrow Wilson, and Lloyd George. They joined forces to defeat Germany. In Paris in 1919 they redrew the map of Europe.

10. (*above left*) Matthias Erzberger. He negotiated the armistice for Germany.  11. (*above right*) Friedrich Ebert. First President of the Weimar Republic. His two sons were killed in the First World War, yet his republican Government was regarded by many Germans as anti-patriotic.

12. (*below left*) Rosa Luxemburg. Revolutionary Jewess, murdered while trying to seize power in Berlin in 1918.  13. (*below right*) Wilhelm Groener. A general who cooperated with socialists and thus preserved the Weimer Republic from revolution.

14. Leon Trotsky. The Red Army was his creation.

15. Vladimir Lenin. He returned from a Swiss exile to lead the revolution in 1917.

16. Joseph Stalin. The first act of the future autocrat was to sign Finland's independence.

17. Pierre Laval. He wanted
smooth relations with France's
enemies.

18. (*top right*) Léon Blum, France's
first socialist Prime Minister.

19. Raymond Poincaré. He feared
a Germany strong enough to
make war again.

anti-Bolshevik crusade, murdered him and his family. By this act Bolshevism was utterly discredited in the eyes of Europe. Kolchak and the Czechs occupied Ekaterinberg and swept on to Kazan and Samara on the Volga. In Moscow an attempt was made to assassinate Lenin, who was severely wounded. A prominent Bolshevik leader was murdered in Petrograd. As a reprisal 500 people were shot. On 6 August 1918 the Bolsheviks withdrew behind the Volga. Trotsky hurried towards the front, issuing a strident warning: "No quarter will be given to the enemies of the people, the agents of foreign imperialism, the mercenaries of the bourgeoisie. ... The Soviet Republic will also punish its sluggish and criminal servants no less severely than its enemies. ... The Republic is in peril! Woe to those who directly or indirectly aggravate the peril."

Under Trotsky's energetic leadership battle was joined. The Bolsheviks, or "Reds," pushed the anti-Bolshevik "Whites" away from the Volga. Commissars were attached to each regiment to provide political leadership. Trotsky himself kept close control of every action and fell harshly upon all who wavered. In one regiment the commander obtained the approval of the commissar to retreat. Trotsky ordered them both to be shot. "I issue this warning," he announced, "if any detachment retreats without orders, the first to be shot will be the commissar, the next the commander." Such ruthlessness was effective. Those who had argued most strongly for peace in 1917 were forced to resort to war to preserve their revolution. Trotsky's victory on the Volga proved that the Republic could defend itself. It gave a stimulus to the Bolshevik troops. It taught the "Whites" that it would not be easy to overthrow Bolshevism.

While Trotsky built up the Red Army, the anti-Bolshevik forces also gathered strength. The British occupied the oil fields of the Caucasus as well as the northern ports of Murmansk and Archangel. The French occupied Odessa. An Allied blockade deprived the Bolsheviks of all food supplies or arms from abroad—a further step in their attempt to overthrow Bolshevism altogether. In the Caucasus another "White" general, Denikin, was building an army to join with Kolchak. In August 1918 Japanese and American troops joined the British in Vladivostok. The Bolsheviks had no power east of the Urals, except in Omsk. In November 1918 Kolchak assumed the position of "Supreme Ruler" of Russia, and the British helped him organize his army. On 18 November he seized Omsk. A popular Siberian song described his army: "Uniform British, boot French, bayonet Japanese, ruler in Omsk." The western Allies and Japan had become the shields behind which the "Whites" gathered.

At this tense moment President Wilson suggested a peace conference between the Bolshevik and anti-Bolshevik leaders, under Allied supervision. Lenin, realizing the desperate condition of his regime, agreed. But the anti-Bolsheviks answered Wilson scornfully: "Moral considerations do not permit us to confer on an equal basis with traitors, murderers, and robbers." The conference, planned for February 1919, did not take place. This obstinacy did the "Whites" no harm. The French promised to continue to support them despite their refusal to contemplate compromise. The armies of Kolchak and Denikin pressed in upon the Bolsheviks.[3] The civil war was brutal and demoralizing.

The Bolsheviks murdered their prisoners; the "Whites" gained popular support by setting their followers against the Jews. The fact that many of the Bolshevik leaders were Jewish gave a new excuse for an old evil. A further enemy challenged both armies, typhus, against which Red commissars and White cavalry were equally impotent. Lenin, almost desperate now for a compromise, asked the Americans in March 1919 to put forward further peace proposals. Lenin was prepared to allow Kolchak his Siberian kingdom, Denikin the Crimea, and northern Russia a separate state ruled from Archangel in return for the Petrograd-Moscow-Astrakhan area remaining under Bolshevik rule.

Unfortunately the Americans received this offer at the very moment when the advance of Kolchak's army towards Astrakhan gave the "Whites" a new incentive to continue the war until the destruction of Bolshevism. At the same time the communist revolution in Hungary, although short-lived, reminded the Allies that communism was not an ordinary manifestation of nationalism, but a concept of world-wide revolution and a call for the overthrow of all bourgeois governments. Lenin's offer was therefore ignored. On the map his position looked hopeless. By the autumn he and his regime might well have ceased to exist.

---

[3] Winston Churchill, the British Government's most ardent supporter of intervention, summarized British aid to Denikin as follows: "A quarter million rifles, two hundred guns, thirty tanks, and large masses of munitions and equipment."

Yet dissension among the "White" forces and a growing lack of enthusiasm among the Allied interventionists favored the Bolsheviks. In the autumn of 1919 the Red Army, which Trotsky had molded into an efficient fighting force, took the offensive. The "Whites" were in a wide circle. The Red Army, pushed thus in a compact mass, could strike from Moscow at every sector of the anti-Bolshevik front. In the winter of 1919-20 Kolchak's army collapsed. In January 1920 he abdicated in favor of General Denikin. In February he was captured by the Bolsheviks and shot.

In May 1919 Denikin advanced, supported by the French at Odessa, into Kiev. His advance was marked by anti-Jewish violence which nauseated his western supporters and rallied most Jews to Bolshevism. The local population welcomed the opportunity to loot Jewish shops and attack Jewish women. Naturally, if this was what Denikin allowed them, he could rely on their wholehearted support. A Kiev writer gave a contemporary account of the pogroms: "A dreadful medieval spirit moves in the streets of Kiev at night. In the general stillness and emptiness of the streets a heartrending cry suddenly breaks out. It is the cry of the Jews, a cry of fear. In the darkness of the street appears a group of armed men. At this sight large five- and six-floor houses begin to shriek from top to bottom. Whole streets, seized with mortal anguish, scream with inhuman voices."

The anti-Bolshevik forces in western Russia gained their greatest successes in September 1919, when they pressed in upon Petrograd. One general, being offered field glasses in order to see the city, declined them. "Tomorrow," he said, "I will be walking along the boulevards." Trotsky dispelled the general's dream. With the counter-attack of the Red Army on 21 October 1919 the cause of anti-Bolshevism was doomed. In November the Bolsheviks captured Orel, thus saving Moscow from the danger of a breakthrough from the south. During the winter Denikin was driven back to Rostov. Typhus spread through his armies. The peasants, their land ravished by civil war, could yield no more food. The townsmen could find no more enthusiasm for war. The Jews prepared to welcome the Bolsheviks as their liberators. The Allies admitted that Bolshevism could not be overthrown, and lost interest in the anti-Bolshevik cause. On 16 January 1920 the Allied blockade was abandoned. On 25 February Denikin's army was shattered outside Rostov. The Bolsheviks swept forward, driving him to the sea at Novorossisk and capturing

22,000 prisoners. Denikin resigned his position as Commander-in-Chief of the defeated White Army. His successor held out in the Crimea. But the "Whites" could no longer take the offensive. In November 1920 they were finally defeated.

Once the Great War had ended, in November 1918, the drive behind the Allied intervention weakened. It then ceased to matter whether Allied supply dumps remained on Russian soil, as there was no German army left to take advantage of them. Before the war ended the intervention was not entirely aimed at crushing Bolshevism. In Murmansk the Bolsheviks had at one moment actually joined forces with the British interventionists in order to prepare against an expected German attack through Finland.

With Germany no longer the enemy, the interventionists transferred their support to the "Whites." But whereas the interventionists were primarily defensive, and numerically small, the "Whites" were aggressive, and did not appreciate the importance of these small rearguard pockets of Englishmen and Frenchmen. Before the "Whites" had been finally defeated the interventionists withdrew. A few extremists in Britain and France wanted to inaugurate a full-scale war against the Bolshevik regime, but were overruled.

The "Whites" failed, not because the interventionists neglected them, but because they represented the old, discredited ruling class, the men who had gone to war in 1914, the men who ill-treated their subordinates and were intolerant of criticism. These gray, unpleasant men found it hard to pose as crusaders. For many Russians Bolshevism was something new, invigorating, and constructive: the Russia of the future. Bolshevism was also the existing power, the overthrow of which would involve continual civil war and the ravaging of the countryside. The "Whites" were willing to accept this price; the Russian peasant was not. He wanted peace. Lenin had given him peace in 1917. He did not want a Kolchak or a Denikin to take it away from him.

In April 1920 the Poles, who were anxious to take the Ukraine from Russia and build up a Polish super-state in central Europe, invaded Russia and seized Kiev, the Ukrainian capital. Trotsky at once appealed to the Red Army to strike a blow against the Poles "which would resound in the streets of Warsaw and throughout the world." It was no longer a question of Russians fighting Russians to decide the internal form of government; this new war was a war of national defense, to protect Russia against the hereditary enemy, a former subject people, the "pestiferous Poles."

The Polish invasion rallied the anti-Bolsheviks to Trotsky's banner. General Brusilov, the last great tsarist Commander-in-Chief, placed his services at Trotsky's command. The Red Army was transformed into a national army. It swept forward into the Ukraine. Polish behavior had alienated the occupied territories; Polish landlords had been reestablished in their former properties, prisoners of war were shot, anti-Jewish pogroms were encouraged. Trotsky forbade retaliation. In a stern order-of-the-day he said: "Let the hand be cut off any Red Army man who lifts his knife on a prisoner of war, on the disarmed, the sick, or the wounded."

On 12 June 1920 the Red Army entered Kiev. It moved westwards to the Polish frontier. At the frontier Trotsky called a halt and urged Lenin to accept a British offer of mediation between Poland and Russia. Lenin refused; he rejected all ideas of British mediation and ordered Trotsky to advance into Poland. For Lenin, Poland was nothing but an obstacle between his own Russian revolution and world revolution. If the Red Army could cross Poland and appear on the German border it would, he argued, act as a signal to the German revolutionaries to seize power in Berlin. Trotsky disagreed. Poland, he said, would never allow Russia to pass through so easily. The Poles had been under Russian rule for over a century; they had been independent for only two years. They were not likely to welcome a new Russian army, however anxious that army might be to press on to Berlin.

The Red Army advanced towards Warsaw. But, as Trotsky realized, its presence was resented by the Polish workers and peasants. Appeals to working-class solidarity did not impress them: the poorest peasant was a Polish patriot; the most persuasive commissar was an odious conqueror.

On 13 August 1920 the Red Army reached a town fifteen miles from Warsaw. They pressed towards the capital. But after four days of intense fighting they were driven back. The world revolution was thrown on the defensive. Trotsky, who had deprecated the whole venture, refused to go to the front in order to rally the troops. He saw no sense in attempting aggression westwards. He knew that all Russia's skill was needed to repair the ravages of civil war and to build up a communist society. He refused to waste men and materials in revolutionary ventures that were bound sooner or later to provoke a further intervention from Britain and France.

The Poles took the initiative and advanced deep into Russian territory. On 12 October 1920 Russia signed a provisional peace with Poland. The Russian generals urged Lenin to undertake a new offensive but Trotsky demanded peace. Only after Trotsky threatened to appeal to the Communist Party against Lenin did his view prevail. At the Treaty of Riga in March 1921 the Russians accepted an extension of Polish sovereignty in White Russia, while maintaining their own control over most of the Ukraine.

Peace came to Russia in 1921. The last of the "Whites" had been driven out of the Crimea and the Polish-Russian frontier had been fixed by treaty. It was seven years since peace had last graced Russia with her presence. Those seven years had drained resources and weakened morale. With peace came weariness, not rejoicing; a desire to sleep rather than the energy to create a new society.

Yet Russian society in 1921 was in a state of chaos. The Bolsheviks, under the pressure of war and civil war, had instituted a policy of "war communism" which had destroyed the old *laissez faire* economy and put in its place the requisitioning by the state of all food supplies and the prohibition of private trade. This rough action was not intended as the inauguration of an egalitarian society, but as an emergency measure to help Russia survive the terrible dislocation of war. But "war communism" could not combat the famine which followed in the wake of war, nor could the officials who put "war communism" into practice eliminate the vast black market which ensured the continuance of private trade and crippled the efforts of the state to centralize supply and distribution. The very attempt to introduce discipline and cohesion in the national economy led only to anarchy. The famine became so severe that Lenin appealed to Europe and America for help, which was sent on a vast scale. The complex and ill-thought-out "war communism" was abandoned. Under the "New Economic Policy" the small trader and the peasant became their own masters again.

Economically, communism was put on one side. Politically, it was severely challenged. A Workers' Opposition Party gained strength by defending the trade unions against communist encroachment. In March 1921 there was a naval rebellion at Kronstadt. The cry "Down with Bolshevik tyranny!" echoed throughout Russia. Trotsky hurried to Petrograd to quell the rising. He failed; his promise of mercy for those sailors who surrendered was howled down. The rebels were crushed only by fighting whose violence equaled the worst excesses of the civil war. The only coherent program the sailors formulated was for free elections. This the communists could not allow. The New Economic Policy gave too much freedom already, according to communist ideology, to bourgeois merchants and property-loving peasants. Politically no such leniency could be allowed. The Bolsheviks had no intention of being outvoted. "We might have a two-party system," one of them remarked, "but one of the two parties would be in office and the other in prison."

Trotsky took the lead in challenging the Workers' Opposition Party. The Communist Party, he urged, should "substitute" itself for the working class. The party should take over all the responsibilities, the very thought process, of organized labor. The party should decide, through its own wisdom and experience, what policies were best for the people. Before the Revolution Trotsky had himself predicted how this process would end when he wrote: "The party organization would first substitute itself for the party as a whole; then the Central Committee would replace the party organization; and finally a single dictator would impose his own will upon the Central Committee." But it was on neither Lenin nor Trotsky that the mantle finally fell.

For the theological seminary in Tiflis, high in the Caucasus mountains, the late nineteenth century was a time of troubles. In 1886 an expelled student assassinated the principal and the seminary was closed for two months. Six years later there was further unrest when the students went on strike and demanded the removal of several monks. Again the seminary was closed; eighty-seven pupils were expelled. Among the new intake of 1894 was the fifteen-year-old son of a former serf, turned shoemaker. This young man wrote poems and read Victor Hugo's novels. The monks sought to tighten religious discipline and intensify religious instruction, but they could not compete with the influence of the books in the cheap lending library in Tiflis. The young man was frequently caught reading forbidden books. "Today," wrote one of the monks in November 1896, "I confiscated Victor Hugo's *Toilers of the Sea.*" The principal commented: "Confine him to the punishment cell for a prolonged period. I have already warned him once about reading an unsanctioned book." But the punishment had no effect, nor were the teachings of pious monks able to draw the student away from his clandestine reading. In 1898 his behavior grew worse. The monks noted that he "is generally disrespectful and rude towards persons in authority." On 29 May 1899 he was expelled. Five years of religious instruction had failed; aged twenty, he was educated, discontented and unemployed. He joined the socialist underground movement, became a Bolshevik, and came to Lenin's attention as one of the few convinced Bolsheviks in the Caucasus. He represented Caucasian Bolshevism at conferences in Finland (then a province of Russia) and in Sweden. He visited London in 1907 for the Social Democratic Congress. He organized a great strike in Baku. He was arrested, imprisoned, and banished from the Caucasus. He changed his name as frequently as his abode. In 1913 he went to Vienna, to write on Lenin's suggestion an essay on the "Problem of Nationalities." He signed it, for want of a better name, "Stalin," or "man of steel." On his return to Russia he was again arrested and banished to Siberia.

After the February Revolution in 1917 Stalin returned to Petrograd from Siberia. Lenin was still an exile in Switzerland. Stalin took over the editorship of the Bolshevik newspaper, *Pravda*. For three weeks, until Lenin returned, Stalin wrote about the coming revolution. He expressed doubt about the need to overthrow the Provisional Government. After three years of exile and isolation it is not surprising that he was uncertain of the party line. As soon as Lenin returned Stalin rallied to the slogan "All Power to the Soviets." He remained editor of *Pravda*. His loyalty to Lenin was impressive. But he was overshadowed by the fiery Trotsky, who, in July 1917, joined the Bolsheviks.

During the October Revolution Stalin was in the background, loyal, but not a leader. The seizure of power was unexpected; most of the names of the revolutionary government which were read out on 7 November 1917 were unknown to those that heard them. It is doubtful if many people knew who Stalin was when his name was announced as "Chairman of the Commissariat for Nationalities." Stalin went rapidly to work, his Ministry a single room with a small desk. Within a week he was in Helsinki, granting the province of Finland its full independence. The decree giving Finland independence was signed jointly by Lenin and Stalin. Thus the "man of steel" first came into prominence as a liberator; the benefactor of small nations struggling to be free.

Stalin was at once attacked for his liberal policy. His critics pointed out that it was the bourgeoisie of Finland, not its proletariat, who benefited from Russian magnanimity. Now all the provinces of Russia were demanding independence. Yet they were all strongly anti-Bolshevik. Stalin had to admit that he was wielding a rope with which he could hang the revolution.

In January 1918 Stalin announced that self-determination ought to be "subordinated to the principles of socialism." But he also advocated a federal structure for the new Russian state, the most important result of which was the establishment of a federal Ukraine under Christian Rakovsky, the Balkan Social Democrat leader who had come to Russia in 1917 and was a zealous advocate of federal autonomy.

During the civil war Stalin became a political commissar, supervising the activities of the southern Bolshevik army. When the attempt on Lenin's life was made Stalin reported that he and the commander of the southern army, "having learned about the wicked attempt of capitalist hirelings on the life of the greatest revolutionary . . . answer this base attack with the organization of open and systematic mass terror against the bourgeoisie and its agents." Thus, under the stress of civil war, the liberator of nationalities became the persecutor of opponents. He also began to fight against his rivals. On one of Trotsky's army orders he wrote: "To be disregarded."

After the civil war, to whose prosecution he had devoted great energy, Stalin returned to his Commissariat for Nationalities. His native Georgia had declared its independence in 1918, supported by Britain, which sent a diplomatic representative to Tiflis. Its independence was a serious blow to Russia, which needed Georgian mineral resources. Tsarist Russia had received two-thirds of its oil from the Caucasus. In 1920 the communists captured Baku on the Caspian Sea. Stalin sent his own envoy to Tiflis and occupied Armenia and Azerbaijan. Georgia was surrounded. In November 1920 Stalin addressed his fellow-countrymen thus: "Georgia, which has entangled itself in the snares of the Entente . . . Georgia, which has transformed itself into a principal base of imperialist operations . . . this Georgia completes now the last days of her life."

Lenin, who was seriously ill after a stroke, tried to oppose the invasion of Georgia. The Georgian Government was regarded with respect by the western nations, whom Lenin, now the civil war was over, wished to placate. At the same time, he knew that the Georgian communist movement was weak and unpopular. He did not relish incorporating into Russia people unappreciative of communist practice and hostile to communist ideas. Trotsky supported him. But Stalin, though unauthorized to do so, went ahead with his plans, engineered a rising on the Georgian border and launched a full-scale attack on Tiflis. Lenin ordered the immediate cessation of hostilities. Stalin ignored him. When Tiflis was occupied Lenin gave way. Against his wishes communist Russia had extended its borders. The leading members of the Georgian Government, who had appealed in vain to the West for help, boarded an Italian steamer at Batum and sailed across the Black Sea to Constantinople and exile.

It was not as Commissar for Nationalities that Stalin had been able to flout Lenin's wishes. That post was intrinsically a subordinate one.[4] But on 3 April 1922 he had been appointed General Secretary of the Central Committee of the Communist Party, a position superficially bureaucratic, but enabling him to control more and more of the party's business. In creating the post of General Secretary Lenin sought only to reduce the muddle and inefficiency which had grown up as a result of the complexity and proliferation of party organizations. He did not foresee the day when the General Secretary would, by his very ability to coordinate diverse activities and adjudicate between conflicting bodies, become not only indispensable but omnipotent. Stalin slowly, unostentatiously and with caution increased his personal power. In an overcentralized government he made himself the center. He supervised the "cleaning out," or purging, of politically hostile officials. He ensured that loyal supporters filled important posts. He cared nothing for public acclaim. He worked in silence and secrecy. He worked his way into every activity of the state. Trotsky, after his magnificent efforts during the civil war, allowed himself to be pushed aside. In May 1922 Lenin suffered his second stroke and for three months was a total invalid.

It was while Lenin was ill Stalin had taken the initiative in the conquest of Georgia. Although Lenin acquiesced in the final annexa-

---

[4] Even so he had been in charge politically, through this seemingly peripheral post, of 65,000,000 people—just under half the total population of Russia.

tion he had not been silent about what he regarded as a rash and ill-conceived project. "I think," he wrote on 30 December 1922, "the hastiness and administrative impulsiveness of Stalin has played a fatal role." On 4 January 1923 Lenin was even more outspoken in the postscript to his will: "Stalin is too rude, and this fault . . . becomes unbearable in the office of General Secretary. Therefore I propose to the comrades to find a way to remove Stalin from that position and appoint to it another man . . . more patient, more loyal, more polite, and more attentive to comrades, less capricious. . . ."

Lenin prepared a public criticism of Stalin. He published an attack, in *Pravda,* on one of the organizations which Stalin controlled. He said it was guilty of "ridiculous swank." Stalin managed to postpone the appearance of this article for a month, but on 4 March 1923 it appeared in print. Five days later Lenin had a third stroke. He was almost completely paralyzed. Though he lived on for ten months he was unable to affect policy. He had failed to oust Stalin from his position of power. Stalin was able to persuade Trotsky that Lenin's criticism of his Georgian policy should remain unpublished. Lenin's influence was dead; his opinions were pushed aside.

In April 1923 the Twelfth Party Congress assembled in Moscow. Stalin was anxious to achieve an important measure of centralization by the establishment of a Union of Soviet Socialist Republics. The republics in this union, if Stalin had his way, would take their orders from Moscow. The federal structure of Russia, which gave each state a large measure of autonomy, and of which he himself had earlier approved, would disappear. Now, having subjugated Georgia and avoided Lenin's open censure, he prepared to break away altogether from "national self-determination," the ideal of his younger days. Stalin insisted upon the need to subordinate nationalist considerations to political ones. Centralization, he claimed, was the essence of communism. Nationalism, leading to fragmentation, was bad doctrine.

Stalin was in a strong position from the theoretical standpoint. His opponents therefore challenged him on practical grounds. They pointed out that in the borderlands Russians had been given preference over local nationals. One delegate cited the case of the Red Army: "The Army still remains a weapon of Russification . . . of all the minority peoples." The dominance of the central government over schools and higher education was criticized equally severely.

Stalin answered these questions of detail by an appeal to the need for overall discipline. The party members, well drilled by the General Secretariat which Stalin controlled, applauded his call for centralization. But one delegate was determined to criticize the whole concept of the proposed Union of Soviet Socialist Republics. He was Christian Rakovsky, head of the Ukrainian Government.

Rakovsky had entered into the federal concept of government with zeal and imagination. He had conducted a Ukrainian foreign policy and sent Ukrainian consuls to Berlin, Vienna, and Prague. He had conducted negotiations and signed treaties with neighboring capitalist states. Internally he had resisted the encroachments of the General Secretariat, and inspired loyalty to Kiev rather than Moscow. Rakovsky pointed out that it was the bureaucratic state apparatus, not the independent-minded federal governments, which went against Leninist teaching. It was the central authority, bristling with demands and armed with privileges which formed "an aristocratic and bourgeois remnant, anointed with Communist oil." By dominating the minority nationalities, Rakovsky argued, the central machinery was advancing the supremacy of Russians over Ukrainians, Georgians, and others, who had a right to unfettered, representational sharing of Soviet economic and political life.

Rakovsky challenged Stalin, but the General Secretary had not built up his party apparatus to be outwitted by an intellectual, a man, Stalin sneered, more at home in Paris than Kiev. Rakovsky proposed an amendment to Stalin's Union Constitution, hoping to restrict the representation of any republic, including the central republic, to two-fifths of the whole. Stalin mocked at this proposal as "administrative fetishism." Rakovsky was voted down. On 6 July 1923 the Union of the Soviet Socialist Republics was approved. The Soviet Union was henceforth to be ruled from Moscow. And in Moscow Stalin was supreme.

In November 1923, with Lenin still alive but unable to play any part in events, Trotsky proposed a relaxation of government pressure. He argued that as communism was firmly established, minority criticisms should be heard. He also insisted that greater frankness on behalf of the government would arouse greater enthusiasm for what it was doing. Coercion, he claimed, could not remain forever the basis of state control. Trotsky appealed to the youth, pointing out that revolutionary "old guards" frequently degenerated into bureaucrats. Stalin quoted Lenin's precept that communism's greatest enemy was faction within party ranks. The cult of Leninism was thus born. On 21 January 1924 Lenin died.

Stalin used Lenin's death to build up his power still further. Trotsky was ill in the Caucasus. In Gorky, where Lenin had died, and in Moscow, to which his body was brought, Stalin organized an elaborate ceremony. For four days Lenin lay in state in Moscow, Stalin standing in the guard of honor at the bier.

Five days after Lenin's death Stalin read out an oath of allegiance which was deeply religious in its phraseology and mystical in its implications:

"In leaving us, Comrade Lenin ordained us to hold high and keep pure the great title of member of the party. We vow to thee, Comrade Lenin, that we shall honorably fulfill this thy commandment. . . .

"In leaving us, Comrade Lenin ordained us to guard the unity of our party like the apple of our eye. We vow to thee, Comrade Lenin, that we shall fulfill honorably this thy commandment, too. . . .

"In leaving us, Comrade Lenin ordained us to guard and strengthen the dictatorship of the proletariat. We vow to thee, Comrade Lenin, that without sparing our strength we shall honorably fulfill this thy commandment, too. . . .

"In leaving us, Comrade Lenin ordained us to strengthen with all our might the alliance of workers and peasants. We vow to thee, Comrade Lenin, that we shall fulfill honorably this thy commandment, too. . . .

"In leaving us, Comrade Lenin ordained us to strengthen and broaden the Union of the Republics. We vow to thee, Comrade Lenin, that we shall honorably fulfill this thy commandment, too. . . ."

After these religious incantations Stalin organized an elaborate funeral. Despite the protests of Lenin's widow and of leading Bolsheviks, Lenin's body was embalmed and then deposited in a mausoleum in Moscow's Red Square, under the Kremlin walls, where it has remained to this day.[5] As Isaac Deutscher, Stalin's biographer,

[5] Stalin, who joined Lenin in the Mausoleum after his death in 1953, was removed from the public view ten years later, after Nikita Khrushchev, his successor, had attacked the "cult of personality" in general and Stalinism in particular.

has written: "To myriads of peasants, whose religious instincts were repressed under the revolution, the Mausoleum soon became a place of pilgrimage, the queer Mecca of an atheistic creed, which needed a prophet and saints, a holy sepulcher and icons. Just as original Christianity, as it was spreading into pagan countries, absorbed elements of pagan beliefs and rites and blended with them its own ideas, so now Marxism, the product of western European thought, was absorbing elements of the Byzantine tradition, so deeply ingrained in Russia, and of the Greek Orthodox style. The process was inevitable. The abstract tenets of Marxism could only exist, in their purity, in the brains of intellectual revolutionaries, especially those who had lived as exiles in western Europe. Now, after the doctrine had really been transplanted to Russia and come to dominate the outlook of a great nation, it could not but, in its turn, assimilate itself to that nation's spiritual climate, to its traditions, customs, and habits."

Stalin outmaneuvered all his opponents. Rakovsky was sent from the Ukraine as Soviet Ambassador to London, then to Paris. Trotsky was discredited in 1925 when Stalin won party support for his own slogan, "Socialism in one country," as against Trotsky's pre-1917 thesis, "permanent revolution." Stalin appealed to both national pride and the desire for security with his advocacy of "socialism in one country." Trotsky's "permanent revolution" sounded too much like an incentive to further war. No one in that war-weary land wanted to challenge further the capitalist West; Stalin played on the people's fears. The Russian revolution, he claimed, was self-sufficient. It needed no external allies. It needed no spectacular foreign conquests.

In 1925 Stalin forced Trotsky to resign from the Commissariat of War. Trotsky's only means of saving himself was to use the army to seize power. This he would not do: his loyalty to the Revolution was deeper than his hatred of Stalin.

Slowly Stalin edged the other Bolsheviks out of positions of power. In 1926 he expelled Trotsky from the Government.

In 1927 Trotsky made a serious attempt to offer an alternative to Stalinism. Stalin's Government, he said, lacked foresight, efficiency, and ability. If danger ever threatened Russia, he would offer himself as an alternative ruler and raise the nation from its present lethargy to the needed efficiency. On the tenth anniversary of the Revolution,

7 November 1927, Trotsky led his followers through the streets of Moscow carrying banners. He was at once expelled from the Communist Party. Rakovsky hurried back from France and at the Party Congress in December pleaded with the delegates for the need of an opposition party. He was howled down. He rose again arguing brilliantly in favor of criticism as an incentive to good government. Stalin could stand no more: "Enough, comrades," he shouted, "an end must be put to this game." Trotsky was deported to Alma Ata, Rakovsky to Astrakhan. Stalin's other critics capitulated. The voices of reason, caution, experience, and wisdom were silenced. For the next twenty-five years Russia lay in a darkness, imposed by an autocracy which offered the alternatives of obedience or death.

Between 1936 and 1939 all of Stalin's leading opponents were put to death, with the exception of the sick and aged Rakovsky who was sentenced to twenty years' hard labor, and Trotsky himself, an exile in Mexico, who was assassinated on Stalin's orders in 1940. Inside Russia Stalin built up a complex and efficient police state, controlling not only all political opinion, but also all artistic activity, academic study, and association between individuals. In 1939 he supervised the writing of a history of the Communist Party in which his own revolutionary role was given absolute prominence, and everything Trotsky had done interpreted as a crime. Having glorified Lenin in 1924, he proceeded to glorify himself under the slogan "Stalin is the Lenin of today."

Russia's internal problems and her ambition to be the spearhead of world revolution both handicapped her foreign policy in the years immediately following 1917. The near success of the Allied intervention created profound Russian bitterness against Britain, France, and Japan. The severe terms demanded by Germany at Brest-Litovsk gave a hint of German ambitions in the East. Russia had no friends. She suspected all her neighbors of designs upon her integrity. Her neighbors feared an excess of revolutionary zeal which might put an end to their own independence.

In the 1920s Russia needed trade and therefore sought international recognition. Her first tentative agreement was with Germany at Rapallo in 1922. In 1923 Rakovsky persuaded Britain to recognize Russia. Then he moved on to Paris where he obtained French recognition for Russia in 1925. Stalin ceased to encourage the Com-

munist International, or Comintern, whose declared aim was world
revolution, and whose base and inspiration was Moscow.

With the triumph of his "Socialism in one country" policy Stalin
withdrew from European diplomatic activity. Western hostility to
Bolshevism proved too strong to enable constructive diplomatic con-
tacts to be established. Russia, like America, lapsed into isolation.
Few Europeans visited Russia. Almost the only Russians to reach
Europe were refugees from Stalinist oppression.

Far Eastern events were Russia's greatest incentive to enter into
diplomatic relations with Europe in the 1930s. Ever since Japan had
defeated Russia in 1905 she had represented a potential danger to
Russian sovereignty east of the Urals, the more so after her active
part in the intervention. When Japan occupied Manchuria in 1931
Soviet fears were revived. In 1937 Japan invaded China. Although
Chinese resistance continued for eight years, much of China was occupied. Japan's advance was a constant threat to Russia. Only by
security on her European frontier could she hope to maintain
enough strength in the Far East to counter a Japanese invasion. She
could not face a war on two fronts.

When, therefore, Mussolini began to disturb the peace of Europe
in 1935, Russia was anxious to join Britain and France in a system
of mutual security. When, in 1936, the Italians gave military help to
General Franco, who was attempting to overthrow the Spanish Republican Government, Stalin intervened by sending military aid to
the Republic. Britain and France were alarmed; it seemed to them
that international communism was on the move again. They wanted
to confine the Spanish civil war to Spain, and although they failed to
stop Italian aid going to General Franco's forces, they applied a self-
denying ordinance, nonintervention, to themselves, and wanted Russia likewise to stand aside. The Russians refused to do so, and regarded British and French reluctance to be involved as insincere. It
seemed to Russia to be hypocritical of the West not to come to the
aid of the Republic.

In 1937 German rearmament gained momentum. In March 1938
Austria was annexed to Germany. The Russians at once proposed
further pacts of mutual defense. Britain and France were hostile to
these proposals. They disliked Russia's continuing support for the
now almost defeated Spanish Republic; they regarded the purges in
Russia as a sign of evil no less pronounced than Nazi evil; they did

not trust Stalin, and were unwilling to rest their security system upon his pledges.

When Germany threatened Czechoslovakia in the autumn of 1938 Russia again offered to join France and Britain in defending Czechoslovakia. She even hinted at being willing to defend Czechoslovakia alone. Britain and France preferred to settle the matter with Germany direct. They did not welcome the appearance of Russia in their inner councils. Russia, on being disregarded, began to suspect that Britain and France wished to encourage a German-Russian war. Why else, they asked, did Germany open trade negotiations with Britain? Was this not a cover for deep political plots? Suspicion of double-dealing had become commonplace in Soviet domestic affairs. Stalin projected it into international relations.

In March 1939 Germany occupied Prague. Stalin was afraid that Russia would soon be threatened. He asked Britain for an alliance. His request was abruptly turned down. Instead, Britain allied herself with Poland, Russia's enemy. When negotiations finally began for an Anglo-Russian agreement it was Poland who sabotaged them, by refusing to allow Russian troops to cross Polish territory for the purpose of attacking Germany. Stalin suspected that Britain only paid attention to Polish demands because she didn't want an agreement with Russia. The British suspected that Russia only wanted agreement in order to enable her to advance her frontiers westwards and regain the territory lost at Brest-Litovsk. Mutual suspicion gave Hitler his chance. He planned the invasion of Poland knowing that Britain and Russia would not combine against him. Stalin, motivated more perhaps by panic than by calculation, decided to make what terms he could with Germany, and at the end of August 1939 signed a nonaggression pact with Germany. As a result, Hitler invaded Poland without fear of Russian retaliation;[6] as a result, Britain and France fought Germany without the benefit of an Eastern ally. France fell and Britain was isolated. Only Germany's stupidity in invading Russia in 1941 forced Russia into the war as the ally of Britain and France.

[6] Russia received a reward for her nonintervention. She was allowed to occupy the eastern part of Poland.

# MUSSOLINI
# AND ITALIAN FASCISM

ITALY BETWEEN THE WARS was an unhappy land. Despite the beauty of its landscape, the antiquity of its culture, and the grace of its cities it knew neither security nor contentment. The violence in Europe after the first war can be traced to many causes: in Germany, to the shame of defeat; in Russia, to the aftermath of revolution. But Italy was a victorious nation in 1918 and though torn by civil strife was spared the savage disruption of revolutionary upheaval.

Italy's weakness was that she was a young nation. Although her civilization was old and magnificent, her institutions were new and inexperienced. Before 1860 Italy had consisted of many kingdoms, ruled primarily by a landed aristocracy whose interest in social reform and liberal political institutions was small. Italy was a quarrelsome collection of separate states; nationhood a concept known mainly to her poets and revolutionaries. The geographic unit consisted of political fragments. Venice was ruled by Austria until 1866, Rome by the Pope until 1870; Piedmont was powerful in the north, Naples proud and independent in the south.

Politically, Italy was united by Count Camillo di Cavour, who became Prime Minister of Piedmont in 1852. Piedmont was his model for a united Italy: ecclesiastical immunities in courts of law were curtailed; liberals from other parts of Italy were encouraged to settle there; industrial credits were granted to new industries; railways were extended and a system of canal irrigation begun. All this encouraged foreign investors. But it antagonized the more conservative Piedmontese politicians. Liberalism inspired idealists, but, however sincere they might be, they were always a minority. Cavour opposed measures which would create too deep a gulf between conservatives and reformers. He looked askance upon the expedition of the guerrilla leader Garibaldi's expedition to Sicily; he gave no immediate help and was openly skeptical of Garibaldi's chances of conquest. When Garibaldi entered Naples, Cavour sent a counterexpedition into the Papal States; then he advanced southwards and forced Garibaldi to give up Naples and Sicily, which Cavour united with Piedmont. Thus, by a defensive measure, Italy was unified. Garibaldi had taken the initiative, Cavour the advantage.

In 1866 Italy allied with Prussia to defeat Austria, and conquered Venice. In 1870 Rome was captured and the temporal power of the Pope annulled. The Pope became a prisoner in the Vatican. To his disgust a Protestant church was built in Rome in 1873, a masonic temple two years later. Rome became Italy's capital, even though it was a divided city. But this capital in the middle of Italy could not hide the division between the industrious, politically adventurous north and the conservative, indolent south. Not even the king could create enthusiasm for a united policy.

In the fifty-five years between Italy's achievement of unity and her entry into the Great War, domestic politics were troubled and imperial adventures fraught with difficulty. The King had little influence over policy, Parliament lacked independence, a skillful Prime Minister could determine the distribution of votes by deployment of his patronage, opposition voters were often arrested on the eve of elections, and on occasion criminals were released from prison to vote for the official candidate. Those who were government employees, including schoolmasters, university teachers, magistrates, and railwaymen, could be threatened with dismissal or removal to an inhospitable region if their politics were contrary to those of the Government.

Once in Parliament, a deputy, who received no official payment, could find himself rapidly drawn into some financial swindle. So strong did vested interests become that in 1895 men who represented companies receiving government contracts were made ineligible for election.

There was no political cohesion among the deputies. Groups, each with its particular leader, vied with one another for positions in new ministries. The basis of an administration was seldom if ever political principle. The ability to accommodate as many groups as possible in one's ministry was the mark of a successful politician. In seventy-four years sixty-seven ministries held office. This was not conducive to good government. A rhetorical style and demagogic content pervaded the debates. Calm judgment and mature expression were rare and ill-rewarded virtues.

Italy was potentially a great imperial power. Of all the modern states which bordered upon the Mediterranean she was certainly the most exposed to, and reliant on, the sea. Her marine frontier was 4,100 miles long, and vulnerable; her land frontier 1,290 miles long, and guarded by high mountains. The dictates of geography were an incentive for empire-building.

Unfortunately for Italy, Italian ambitions in the Mediterranean were forestalled in 1882 when Britain occupied Egypt, and France took Tunisia. Under the pressure of damaged pride Italian politicians pointed to the Red Sea as the best area for imperial adventure. It was an ill-chosen area, as dangerous politically as it was unhealthy climatically. Conflict with Ethiopia led to war, and the establishment of Eritrea as an Italian colony. This success spurred Italy to further conquests, her aim the subjugation of Ethiopia. "Italy," said Bismarck, "has a large appetite but poor teeth." He was right: in 1895 the Ethiopians defeated the Italians at Adowa; 6,000 Italians were killed in a single day and the conquest of Ethiopia had to be abandoned. Italy appeared ridiculous to imperial Europe.

The British victory over the Boers in 1902 revived Italian interest in Africa. The success of the Young Turks in overturning the corrupt government at Constantinople in 1909 aroused fears that the Turkish Empire would revitalize itself. Part of its territory, Libya, was coveted by Italian imperialists. Economic penetration, begun seriously in 1905, might easily be halted by a vigorous Turkish Government. Italians noticed with alarm that the new Turkey preferred to give its best contracts to German rather than Italian firms. In 1911 French troops entered Morocco. Italy was in danger of losing any chance of a foothold on the North African coast. In October 1911 she therefore declared war on Libya and in November annexed Libya by royal decree. But the war went on despite the decree and for over a year the Turks held out, depleting Italian strength and depressing those who dreamed of rapid conquest. To hasten their victory the Italians resorted to aerial bombardment, a new form of warfare. But on a population of desert dwellers bombs were of little practical effect. Atrocities by Italian soldiers were given wide publicity in Europe and the slow tempo of conquest made the Italian action look rather absurd in the eyes of Europe. When, in 1912, the Turks agreed to cede Libya, a large Italian payment into the Turkish treasury looked too much like an indemnity for Italians to feel that Turkey had really been beaten. Nevertheless, the conquest of Libya revived national pride, so seriously damaged at Adowa, and under the impetus of the new conquest a ministry of colonies was established. Rejoicing and boasting helped to hide the fact that emigrants found more opportunities in French Morocco and America than in the new colony. By 1928 only 2,800 Italians had settled in Libya. Besides being a colony almost without colonists it was badly administered and starved of funds by a government with no money to spare from its always impecunious treasury.

In 1914 Italy remained neutral. Although Austria was her ally the relations between the two countries were strained. There were so many Italians living under Austrian or Hungarian rule that Italy sought an opportunity to go against Austria: a war of liberation. In September 1914 a group of Futurists, artistic extremists who believed in the nobility of war, interrupted a performance of a Puccini opera in Rome in order to burn an Austrian flag on the stage. War, they said, would rejuvenate the Italian spirit, as well as freeing Italians from alien rule. These views were echoed by people in all walks of life, including the socialists. They received encouragement from Britain with whom, on 26 April 1915, Italy concluded a secret treaty.

The Treaty of London is worthy of close inspection. In 1914 the nations of Europe went to war on impulse. None formulated specific war aims. All liked to think that their actions were primarily defensive. All denied territorial ambitions. With Italy it was different. In the Treaty of London she revealed her interest. She was promised a fair share in any distribution of German colonies after the war and was promised a territorial settlement in the Tyrol and along the Dalmatian coast strongly in her favor. In return she agreed to make war on Austria within a month of signing the treaty.

The war went badly for Italy. Towards the end of 1917 the army was defeated by the Austrians at Caporetto. With the collapse of Germany and Austria-Hungary in 1918 Italy found herself among the victors. But the price of victory was high; the country was impoverished and downcast. Caporetto was an even greater disaster than Adowa. At the Peace Conference Italy found her Dalmatian claims eaten into, despite the Treaty of London, by the counterclaims of a new state, the Union of Serbs, Croats, and Slovenes (later Yugoslavia) which was favored by the Americans as an example of national self-determination. In Africa Britain took Germany's colonies for herself; in the Near East she shared them with France. Though Italy made small territorial advances along her eastern border, they neither elated nor satisfied the Italian spirit.

Postwar Italy was a breeding ground of discontent. More than a hundred and fifty thousand deserters from the army roamed the countryside, hiding from the authorities and living by charity and brigandage. Demobilization was completed long before industry could be reorganized to receive the men. One precious avenue of emigration was closed: America no longer wanted to absorb Europe's surplus population. Politically, the prewar chaos remained. Parliament failed to provide men or policies capable of dealing with the postwar emergency. Italy needed a man of vision, ability, and reforming zeal. It obtained a leader who possessed all these things, but had also a touch of evil. Benito Mussolini's bad qualities flourished alongside, and finally overcame, the good.

Mussolini was born in 1883, the son of a socialist blacksmith. Like Joseph Stalin, he received a religious education. He was a pupil at a Catholic seminary. Like Stalin he was expelled, but not for disobedience, for violence. Mussolini had stabbed a fellow pupil.

Leaving school, Mussolini became a schoolmaster and, in order to avoid conscription, emigrated to Switzerland in 1902. He started many jobs but kept none. He was arrested for begging in Lausanne and as he had a false passport was expelled from canton to canton. He regarded himself as an intellectual and told an acquaintance that he meant, one day, to write a book more horrific than anything by Edgar Allan Poe. He would call the book, he said, "Perversion."

In 1904 Mussolini returned to Italy to do his military service. On demobilization he became a journalist and was active in his local Socialist Party. In 1911 he was imprisoned for opposing the war against Libya. He unwisely described the Italian flag as "a rag to be planted on a dunghill."

Prison stimulated his literary talents; on his release he edited a would-be Marxist magazine called *The Class Struggle*. His position in the Italian socialist movement was curious: he was more interested in the seizure of power and the establishment of autocratic rule than in social reform. In 1912 he became editor of the official Socialist Party newspaper, *Avanti*. When war came in 1914 his immediate reaction was to oppose it. On 8 September 1914 he wrote: "It is our right and duty to urge the revolt of the working classes against today's event." But within a month he decided to support the war. His socialist colleagues were outraged. He gave up the editorship of *Avanti* and launched a new daily paper, *Il Popolo d'Italia*, which advocated Italian participation in the war: "Germany must be crushed. And she can be crushed quickly with the help of Italy. . . . What an historic day it will be when the factories of the pederast Krupp go up in flames that will illumine all of Europe and purify Germany. . . . Essen, city of guns and cannons, must be razed to the ground. Only then will the pillaging and murderous Germans reacquire the right of citizenship in humanity."

For a short while Mussolini served in the army. He became a corporal, doubtless because of his military service experience. But he was invalided out after being wounded during grenade practice. He later claimed that he was wounded in battle, adding, characteristically: "One of the newspapers had mentioned where I was laid up. Thereupon the Austrians shelled the hospital."

After the war Mussolini, discontented with socialist lethargy and disillusioned by socialist pacifism, formed a new party, the fascist party, in Milan. Its program was still basically socialist, and included an 80 per cent tax on war profits, workers sharing in industrial management, the annexation of Dalmatia, and the confiscation of ecclesiastical property. The fascists said they would launch a revolution and rebuild a new, strong, proud, and respected Italy. The voters of Milan listened to this strange doctrine, but gave it only 4,000 votes. The socialists polled 170,000. It seemed that Italy was weary of drama in politics.

In September 1919 a small but extraordinary incident hit the headlines of Europe. A one-eyed, sixty-year-old poet invaded the Dalmatian port of Fiume. The port's sovereignty had not been decided upon at the Paris Conference. The poet, Gabriele D'Annunzio, hoped, by seizing the town, to show that Italy could still assert her rights without deference to compromise. For over a year D'Annunzio ruled in Fiume. The Italians found themselves enthusiastic for his bravado. Members of the Italian royal family paid him visits. He developed a new style of speech, the balcony question with crowd responses:

> "Whose is Fiume?"
> "Ours!"
> "To whom the future?"
> "To us!"

D'Annunzio encouraged horseplay and sneered at convention. On one occasion he flew over Rome and dropped a chamber pot full of carrots on the parliament building. He offered documents legalizing divorce, at a price. Many Italians delighted at this sudden emergence of an anti-Catholic authority. But in December 1920 the Italian Government decided to dislodge him. There was an armed clash. D'Annunzio declared war on Italy, then surrendered. He retired from public life, rich and admired. His slogan "Fiume or death" was forgotten. But the success of his banditry and the exhilaration of his wildness was long remembered. He had been a comic-opera leader. Mussolini determined to emulate him in more serious style.

Violence became the hallmark of Italian domestic politics. Land which during the war had been promised to soldiers as a reward for their service was seized by the poor peasants. Rich peasants descended upon these illegally held plots and took them for themselves. In industry the breakdown of wage negotiations led to the factory owners declaring a lockout. The workers retaliated by seizing the factories. The red flag flew for a while from factory roofs. But the seizure was ill-organized and had no political objectives. When the Government offered a compromise the occupation of the factories was abandoned.

But violence continued. Even if the socialist strikers were peaceful, there were always men willing to provoke them. Mussolini was a master of provocation. He knew that if he could involve the socialists in street battles he could appeal to the nation as its savior against red revolution. "Respectable" people were afraid of communism and could not conceive of revolution as coming from anywhere but the Left. Russia was a constant example of a communist victory. If Mussolini's bands of thugs were able to defend Italy from the "red peril" what could one say against them?

The Government was further discredited in the eyes of all but the few moderates when they abandoned all hope of establishing Italian sovereignty over Albania, which they had in part occupied during the war, and withdrew their troops. Worse still as far as nationalists were concerned, Italy came to an agreement with Yugoslavia, renouncing Italian claims to Dalmatia and accepting Fiume as an independent state, or Free City. Compromise is the essence of international amity. But the Italians, suffering from a sense of inferiority, did not approve their Government's wisdom.

The Prime Minister, Giolitti, having won four elections in his political career, decided to attempt a fifth in May 1921. In order to reduce the number of socialist and Catholic deputies he organized a "national bloc" and invited the fascists to join him. They agreed and as a result found their antisocialist hooliganism unchastised by the police. On polling day dozens of their opponents were clubbed to death, but Giolitti did not denounce his new allies. He needed the fascist vote. As a result of the election thirty-five fascist deputies were elected, in a total house of 535. It was a small number, but they were noisy men, and Parliament had long been recognized as a useful platform for demagogic utterances. Mussolini, having been elected as a result of an alliance with Giolitti, made his first speech an attack on the Government. Giolitti's "national bloc" had failed to win a majority vote in the election and, as the defections, led by Mussolini, mounted, Giolitti resigned.

Fascism was a creed of violence. Its main activity was street warfare. It encouraged brutality. Socialists, after appealing in vain for government protection against fascist thugs, took matters into their own hands. Italy was reduced to a state of civil war. The fascists controlled more and more towns and represented more and more interests. In Trieste they were anti-Slav, elsewhere they were anti-peasant; some were republican, others monarchist. Most were anti-intellectual. All applauded violence.

By his ability to organize violence Mussolini made himself indispensable. Since the only alternative to fascist force was socialist force, the lovers of order and discipline, conservatism and patriotism, accepted fascism. In July 1922 the socialists, as a futile gesture of defiance, declared a general strike. The myth of the general strike, the belief that power could be wielded by those who directed such a strike, was cruelly shattered. Mussolini moved his thugs into Ancona, Livorno, and Genoa, destroying socialist headquarters and beating up strikers. On 4 August 1922 his men entered Milan. The strikers battled with them for three hours but were beaten. The fascists destroyed the printing presses of *Avanti*, Mussolini's old newspaper. D'Annunzio appeared on the balcony of the town hall and gave his approval to fascism. The fascists ran the trams and trains which the strikers had immobilized, thereby gaining the gratitude of respectable citizens. Strikebreakng, even in the brutal form practiced by Mussolini, was applauded as a commendable example of state patriotism. It was the strikers who, by deserting the municipalities, appeared as traitors, but it was not considered treachery to smash them.

Mussolini was supported by the industrialists, who applauded his plea for labor discipline. His violence was left undisturbed by the Government, who feared that it would be turned against them if they challenged it. The more Mussolini acted, however squalidly, the more it appeared that he alone could control events. In October 1922, having obtained the mastery of Ferrara, Cremona, Parma, and Ravenna, and forced the socialist prefect to flee from Bologna, Mussolini directed the capture of Fiume. Its antinationalist government was driven out and fascists ruled in its place.

Mussolini planned the final stroke, a march on Rome. His men were assembled on the outskirts of the capital. The Government urged the King to grant full powers to resist Mussolini. But the King was unwilling to risk civil war. He agreed to give Mussolini the powers he wanted. Mussolini was in Milan. He stayed there until he learned by telephone that the King would accept him as Prime Minister. He then insisted on confirmation by telegram. The telegram was duly sent. Thereupon Mussolini took the night train, arriving in Rome by sleeping car on the morning of 30 October 1922. His followers were still on the outskirts of Rome, waiting to march. But when they received the order to come into the center of Rome that order was signed, not by a violent desperado seeking power but by the Prime Minister of Italy, Benito Mussolini. Aged thirty-nine, he was Italy's thirty-ninth prime minister and the youngest in Italian history.

Mussolini made his first speech as Prime Minister in the Chamber of Deputies on 12 November 1922. He told the deputies that as he had formed his government without reference to them he did not regard himself as responsible to them. He poured scorn on parliamentary institutions. Most of the delegates acquiesced like chastened schoolboys, caught in the illegal game of democracy, but one moderate socialist, Giacomo Matteotti, was bold enough to cry out : "Long live Parliament!"

Mussolini quickly obtained the right to exercise emergency powers for twelve months. The liberal parliamentarians were delighted that someone should take responsibility out of their hands. One liberal senator declaimed: "Mussolini has given to the government freshness, youth, and vigor. . . . He has saved Italy from the socialist danger which has been poisoning our life for twenty years."

Support for the fascists had come from many quarters; many people therefore expected to reap some benefit from the fascist victory. Thuggery which had spread terror through most of the northern cities of Italy was legalized: the thugs became a party militia into whose organization the resources of the state could pour. The old special militia, the Royal Guard, was dissolved. Though its members attempted to resist their dissolution, they were no longer on the side of the law. Mussolini knew how to sustain the enthusiasm of his own fascist militia, offering them good quarters, a uniform (distinguished as in street-fighting days by the black shirt) and increased pay.

To please the southern agrarian magnates Mussolini suspended all land-reform legislation. He did not mind alienating the peasants if he could win their overlords to his side. Industrialists were particularly well cared for. Death duties were halved and a commission of inquiry examining wartime profit scandals was dissolved. Every incentive was given to private enterprise. The profitable state telephone system was handed over to competitive firms; the government monopoly of life insurance was abolished. Mussolini became the champion of industrial *laissez faire.* He was being, for once, consistent with his earlier sayings after his break with socialism: "I am for the individual and against the state. . . . Down with the state in all its forms and permutations."

Mussolini's criticism of Parliament took a practical form. He proposed, at the end of 1923, that the party obtaining the largest number of votes, if over 25 per cent, should automatically be given two-thirds of the seats in the Chamber of Deputies. Many liberals were delighted at this brilliant solution to the problem of government instability. Mussolini put his scheme to the vote, sensing that Parliament would be willing, albeit with a few protests, to destroy itself. His plan was carried by 235 votes to 139. Over a hundred deputies abstained. In the gallery sat the blackshirts, toying with their pistols and cleaning their nails with the points of their daggers. If it was not "coercion" it was at least "suggestion."

Mussolini, knowing that he could now dominate Parliament even if only 25 per cent of the electorate supported him, held an election in April 1924. He already had much in his favor: the King had invited him to become Prime Minister, both the Senate and the Chamber of Deputies had approved his parliamentary reforms, and he had inaugurated an economic policy favoring free enterprise, speculation, and the growth and maintenance of private capital.

He also had his legal militia which kept order at the polling booths. They had not forgotten the success of their brutal methods as practiced on opposition groups before 1922. Opposition newspapers tried in vain to arouse antifascist feeling. Armed raids were made on their premises, their presses were smashed and their stocks of newsprint burned. To the accompaniment of such violence Mussolini's fascist and coalition parties obtained 65 per cent, or four and a half million votes. No Prime Minister since Cavour had received such a large majority. His plan for augmenting a minority vote proved unnecessary.

Violence did not cease with electoral victory. The very existence of parliamentary security gave the blackshirts a feeling of omnipotence. Mussolini encouraged the settling of old grievances against recalcitrant opponents. In June 1924 Matteotti, the moderate socialist, accused Mussolini of preparing to use force if the election failed. Within a week Matteotti was murdered.

The death of Matteotti shocked a number of fascists: it seemed to be an act of extremism no longer necessary after parliamentary dominance had been won. But this intellectual criticism was ignored by the rank and file of the movement, who did not equate entry into Parliament with respectability. Mussolini expressed his sorrow; the Senate passed a vote of confidence in him of 235 against 21. The King preferred the death of a single socialist to socialist rule, and told a deputation of army veterans who protested to him about fascist crimes: "My daughter shot two quail today." Against such indifference the deputation pleaded in vain. Even more futile was the withdrawal of the opposition deputies from Parliament in June 1924. They realized that they could not hope to outvote Mussolini and planned their withdrawal as a gesture of moral disapproval. But it left Mussolini even less hampered than before. Not a single hostile word would cross the parliamentary floor. The leader of the withdrawal had already been beaten up by blackshirts in 1923; he died from wounds received in a second ambush in 1925.

In December 1924 evidence was published in Italy implicating Mussolini in Matteotti's murder. Shocked by this a number of his supporters openly renounced fascism. It was rumored that Mussolini would resign. On 3 January 1925 he made a speech in which he accepted responsibility for the murder, and continued: "If fascism has turned out to be only castor oil [1] and rubber truncheons, instead of being a superb passion inspiring the best youth of Italy, I am responsible." He appealed for a vote of confidence in his powers to rejuvenate Italy: with 123 hostile deputies no longer in Parliament he naturally received that vote. As 1925 progressed he destroyed Italian liberties with ease and swiftness. One by one hostile newspaper editors were imprisoned and their premises taken over; whole issues of critical newspapers were seized in order to disrupt their sales; newspaper owners were persuaded to dismiss liberal editors and replace them by fascist nominees.

In December 1925 Mussolini relieved the King of his right to nominate and dismiss ministers; in January 1926 he announced that henceforward all edicts issued by him would have the full force of law. A Grand Council of Fascism was set up, which alone was empowered to choose Mussolini's successor in the event of his death. The secretary of the council was also secretary of the fascist party. The composition and agenda of the council were determined by Mussolini himself. Socialist powers of organization were broken in 1926 when the right to strike was abolished and labor disturbances became punishable by long terms of imprisonment.

In order to consolidate his power Mussolini reversed the economic policy favoring private enterprise. The state became the "corporate body" for which undivided loyalty was demanded. Unfortunately for Mussolini the theory of a central directing authority was not easily transformed into practice. Corruption and inefficiency were the most obvious results of state supervision. Though all workers became state employees and paid compulsory annual subscriptions for the privilege, the bosses could keep their independence by a certain amount of well-directed bribery. Loyal bosses willing to help party

[1] A particularly unpleasant form of fascist activity was to force spoonfuls of castor oil down the throats of opponents, thus destroying their digestive organs.

funds were naturally not hindered when they decided to squeeze out less influential competitors. The state, instead of offering protection to all industrial enterprises, in fact shielded those who took the initiative in monopolistic activity. The party officials, most of them men of mediocre talents, enjoyed the sense of power which a complex system of bribery gave them; titles of nobility and honorary degrees were among the incentives offered to citizens whose loyalty to fascism might be wavering.

The fascist leaders did not see themselves as crusaders or purifiers; they did not believe they were leading an Italian renaissance: they were interested only in the power to swagger and give orders, the power to make people admire them, the power to become rich and indolent. Despite its glorification of violence, bravery, and war, fascism encouraged lethargy, incompetence, and irresponsibility.

It was Mussolini who gave the regime its vigor. His boasting was more important than his performance. His few small achievements were transformed into miracles in the minds of both Italians and foreigners. The very fact that he made the trains run on time brought forth gasps of amazement from other Europeans. When he built a fast motor road or drained a marsh, put up a gaunt marble office block or pinned medals on the chests of heroes of national production (farmers who produced more grain, or women who produced more babies), he seemed to embody the new, efficient, modern statesman. But this was largely bluff. Production fell in most industries; exiles exposed fascist malpractices in the foreign press; the absurdity of the plethora of gold-braided fascist uniforms was the butt of many jokes. The abolition of the handshake and its replacement by the arm-length salute was typical of the absurd, and at the same time annoying, changes introduced. When, in 1936, it was clear that no effort on Mussolini's part would raise the Italian standard of living and that foreign wars would further weaken the economy, Mussolini brazenly declared: "We must rid our minds of the idea that what we have called the days of prosperity will return. We are probably moving towards a period when humanity will exist on a lower standard of living."

Fascism was a theoretical shield held in front of the inefficiency, corruption, and bluster of Mussolini's Italy. It was a glistening shield, hiding the shambles that it guarded. It elevated the state to the level of a deity, but thinking Italians knew this deity to be a sham. "The fascist conception of the state," wrote Mussolini, "is all-embracing, and outside the state no human or spiritual values can exist." Questioning authority became a crime. Only that which the state encouraged was said to be worthy of imitation. The books which Italians might read, the films they might see, the opinions they might hold, were all carefully defined. Yet, without Mussolini himself this vast apparatus of state control would undoubtedly have collapsed. He alone provided a focal point, an apparent justification, a "reality" to contrast with the chaos of dogma. The slogan on every prominent wall, "Mussolini is always right," made it clear that Mussolini, not the state, was the real master. As children in classes for eight-year-olds throughout Italy were taught in 1936:

"The eyes of the Duce are on every one of you. No one can say what is the meaning of that look on his face. It is an eagle opening its wings and rising into space. It is a flame that searches out your heart to light there a vermilion fire. Who can resist that burning eye, darting out its arrows? But do not be afraid; for you those arrows will change into rays of joy."

Mussolini enjoyed playing the part he had designed for himself; he enjoyed speechmaking and was thrilled when interviewed by foreigners, to whom he could talk at great length about himself and his regime. He understood the impact of his own position, of his boasting and swagger, and of his power of coercion. "The crowd loves strong men," he told a visitor, "the crowd is like a woman." Mussolini used the Italians as a negligent Casanova uses women; he loved himself, not them, and in using them he destroyed them. He took from Italy her goodness, her warmth, and her diversity. In their place he put regimentation and crudity. He brought a civilized, gentle people to their knees, encouraged brutality, cynicism, and vainglory, and made a mockery of Italian culture. That he could be accepted at all was a sign that the culture of many generations had by-passed the spirits of men born to an age of social unrest and war.

Fascist theory was consistent in one thing only, the glorification of war. Fascism asserted that only by physical conflict could men achieve their full stature. War was the best means of asserting a nation's greatness and maintaining its supremacy. The shame of Adowa and Caporetto could not be forgotten; the stirring example of D'Annunzio's seizure of Fiume provided a model for other annexations. Acts of brigandage were elevated to the status of deeds of valor.

In 1923, before he had formulated his theory of war, Mussolini took the initiative in foreign affairs. A military commission which was fixing the boundary between Greece and Albania was massacred on Greek territory by persons unknown. The commission's chairman, two assistant officers, and chauffeur were all Italians. Within twenty-four hours of hearing of the murders Mussolini sent an ultimatum to the Greek Government, as follows:

1. An apology in the fullest and most official manner to the Italian Government.
2. The celebration in Athens of a Mass in honor of the victims, to be attended by the Greek Government.
3. The Italian flag to be saluted by a Greek fleet at Phalerion, the salute not to be returned by the Italian fleet until sunset of the same day.
4. A strict inquiry at the scene of the massacre, with the assistance of the Italian Military Attaché.
5. The inquiry to be carried out within five days.
6. All persons found guilty to be sentenced to death. The Greek Government to pay an indemnity of fifty million lire.
7. Solemn military honors to be paid to the bodies of the victims. The reply to be received within twenty-four hours.

The Greek Government replied within the time limit. It objected to demands 4, 5, and 6, but declared itself willing to pay an "equitable indemnity" and to negotiate on the disputed points. If Italy still felt aggrieved, said the Greeks, they were willing to appeal to the League of Nations, of which both were members, for a judgment.

A day later, without replying to the Greeks, Mussolini ordered the occupation of the Greek island of Corfu. The island was undefended; its citizens, living far from the scene of the murder, were bombarded, and many were killed. An Italian ship set sail with a cargo of cement and bricks to build barracks on the conquered island.

Having taken the initiative, Mussolini allowed the Conference of Ambassadors in Paris, which had despatched the Boundary Commission in the first place, to adjudicate. He refused to allow the League to pass judgment. It was a blow for the authority of the League, which had every reason to censure Italy for its hasty, unnecessary, and murderous actions. The Conference of Ambassadors was less concerned to criticize Mussolini. Italy was, after all, one of the victorious nations of the war, and among allies a sense of solidarity remained. France, especially, was unwilling to antagonize Italy, whose support she needed in her continuous duel with Germany.

The Conference of Ambassadors decided that Greece should pay the full indemnity demanded, in return for an immediate Italian withdrawal from Corfu. Mussolini agreed; the ship carrying building materials turned round and the soldiers withdrew. The incident made Mussolini look ludicrous, even wicked, in the eyes of Europe. Irresponsibility such as he had shown was frowned upon by those statesmen who were trying to build a peaceful postwar world. Mussolini tried to explain his action: "You must not believe that the occupation of Corfu was carried out only as a means of forcing Greece to accept our terms. It was also carried out to increase the prestige of Italy."

From the excitement of this little episode, Mussolini appeared to draw inspiration, for by 1931 he had developed a clear if frightening concept of the meaning of war. In the *Italian Encyclopedia* he wrote: "Perpetual peace would be impossible and useless. War alone brings all human energies to their highest state of tension, and stamps with the zeal of nobility the nations which dare to face it."

Mussolini tried to fill Italy with enthusiasm for war. But the wars which he embarked on after 1934 did not arouse great enthusiasm. The basis of fascism was intended to be legalized violence, drilled brutality, systematic conquest. But the Italian is not a warmonger. He joined in the battles because he was forced to, not because he delighted in war. Fascism was an effective sergeant-major, but it did not penetrate the souls of the people.

In the four years before the outbreak of the Second World War Mussolini sent his armies into action three times. Thrice he added to the climate of international violence inaugurated by the Japanese in their attack on Manchuria in 1931. By invading Ethiopia and using all the military means at his disposal, including poison gas, to subjugate the Ethiopian people, he put himself internationally, as he had already put himself internally, on the side of brigands, villains, and tyrants. In vain did Ethiopia appeal to the League of Nations, of which both she and Italy were members. The League nations could not agree among themselves to take action of a military nature against Italy, or to impose severe economic sanctions upon Italy, such as the refusal to sell her oil, in order to force Mussolini to withdraw. The League, in failing to come to the aid of Ethiopia, revealed its basic weakness: it could not enforce Article 16 of its Covenant, an article which had heretofore been believed capable of holding back aggressively minded nations from the brink of war.

Article 16 stipulated: "Should any member of the League resort to war in disregard of the Covenant . . . it shall *ipso facto* be deemed to have committed an act of war against all other members of the League."

Provision was laid down in the Covenant for the combined imposition of military, naval, or air action against the offending power. Yet the League did nothing effective against Mussolini. It thus showed itself to be a false guardian of European security. Potential aggressors saw that they could flout it with impunity. Threatened nations realized that they could not hope for protection from the League: their only security was what they themselves could provide. This was a bleak prospect for Europe.

Mussolini's action shattered what remained of Europe's confidence in the effectiveness of collective security. The conquest of Ethiopia, the only large African state not ruled by a European power, cast a shadow upon the independence of all weak nations. For most of them that shadow was to become a machine gun within five years.

Britain and France helped to make a mockery of the League's search for effective sanctions against Italy by agreeing in December 1935 to a "partition" of Ethiopia which they hoped would satisfy both Italians and Ethiopians. This, the "Hoare-Laval" plan, was unacceptable to Italy, who wanted more than it offered them. It was also an insult to Ethiopia, which could not accept such a severe reduction of its sovereignty.

Mussolini continued with his conquest of Ethiopia, which proved a more complicated and more costly enterprise than he had imagined. The Ethiopians, though ill-equipped, resisted their would-be conquerors with fanatical vigor. Mussolini telegraphed to the commander of the invading army on 29 March 1936: "Given war methods of enemy, renew authorization use gas, of any kind, on any scale." Flame throwers, drenching the defenders in burning oil, were another effective weapon in the Italian armory. When the war ended there were an estimated 28,000 Ethiopian dead. Only 1,305 Italians had lost their lives. Mussolini lamented that, for Italy, the war had been won at too small a cost, that it had failed to harden the national character or to create enthusiasm for imperial conquest.

By this conquest of Ethiopia Mussolini became an emperor. But in Europe the new colossus was Hitler, not Mussolini. Hitler's violence, being more systematic, was more feared; Hitler's ambitions, being

European, were taken more seriously. Few people regarded the subjugation of an isolated African kingdom as either impressive or exciting. Yet Mussolini wanted to be admired. He needed a victory in
Europe which would turn the eyes of Europe from Berlin to Rome.

In 1936 Francisco Franco, a general in the Spanish Army, decided
to overthrow the Spanish Republican Government. He planned an
invasion of Spain from Spanish Morocco. Mussolini offered Franco
military aid, in the form of airplanes and blackshirts, hoping that as
a result of a swift victory Franco would be his debtor, a friendly
fascist regime would be established in Spain, and Italian valor would
have been demonstrated on European soil.

None of Mussolini's hopes were realized. Far from gaining a swift
victory, Franco found himself engaged in a prolonged battle with
the Republic, which countered his Italian aid with aid from Russia.
Mussolini's troops were unable to march in triumph through the
cities of Spain; they sustained a morale-shattering defeat at Guadala-
jara. Mussolini was forced to send his most modern, and scarcest,
military material to combat the high-quality Soviet aid, and had to

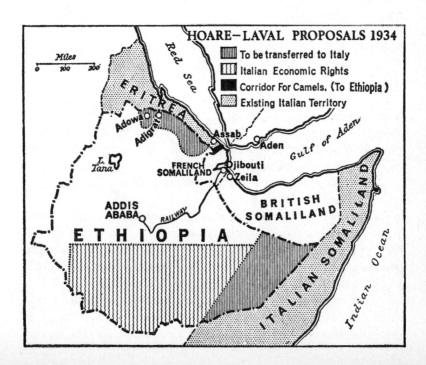

send men from the regular army to reinforce the amateur black-shirts. The intervention proved a costly economic drain and tied down 70,000 Italian soldiers. Instead of enhancing Mussolini's prestige in the eyes of his fellow dictator it made him unpopular and despised. His army was clearly mediocre, and if tied down in Spain, could not play an effective part in the European balance of power. It could neither check Hitler nor reinforce him. Hitler could therefore ignore it. This was hardly to Mussolini's liking.

The Spanish civil war lasted for three years. Although fascism was established in Spain, it left the country embittered and exhausted. Spain could no longer act as an effective ally in the event of a European war. Mussolini had failed to alter the Mediterranean balance of power in his favor. But in his now weakened position he needed active allies. By intervening in Spain he had aroused the anger of Britain and France. He had also shown Hitler that Italian strength was a sham. As a result Hitler, while paying lip service to Mussolini as an ally, ignored him when it came to power politics.

When Hitler annexed Austria in March 1938 Mussolini had to acquiesce, even though four years earlier he had warned Hitler not to tamper with Austrian independence. When Hitler occupied Prague in March 1939 Mussolini was again offended. He had hoped that Central Europe would remain in the Italian sphere of influence. This was clearly not to be, nor had Hitler informed him in advance of his plans. In April 1939, on Good Friday, as a last futile gesture of independence and strength, Mussolini invaded Albania. Although this isolated feudal state was quickly overrun, military difficulties arose during the conquest which convinced Mussolini that he could not afford to enter a European war until 1942 at the earliest. Ethiopia, Spain, and Albania had weakened his exchequer and his army. Hitler, learning of this weakness, knew that he must act alone in any European war. When Germany invaded Poland in September 1939 Italy declared her neutrality.

German Nazism did not appeal to Mussolini. Yet he realized that the systematic brutality and military success of Nazism were what he had wanted of Italian fascism. Like an envious child he emulated Hitler where he could. This imitation was seen at its most grotesque over the Jewish question.

There were 50,000 Jews in Italy in 1931. They formed a respected, if small, section of the population. In the *Fascist Encyclopedia* Mussolini had boasted that there was no racial problem in

Italy. The article on "anti-Semitism" in the *Encyclopedia* was actually written by a Jew. Mussolini was known to be a critic of Hitler's anti-Semitic policies.

In May 1938, pandering to his northern ally and hoping to impress on Hitler that Italians too could be ruthless if they wanted, Mussolini introduced anti-Jewish legislation in Italy. Jewish professors were dismissed from the universities, Jewish generals from the army, Jewish admirals from the fleet. Mussolini himself had to change his dentist. Jewish children were expelled from state schools; Jews were banned from becoming teachers or journalists.[2] Italians resented the barbarity of these laws and as a result they were only partially enforced. Italians still gave shelter to Jews escaping from Hitler. Fascists resented the fact that the anti-Jewish laws were the result of German pressure. Once again Mussolini had succeeded in making Italy look absurd and wicked abroad, and had humiliated the Italian people.

There was much wisdom, if also some self-justification, in the opinion of Benedetto Croce, philosopher, liberal, and supporter of Mussolini until the murder of Matteotti, when he wrote: "There was a deep and important distinction between Nazism and Fascism, because the first was a terrible crisis which had been brooding through centuries of German history, and the second was an excrescence quite alien to the history of Italy. . . . Nazism had a tragic and diabolical aspect, but Fascism kept an incorrigibly clownlike appearance even in the crimes it committed, and anybody could see as much at a glance by contrasting the appearance of the two chiefs."

It was true that Hitler was serious in his persecutions, sincere in his denunciations, and successful in his foreign wars and domestic persecutions. Mussolini, in contrast, made only the noises of a lion. His actions were never as successful as his plans. His plans were never as grandiose as his opinions. And even his opinions eventually became the laughingstock of Italy. Thus in 1935 a British diplomat, Sir Robert Vansittart, could rightly call Hitler "Dictator Major" and Mussolini "Dictator Minor." By 1939 it was clear that after seventeen years as an autocrat Mussolini had captured neither the imagination, the respect, nor the support of the Italian people.

---

2 Enrico Fermi (1901–54), one of the world's greatest physicists, whose wife was a Jewess, left Italy in 1938 as a result of the anti-Semitic legislation. He emigrated to the United States and played a leading part in the development of the atom bomb.

# POLITICAL INSTABILITY AND THE WEAKNESS OF FRANCE

On 11 November 1918 France was victorious; for the first time since the days of Napoleon she had defeated Germans in battle. The victory had been bought at a greater cost in lives and resources than she had ever spent before; but it was undoubtedly a victory. As Erzberger put his signature to the armistice agreement, as the guns fell silent along the western front, and as men emerged from the trenches bewildered that their dream had come to pass—at that moment France was undoubtedly and visibly victorious. But neither the elation nor the supremacy felt by Frenchmen that day was to last for long.

France, the victor, was much weaker in 1918 than she had been four years earlier. Her youth had been decimated on the field of battle; her northeastern territory had been devastated and she had defeated a Germany whose population at the end of the war was almost twice her own. French politicians at once realized that their greatest danger was a revived, vengeance-seeking Germany. They therefore set out to hamper and restrict German development as much as possible. At the Peace Conference they demanded a heavy German payment, not a lump sum fixed from the outset, such as Germany had imposed on France in 1871, but an unspecified sum to be calculated on the basis of the actual damage done by Germany. A lump sum, or indemnity, even if heavy would have appeared to Germany as the inevitable price of defeat. But to demand an itemization of specific claims invited exaggeration and a continual raising of the demand.

Economic pressures were not the only ones that France sought to apply; militarily she forced Germany to destroy her army, navy, and air force. In theory France was pledged, in the fullness of time, to disarm down to Germany's level. In practice she had no intention of abandoning the military supremacy which the ability to disarm Germany had given her. She was acutely aware of her numerical inferiority and had learned during the "war of attrition" just how much numbers mattered. Forty million Frenchmen, victors in theory, faced nearly seventy million Germans. If it were to come to war once again France knew she would lose. Realizing that she could not always rely on Britain as an ally, she placed all her hopes in a peace treaty so severe that it would make it impossible for Germany to rise again.

France suffered her first postwar defeat at the Paris Peace Conference. Clemenceau was confronted with a difficult choice. If he insisted upon French control of the Rhineland he would lose British and American sympathy to such an extent that France would not be able to rely upon these powers to help her in the event of a German revival. If, however, he could accept the territorial integrity of Germany and be content with a demilitarized Rhineland under German sovereignty, Britain and America would pledge themselves by separate treaty to defend France if her frontiers were violated. Clemenceau chose to abandon direct French control over Germany and to accept the Anglo-American treaty. The terms of the Versailles Treaty were accordingly drawn far more leniently in their territorial aspects than France had intended. The fragmentation of Germany, which many frightened Frenchmen desired, was abandoned.

French security now rested upon the Anglo-American treaty. But when the American Senate refused to ratify the Versailles Treaty it also rejected this specific American guarantee to France. Britain, whose relations with France were strained owing to constant squabbles over every item of peacemaking, leapt at this opportunity to renounce her own guarantee. France found herself with neither a French-controlled Rhineland state nor the crucial compensatory guarantee from Britain and America. Her isolation and her weakness were complete.

The Treaty of Versailles disappointed France in many ways. Territorially it was Britain who gained most, for Germany's African colonies went mainly to her. The return of Alsace-Lorraine to France was seen, not as a gain, but as recognition of a French right which should have been recognized long before. Its transfer could hardly become a German grievance. The Germans were later taught to denounce Versailles as if it were the embodiment of Allied vengeance, rapacity, and wickedness. In fact the Treaty was lenient towards Germany, allowing her to remain as Europe's largest territorial unit. Owing to the conflict of President Wilson's idealism with Clemenceau's vision of triumph it was France who gained the least. By the destruction of German armed might she gained twenty years' peace: but it was clear to the Allies that if Germany found the means to rearm unchallenged she could swiftly dominate France. The French were told to put their faith in European disarmament. But when the Disarmament Conference began in 1925 it fussed and fumbled and came to grief. A second attempt, in 1930, to agree to a reduction of arms was equally unsuccessful. When a French proposal to abolish bombing aircraft came before the conference, and was widely approved, it was quashed by Britain, who argued that bombs were the only means of inducing wild tribes on outlying imperial frontiers to come to heel. Europe remained armed, except for Germany. When German rearmament began to reach formidable proportions in 1936 there was no argument to answer the German cry: "We must be armed up to the level of France. Otherwise we will come to conference tables as inferiors. Equality of arms is our only hope for justice in other matters." Britain applauded the logic of this plea. France could do nothing but accept the new military power. The Treaty of Versailles was entirely in Germany's interest over disarmament. In the 1930s German politicians frequently cited Clemenceau's promise to the German delegate at Versailles, a promise which, because it was unfulfilled in the decade after the war, was construed after 1930 entirely in Germany's favor:

"The Allied and Associated Powers wish to make it clear that their requirements in regard to German armaments were not made solely with the object of rendering it impossible for Germany to resume her policy of military aggression. They are also the first steps towards that general reduction and limitation of armaments which they seek to bring about as one of the most fruitful preventives of war."

France placed her immediate hopes in reparations. She wanted to force Germany to cover the cost of reconstruction for her. She also hoped that reparations would continue for many years so as to keep

Germany perpetually in debt. According to some calculations Germany would complete payments only by 1940, according to others by 1960. In this way France would ensure her economic dominance over Germany, even if it were a poor exchange for the political dominance which had been denied her by Britain and America.

Had France been able to impose the severe reparations which her statesmen envisaged, and had the reparations payments been rigidly extorted, Germany would indeed have had a grievance against Versailles which her public might bewail. But France's plans were frustrated. The British did not really approve of reparations, and took the lead in reducing them. Increasing economic crises in Europe made it impossible for Germany to pay even the reduced demands. America supported the German economy by loans which helped German postwar recovery as well as enabling Germany to make reparations payments.

When Germany refused to pay reparations Britain was sympathetic. Lloyd George was anxious to help the Germans escape from what he considered an unjust aspect of the treaty. The Germans appealed for a moratorium on payments in 1922. The British supported their request and a conference was convened in London. But Raymond Poincaré, fearful of Anglo-German collusion which would undermine French independent action, refused to sanction a moratorium. He announced that, as Germany was in default of payments, France would occupy the Ruhr.

It is easy to criticize the French occupation of the Ruhr as an act of madness. Such indeed was the contemporary British view. But Poincaré saw that unless he asserted French power quickly, France would be outwitted in every international crisis. He feared, not without reason, an Anglo-German pressure group which would act against France over every issue which arose. Unfortunately for Poincaré, the Germans in the Ruhr adopted a policy of passive resistance. They refused to work in the factories. They refused to serve in the shops. French troops were confronted with a sullen, uncooperative populace.

The British were quick to point out that, by inciting tne closure of the Ruhr factories, France was making it impossible for Germany to produce the very materials from whose sale she could pay reparations. The Americans regarded the French action as a sign of immaturity in the conduct of international relations. Only Mussolini, the new ruler of Italy who dreamed of an Italian empire, gave his grudging approval, hoping, not without reason, that France would later look kindly upon his own adventures.

By the time German resistance was broken the Ruhr had become the scene of acute industrial dislocation. France reluctantly accepted a lower scale of reparations payments. Under Britain's initiative she signed the Locarno Agreement in 1925, which guaranteed her frontier with Germany. She could no longer take unilateral action against Germany. Nor could she treat Germany any longer as an "enemy" power. The distinction laid down at Versailles between "Allied and Associated Powers" on the one hand and "Enemy Powers" on the other was destroyed. Germany could no longer claim that as a result of this Versailles division she was regarded as an outcast by the other European powers. The Locarno Treaty brought to an end this stigma from the Versailles Treaty. Germany had been an "enemy" for less than six years from the day of defeat. And once she became an equal she could treat France much more severely should France contemplate any alteration in the *status quo* unfavorable to Germany.

The Locarno Treaty was intended to obviate any need for a Franco-German war. The crucial clause, Article 2, began as follows:

> Germany and Belgium, and also Germany and France, mutually undertake that they will in no case attack or invade each other or resort to war against each other. . . .

This was supplemented by Article 4:

> In case of a flagrant violation of Article 2 . . . by one of the high contracting parties, each of the other contracting parties undertakes immediately to come to the help of the party against whom such a violation or breach has been directed. . . .

But France did not have much faith in these paper pledges. She knew that they were only meaningful if Germany remained militarily weak. France still hoped to help ensure this weakness by a stern reparations policy. But she had to contend now, not only with German hostility to high payments, but with criticisms from Britain and America, both of whom were urging her to "give Germany a chance" and welcome Germany as an equal in Europe. France was reluctant to forgive so quickly. It seemed to her that Britain had forgotten her own dead, forgotten her anxieties about a revived Germany, and forgotten her desire to support France when danger threatened. Frenchmen noted that English historians were even writing books denying that Germany was responsible for the war. Such "impartiality" offended French susceptibilities. It pointed to a growing British willingness to take the German side in any international dispute, whether historical, political or economic.

The French hopes of continual reparations payments were shattered by the economic crisis which hit Germany in 1930. Germany was unable to pay; France, as a result of the Locarno Treaty, was unable to resort to force. Both sides accepted an American proposal to suspend payments until the crisis was over. France imagined that she would be able to resume collecting reparations within two or three years. But the Germans sensed that the moratorium was the death-knell of French demands. Under British initiative a conference assembled at Lausanne and, on 8 July 1932, an agreement was signed virtually freeing Germany from her reparations payments. The Lausanne Treaty annulled the most critical aspect of the Versailles Treaty.

Though Germany had made many payments between 1919 and 1932, she had paid only a fraction of the amount suggested at Versailles. Now that burden was lifted. The economic crisis, and British sympathies for Germany, deprived France of her most treasured protection against a German revival. It is possible in retrospect to see the absurdity of the extreme reparations demand. But it would be a mistake to ignore French fears and French limitations. Reparations was her only ace; she kept it in her hand as long as she could; but once it was played, and trumped, she was alone. In the eight years that were left between 1932 and her defeat at the hands of Germany, France lacked security, confidence, and power. All she had was her pride, and when that was destroyed by domestic upheaval she was a broken reed.

French domestic politics were bedeviled by economic troubles. The Third Republic, since its inception in 1870, had urged a great deal on its citizens. Between 1870 and 1914 it had championed lay education, opposed anti-Semitism, encouraged the liberal arts, and, in true republican fashion, delighted in parliamentary debate and political flexibility. But it was unable to create a stable basis for government finance. The most obvious answer to economic troubles was to institute an income tax. This was made impossible by the very flexibility of political parties. Any prime minister proposing such a tax knew that his ministry would be outvoted.

Under the extreme financial pressure of war Clemenceau managed to introduce an income tax in 1917. Its rates were low and its loopholes large. The problem which confronted each postwar government was whether or not to increase the income tax and make evasion more difficult.

Poincaré was well aware of the need for a more effective income tax. But he put his budgeting hopes in reparations. For as long as reparations payments continued he considered them a sufficient source of revenue to enable income tax to be forgotten. A double budget gave Frenchmen a false sense of security. Budget "A" showed a regular surplus. Budget "B" showed a deficit three times as large. But Budget "B" was not combined with Budget "A." Instead, it was "balanced" by the hypothetical reparations payments of the future. This large deficit contained the cost of postwar reconstruction. The credits which were to cancel it never came in.

In the election of 1924 the left-wing parties were victorious. The socialists proposed a capital levy. Their political allies, the radicals, rejected this on the grounds that it was a slimly disguised and dangerously dictatorial form of income tax. In panic many Frenchmen invested their capital abroad. The value of the franc fell. Economic chaos brought political chaos. There were six cabinet crises in nine months. Governments were reconstructed almost as soon as their composition was made public. Such instability made a mockery of Parliament, and the process of policy-making and legislation came to a halt.

To solve this crisis Poincaré was called back to the premiership and held office again from 1926 to 1929. He promised to find an acceptable balance between the "soak the rich" policy of the defeated socialists and the economic anarchy of a taxless, false budgetary system. Under the mandate of emergency he was able to increase income tax. He also raised tariffs by 30 per cent. The peasant gained protection from his more efficient European competitors. As a result, he could afford to pay his taxes, and the franc recovered. It was stabilized at 20 per cent of its prewar value. This meant that those who held 100 francs of prewar government bonds, the staple investment of the cautious middle class, could now redeem their bonds for twenty francs. Some sulked over their loss; others rejoiced that they had saved anything at all. Poincaré, known earlier as *"Poincaré la Guerre,"* gained a new title, *"Poincaré le bien aimé."* His new, stable franc became a symbol of French recovery.

The political implications of economic recovery were not so beneficial. With money in his pocket the voter became less inclined to vote for unknown or revolutionary policies. He wanted no change in his quiet life. Left-wing parties found it harder and harder to gain support for progressive policies. Reform became unpopular. Republicanism lost its verve: it now stood for the *status quo.* Critics of social injustice, of tax inequalities, or of political corruption were considered dangerous for the new gentility. At the 1928 elections the right-center parties were given a majority. Poincaré retired through illness in 1929. He was succeeded by André Tardieu, who headed three governments between 1929 and 1932.

The quick turnover of governments was a constant reminder of the basic instability of the French electoral system. Tardieu was anxious to reduce the complexity of parties and to introduce a two-party system such as existed in Britain and America. His plans to simplify voting procedures and make a two-party system possible alienated the radicals, who prized their ability to ally with either right- or left-wing groups as best suited them. Although this flexibility was one of the causes of parliamentary confusion, it was naturally regarded by radicals as their only guarantee of survival. They suspected, not without reason, that Tardieu wished to force them into his own right-wing grouping. Tardieu appealed to the electorate for a mandate to change the system. The voter remained true to his principles of immobility, caution, and tradition. Tardieu and his plan were defeated. The radicals were given a majority. But although they outnumbered the socialists they could not form a stable government without them. The socialists, whose vote had also grown, showed their strength by refusing a coalition with the radicals. The government passed to them; but the radicals fought back. In twenty months there were six cabinet changes.

At this moment of political instability France was struck by the European economic depression. Though she had avoided it for longer than any other power, she could not avert it forever. To her parliamentary confusion was added the unrest of mass unemployed. In this atmosphere of uncertainty and growing social bitterness there grew up a plethora of popular movements. Some were directly modeled on Mussolini's fascists or Hitler's Nazis, demanding a more authoritarian form of government; others also on the Right wanted to uproot the social system and establish new institutions and a new basis of political power.

It was a financial scandal which gave these popular movements an excuse for action. Late in 1933 a financier named Serge Stavisky was shown to have been engaged in doubtful dealings for over six years. From the evidence of his activities it was clear that the authorities had known of his frauds, and had taken no action. When dates were fixed for legal proceedings the influence of powerful friends postponed them. Innumerable middle-class investors had put their money into his spurious companies. The public outcry was so great that Stavisky was at last sought for by the police. He committed suicide to avoid arrest. It was at once rumored that the police had shot him on orders from the politicians whose reputations were in danger. Shortly after Stavisky's death the body of a government lawyer connected with the case was found mutilated on a railway line. It was announced that he had committed suicide. But rumor had it that he too had been killed because he knew too much. There were riots in Paris every evening for several weeks. In January 1934 a new government was formed by the radical leader Edouard Daladier, in the hope of introducing some discipline to the capital.

On 6 February 1934 the right-wing organizations planned a monster rally in the center of Paris. Their aim was to topple the radicals and show that "France" wanted a right-wing government. Daladier ordered the police to disperse the marchers but the police were unable to do so. First they used water hoses and then bullets. When the mob finally dispersed fifteen dead were left behind; some 1,500 people were injured. Paris had not known such violence since the 1871 Commune. But although there had been bloodshed, there was no organized plot to seize power. Frustration at the incompetence and sluggishness of Parliament, not ambition to establish a totalitarian regime, seems to have been the dominant impetus behind the demonstrations.

The rioters were partially successful. Daladier resigned and a right-wing government, led by Tardieu and including the defender of Verdun, Marshal Pétain, took office. But Tardieu's Government had no intention of overthrowing the republic. Although pledged to efficiency, it had to rely on the same complexity of parties and political alignments as had bedeviled its predecessors. It still needed radical support. When the Prime Minister tried to strengthen his powers as against those of Parliament the radicals withdrew. The Government fell, to be succeeded by another combination of rightists and radicals, led by Pierre Laval.

Laval's ambition was the economic recovery of France. He instituted a deflationary policy in order to reduce French prices and enable French products to compete in the world market. He cut the salaries of state employees, hoping thereby to set an example to private industry. Industrial production was nourished by financial incentives until it began to rise. But these economic advantages were gained only as a result of government controls. The radicals discovered that they did not like such "ruthless" planning. They felt that by supporting Laval they were giving too much power to the Right and sacrificing their independence. They withdrew from Laval's Government, which immediately fell. Laval had been Prime Minister for exactly a year. By French standards his was a long regime.

The effect of the right-wing demonstration on 6 February 1934 did not vanish with the dispersal of crowds. The left-wing parties were alerted. They feared an organized right-wing *coup d'état*. Under the impact of the riots they began to combine. The socialists announced their willingness to work with the communists, their traditional rivals. The radicals began to wonder whether it might not be best for them if they too joined the socialists and pressed for more reforms. Their record as a reforming party had suffered by their association with the Right from 1934 to 1936.

Elections were held throughout France on 26 April 1936. The combined force of the radicals, socialists, and communists campaigned under the banner of the "Popular Front." It was one of the most bitterly fought elections of the Third Republic. The "Popular Front" electors were convinced that if the Right was victorious they would institute totalitarian rule. The enthusiasm behind the "Popular Front" was more than electoral partisanship. The election was in many ways a substitute for civil strife. By casting his vote the man in the street would show on which side of the barricades he intended to stand.

The "Popular Front" was victorious in June 1936. The socialists, with 146 seats, became the largest party in the Chamber of Deputies; the radicals followed with 116; the communists rose from a meager 10 to an impressive 72.

The "Popular Front" Prime Minister was the socialist, Léon Blum. "France is ready for you," said one of his friends. "She awaits you nervously, but her nervousness is that of a young bride." Blum was an energetic husband. Under the Matignon Agreements the employers were brought to the conference table with the unions and a compromise was worked out which improved labor relations. Workers' delegations were set up to deal directly with factory managers. Wage increases from 7 to 15 per cent were negotiated. Blum himself presided over the signing of the agreements. Then he pushed social legislation through the Chamber: a forty-hour week, a guaranteed minimum of overtime pay, a grain marketing board to eliminate speculators, nationalization of the armaments industry to eliminate war profiteers, and, most important of all, holidays with pay.[1]

Léon Blum's reforms invigorated France. But the radicals began to resent so much activity. Planning was not to their taste. A year after he had come to office Blum was overthrown, following the withdrawal of the radicals from his government. Like Laval, he had lasted for a year. It seemed that no man, whatever his merits, could hope for more. Blum became Prime Minister again for a few months in 1938, but it was only the shadow of power. It was the radicals who now held the balance and Edouard Daladier became Prime Minister once more.

Daladier was primarily concerned with foreign policy. The German problem had become so acute by 1938 that it overshadowed all else. As a former history professor Daladier readily submerged himself in Franco-German relations. Domestic policy was left in the hands of Paul Reynaud, a believer in free enterprise as the best cure for economic lethargy.

Reynaud obtained Cabinet approval for the reversal of many of Blum's reforms. The forty-hour week was no longer enforced and the minimum pay for overtime was reduced. Reynaud called his policy an "experiment in liberalism." It certainly benefited the business man and the industrialist. The working class, which had been stimulated by Blum's legislation, and imagined that their interests would

---

[1] After his return from a German concentration camp in 1945 Blum sent a suit to the cleaners. It was returned with a note in the pocket: "Thanks for paid holidays."

be looked after for some time, were bitterly disappointed by Blum's fall. A general strike, labor's "last-ditch" weapon, was organized. But Daladier had no intention of yielding to left-wing popular pressure as he had yielded to the Right in 1934, nor did Reynaud intend to abandon his economic program. The strikers were mobilized for service in the army reserve: refusal to obey was tantamount to treason. The Government let it be known that there would be no delay in setting up courts-martial. The strikers gave way: there was no fighting spirit left. Once the "Popular Front" had gone the workers felt isolated and abandoned. At least they could console themselves that they were allowed to form unions and allowed to complain to their bosses. Such privileges were denied their German, Spanish, Russian, and Italian fellow-workers. They were not to know that soon they would also be forbidden in France.

When Germany began to rearm in 1933 France had to choose between two conflicting policies. She could either strengthen her alliance system with eastern European states such as Poland, Czechoslovakia, and Rumania, in an attempt to isolate Germany, or she could try to come to terms with Germany and accept German mastery in Europe. The alliance system involved the danger of antagonizing Germany and provoking her to aggression. Rapprochement with Germany involved the risk of France being pushed into a position of psychological, economic, and eventually political inferiority.

France had to consider two other problems before attempting to resolve the German issue. She had to decide how to avoid conflict with Mussolini's Italy, which had designs on the French island of Corsica and the French departments of Nice and Savoy. There was also the problem of Britain. It seemed to France that Britain was neither a reliable nor an enthusiastic friend and that in the event of a crisis she might not come to France's assistance.

Between 1934 and 1940 France tried both to woo and to resist Germany. Both policies failed. She also failed to win Italian friendship. Nor was it until 1940 that she found, in Britain, a power even more eager than herself to fight for the traditions of democracy which Germany was seeking to destroy.

In 1934 Louis Barthou became Foreign Minister. He favored the policy of strengthening the eastern alliances and made a series of visits to his eastern allies. He also went to Rome, hoping to find

Mussolini in conciliatory mood. Finally he invited King Alexander of Yugoslavia to France: 1934 was scheduled to become a golden year for French security. But tragedy struck at Marseilles, where both Alexander and Barthou were murdered by a Yugoslav terrorist.

Before his assassination Barthou had initiated a mutual aid pact with the Soviet Union. This his successor as Foreign Minister, Pierre Laval, brought to fruition. But Laval also hankered after the alternative solution, accommodation with Germany. He did not intend to sacrifice French interests in so doing, but he gave an unfortunate impression of being tricky and underhand in his policy. More openly, he continued Barthou's pro-Italian policy. When confronted with Mussolini's Ethiopian ambitions he acquiesced, thinking not unreasonably that if the Italian Army were tied down in Addis Ababa it would be less likely to appear in the streets of the French Riviera.

In March 1936 Hitler occupied the Rhineland. This was not only a violation of the Versailles Treaty, against whose "evils" Hitler fulminated, but also of the Locarno Agreements, which had been entered into willingly and indeed enthusiastically by the German Government. Hitler destroyed France's eastern alliance system, since he made it difficult for France to go to the help of a threatened partner owing to the possibility of German retaliation from the Rhineland.

The French Cabinet discussed a counterattack, but unluckily for France Hitler had struck at a moment of political confusion, and the Prime Minister, the radical Sarraut, had neither the authority nor the energy to act. He sent his Foreign Minister, Flandin, to Britain, to see if the British would support a strong French move. The result was a disappointment: Britain did not intend to take or to support any action against Germany.

France was isolated. Her eastern allies had become more remote; her former partner of the western front had become lethargic. Flandin drew the conclusion that France was no longer capable of independent action and ought to make the best terms possible with Hitler. But Flandin soon fell from office.

When the "Popular Front" came to power in June 1936 a new problem arose: General Franco's attempt to overthrow the Spanish Republican Government. Many of the "Popular Front" supporters wanted to give the Republic active military assistance, to counter Italian aid to Franco, and to assert working-class solidarity. But

Blum refused to intervene in Spain. He still hoped to win Britain to France's side. He knew that if France took part in the civil war, Britain, who was urging the European Powers not to intervene, would be gravely offended. Blum's followers deeply resented his refusal to give aid to Spain. But in standing aside he was acting in France's best interests, avoiding conflict with Italy, avoiding provoking the French Right to violence in favor of Franco, and avoiding British displeasure. Although his policy seemed to underline, even more than the Rhineland crisis had done, the fact that France was broken as a great power, yet some powers of independent action were preserved.

It was Edouard Daladier and his Foreign Minister, Georges Bonnet, who finally subordinated French policy to British. The British Prime Minister, Neville Chamberlain, sought throughout 1938 and 1939 to come to terms with Germany. He urged the French to do likewise. He deprecated the division of Europe into two warring camps. He encouraged Bonnet to seek the benevolent neutrality of Italy. And he took the lead in trying to placate Hitler. Chamberlain failed, and in doing so he humiliated France. He begged France not to contemplate a war against Germany for the sake of Czechoslovakia; he poured scorn on Daladier's attempt to champion the Czechs; he entered into negotiations with Hitler without at first inviting the French to join him. When Chamberlain met Hitler at Munich, Daladier, like Mussolini, was little more than a spectator. Yet Chamberlain had the audacity to suggest that Daladier should fly on to Prague and give the Czechs the details of their required surrender. This Daladier refused to do. He returned to Paris from Munich depressed and angry. He regarded the sacrifice of Czechoslovakia to Hitler's ambitions as a shameful deed. Yet the British had given him only one alternative: to accept it, or to fight Germany alone. Britain had no intention of becoming involved in a Franco-German war on behalf of Czechoslovakia.

Daladier was ashamed at having submitted to British dictation; Bonnet, who had not been so anxious to "stand by Czechoslovakia," minded less. But the independence of French policy was seriously weakened at Munich. When Britain gave her guarantee to Poland, Daladier tried to ensure that the guarantee would be effective. But he could not halt Chamberlain's last-minute efforts to persuade the Poles to make concessions to Germany, nor could he persuade Bonnet to agree to firmness. Frenchmen grew cynical, caring neither to resist German pretensions nor to submit. When Germany invaded Poland the British hesitated to declare war. When they decided to do so, Daladier and Bonnet still held back. They could not bear to commit themselves to war. They knew that many Frenchmen would rather accept Nazi domination than go through the holocaust which, in 1914, had led them to Verdun.

The British declaration of war acted as a temporary stimulus to French morale. France declared war on Germany that same day: 3 September 1939. But the defeatists talked openly of capitulation by the end of the year. Only with difficulty had Daladier obtained a majority for his war policy in the Cabinet. France entered the war disunited and pessimistic. The Germans were now strong, well-disciplined, and bent on conquest. When the news of Poland's defeat reached Paris more than one Frenchman asked himself: "Would it not have been better to have imposed a more severe peace on Germany in 1919? Would it not have been wiser to have resisted Britain's attempts to modify the treaty in Germany's favor? Would it not have been safer to have occupied Germany, and divided her into separate states?" It is not for those who survived the Second World War to mock such questionings.

# ☆ 14 ☆

## THE SUPREMACY OF CONSERVATISM IN BRITAIN

DURING THE Great War the balance of political parties in Britain had been destroyed and government by coalition had been inaugurated, first under the leader of the Liberal Party, Asquith, then under a Liberal Minister, Lloyd George. When the war ended the coalition remained, with Lloyd George as Prime Minister. Many Liberals wished to return to the status of an independent political force and broke away from Lloyd George's leadership. A number of Conservatives disliked serving under Lloyd George and stood aloof. Lloyd George's peacetime coalition was a measure of his personal power and an indication of his political ambition. But it was unpopular with those who wished to return to the two-party system and who regarded the coalition as unnecessary and Lloyd George as personally dictatorial.

Lloyd George and his supporters maintained that the men who had won the war should "win the peace," and that it was only under his dynamic leadership that successful reconstruction could be achieved. The coalition was reelected in 1918. Although the war was won, the peace treaties had not then been signed, and Lloyd George owed much of his electoral majority to the crude anti-German slogans of his supporters, one of whom, Sir Eric Geddes, described their program as to "squeeze Germany like a lemon, until the pips squeaked." It was assumed that Lloyd George, despite the caution of his own utterances, would follow the policy of his coalition and impose severe terms on Germany. He also promised the returning soldiers "Homes fit for Heroes," although, when Bonar Law, the Conservative leader and a member of the coalition, asked what this meant, he was told that Lloyd George did not "think it necessary to discuss in detail how this program is to be carried out." But appeals to soldiers meant little, and they would probably not have trusted Lloyd George with power after the misery and weariness of the war. Fortunately for Lloyd George, perhaps, the soldier's vote hardly mattered. Although an elaborate scheme for postal voting had been worked out for soldiers, the task of drawing up the electoral register was left to an incompetent Minister. The registers were incomplete when election day came, and the majority of serving soldiers never received the vote. As a result of the election Lloyd George's coalition received 478 seats, his opponents, including a number of Liberals, 229.

Lloyd George became a peacetime Prime Minister. The Liberals who supported him sank to 136; the Liberals who opposed him fared even worse, gaining only twenty-eight seats. In this way Lloyd George had destroyed his own party while himself retaining political power. The great Liberal Party, which had ruled England from 1905 to 1915, was dead; a Liberal who wished to be a force in politics had either to become a Conservative or a socialist. Though the party survived, its status never improved.

Lloyd George's new coalition Members of Parliament were not the best that the parliamentary system could offer. The coalition did not enlist men of ideals or vision. Stanley Baldwin, Lloyd George's junior Conservative Cabinet Minister, described the newly elected members as "a lot of hard-faced men who look as if they have done very well out of the war." Idealists looked outside Parliament for inspiration; they hoped that in foreign affairs the League of Nations would provide the leadership and high-mindedness that seemed lacking at home. But for domestic affairs there was no solution. Working conditions were bad, strikes frequent, and arbitration slow. At one sumptuous dinner Bonar Law was asked by his hostess what the strikers really wanted. He pointed to the luxurious spread and replied: "Perhaps they want a little of all this."

The coalition failed to halt the growing industrial unrest. Lloyd George produced an unemployment insurance scheme which proved inadequate: men received 15s a week, women 12s. At by-elections the Liberals began to make small gains. In May 1921 Bonar Law, who had proved Lloyd George's most effective Conservative supporter in the coalition, was forced by ill-health to withdraw from the

Government. In 1922 Lloyd George's list of nominees for peerages created a political scandal. Many of the proposed peers could boast no other distinction than having paid handsome sums into Lloyd George's election fund. One, a South African financier, was considered particularly unsuitable. Even King George V was stirred to write to Lloyd George that he considered his peerage "as little less than an insult to the Crown and to the House of Lords." Lloyd George was prudent enough to sense danger and persuaded the financier to refuse his peerage.

It was over foreign affairs that Lloyd George destroyed himself. The Greeks, seeing Turkey defenseless and friendless as a result of her dismemberment after the war, hoped to make large territorial gains at Turkey's expense. Britain and France had "promised" Greece such gains during the war. An army of 200,000 Greeks advanced ino Turkey from Smyrna. But the Turkish soldier Mustafa Kemal (later Atatürk), who in 1915 had been partly responsible for defeating the British Army at Gallipoli, became President and dictator of Turkey in 1920 and prepared to check Greek ambitions. Kemal was supported by France. The Greeks halted. But in August 1922 Lloyd George provoked a crisis by making so pro-Greek a speech that the Greek King incorporated it in an army proclamation and Kemal, fearing an immediate attack, took the initiative. The Greeks were driven into the sea. The Turks then turned towards Constantinople, which had been under British military occupation since the end of the war. An Anglo-Turkish war seemed imminent. Within the coalition there were a number of antiwar voices, chief among them being those of Lord Curzon, the Foreign Secretary, and Stanley Baldwin. But Lloyd George's principal supporters, Winston Churchill and Lord Birkenhead, argued strongly for war. They did not wish to compromise with Turkey. The coalition, although divided, agreed to face the prospect of war.

Four years after the nation had laid down its arms, it was being asked to take them up again. On 7 October 1922, Bonar Law wrote a letter of protest to *The Times*. In his letter he echoed the feelings of many Conservative supporters of the coalition when he declared that Britain could not police the world alone. It was more important, he wrote, to safeguard the Empire than to march, isolated and unprepared, into a distant, unnecessary war. As Lord Beaverbrook, who was Bonar Law's chief supporter, wrote:

"The people by this time were against war. The Government had failed completely in their efforts to stir up a war spirit. They could not engender any enthusiasm whatever for an adventure in the Near East. It is possible that if the Cabinet had persisted, some headway would have been made in the direction of securing public approval but, as soon as Bonar Law raised the standard of peace, around which people could rally, the whole enterprise was at an end. Some Ministers might still wish to go to war. They could unfurl the banners and beat the drums. But the nation would not march."

Lloyd George had to abandon all thought of war against Turkey. The Conservatives began to fear that his antics and ambition would damage them. They began to dream of an independent Conservative Party. But they did not wish to gain independence from Lloyd George, as the Liberals had done, at the price of division and unpopularity. Conservative refusal to be smothered inside the coalition was reflected in the victory of a noncoalition Conservative at a by-election. Lloyd George's magnet had lost its power. On 19 October 1922 the Conservative Members of Parliament met at the Carlton Club. Stanley Baldwin, President of the Board of Trade, described the Prime Minister as a "dynamic force," so dynamic, he added, that he had destroyed the Liberal Party; sufficiently dynamic still, he concluded, to ruin the Conservatives. Baldwin's argument was effective; the Conservative members voted, by 187 votes to 87, to leave the coalition.

Lloyd George resigned at once and Bonar Law formed a Conservative administration. With the exception of two brief periods when a minority Labour Government was in office the Conservatives retained power until Winston Churchill formed a coalition Government in 1940. Lloyd George's defeat enabled the Conservatives to emerge as the ruling party, cautious and unadventurous, but reflecting the nation's desire for tranquillity. At the general election in November 1922 the Conservatives won 345 seats, Labour 142, Lloyd George's remnant of the coalition 62 and Asquith's Liberals 54. Stanley Baldwin succeeded Bonar Law as Prime Minister in 1923. He promised the nation a "quiet life." Two Labour Governments, in 1924 and 1929, led by Ramsay MacDonald, hardly threatened that quietude. They recognized Bolshevik Russia and raised the income tax. But the Conservatives regained political dominance during the economic crisis of 1931, when they joined and controlled a "National Government" under Ramsay MacDonald's nominal leadership. The Labour Party wished to rule alone. MacDonald lost their support by agreeing to a National Government. They considered him a traitor to socialism. The Conservatives did not feel so strongly: he represented no threat to conservatism, as Lloyd George had done. Two months later the Conservatives triumphed at the poll, winning 473 of the 554 National Government seats. Labour representation fell from 288 to 52.

The Conservative dominance in British political life led to a period of inaction and lethargy. The party, feeling so secure in their majority, had no need of vote-catching policies. They represented the comfortable mean between the wild violence of the fascist right and the growing anger and frustration of the socialist left. The most creditable feature of conservatism in the thirties was that it did not succumb to violence. The Conservatives outlawed the private army of Sir Oswald Mosley, a former Labour politician who had become the leader of the British Fascist Movement. They were equally firmly opposed to a second private army which the Labour politician Sir Stafford Cripps wished to set up to combat fascist acivity. There was no need for private armies: the British people did not approve of street fighting and had no intention of manning the barricades. Stanley Baldwin, three times Prime Minister, was an effective national pilot. Under his gentle guidance the ship of state seemed pleasantly becalmed. The great gales of Europe could not ruffle its sails. Its keel was unaffected by those two powerful currents of political violence, the rise of Nazism in Germany and the growing autocracy of Soviet Communism. While the rest of Europe was tossed and turned, England lay in quiet waters.

Yet the thirties were far from being years of rest and recuperation. England was badly hit by the world economic crisis and in the industrial cities there was widespread unemployment. Baldwin's Chancellor of the Exchequer, Neville Chamberlain, set up four commissioners to investigate the depressed areas. In his 1934 budget he restored unemployment benefits, which had been cut during the economic crisis. Even the income tax was reduced. Yet there was a budget surplus, the envy of all European treasuries. "There are," wrote Chamberlain, "some who think I am overcautious . . . humdrum, commonplace and unenterprising." Like his party and like his nation, Chamberlain rejected violence and exaggeration in politics.

When foreign affairs became more troublesome, Chamberlain failed to see that greater energy was needed to deal with the international crises. But in domestic affairs the relaxed nature of government was in many ways advantageous. There were no dramatic achievements; there were equally no sudden setbacks.

It was in dealing with the Indian Empire that the Government was most active. Indian nationalism, under Mahatma Gandhi's leadership, was vocal and adventurous. Although Gandhi's methods were nonviolent, they caused great inconvenience. A thousand Indians sitting silent at a crossroads or lying like branches across a railway line could be as troublesome as an armed mob. And whereas a rushing mob can be met with gunfire and the subsequent casualties attributed to the inevitability of violence, a squatting crowd can hardly be brutally treated; their very immobility exudes moral rectitude.

The Conservatives had to find an answer to nonviolence. They decided to promise India self-government. It was a courageous decision. Unfortunately Gandhi's followers were not as patient or as conscious of the power of nonviolence as Gandhi himself. In riots in 1930 over 103 people were killed and the British reacted by mass imprisonments amounting to 60,000. But the British were still willing to compromise, and in 1934 the Indian National Congress agreed to accept British protestations of sincerity.

That sincerity was shown in 1935 when the Government of India Act was passed. The Act provided for the setting up of an All-India Federation within which the provinces and states, whether Hindu or Muslim by religion, would have self-government. The Act was debated in the British Parliament for over eight months and it is estimated that fifteen and a half million words were spoken on the subject. Four thousand pages of Hansard, the official parliamentary record, were filled with speeches on India. As Sir Samuel Hoare, the Secretary of State for India who was mainly responsible for seeing the Bill through Parliament, wrote: "Never was there a better example of government by parliamentary discussion. . . . If the essence of democracy is government by debate, Parliament was never exhibited in a more truly democratic light."

The India Act was passed on 24 July 1935, a fine example of imperial magnanimity. At a time when Hitler, Mussolini, and Stalin were imposing severe restrictions upon the liberty of their subjects, the British were lessening the burden and loosening the bonds of empire.

One dissenting voice challenged the India Act and all that it represented. Winston Churchill had been a subaltern in India in the days when British rule was magnificent and its principles unchallenged. He resented the thought that Britain had become incapable of imperial rule and should give way before agitation which he regarded as irresponsible and ungrateful. As a young Minister he had been a Liberal, serving with distinction under Asquith and Lloyd George. After the fall of the coalition he turned to conservatism. He was Chancellor of the Exchequer under Baldwin from 1925 to 1929. He hated the India Act, and tried to rally a Conservative majority behind him. It seemed that he would split the Conservative Party and end the unity achieved by Baldwin. His challenge was resented as much for the harm it could do to the party as for its intrinsic merits or folly. Churchill employed his fine oratorical gifts in a fierce attempt to keep India under British rule. In London in 1935 he said:

"Gandhi-ism and all it stands for will, sooner or later, have to be grappled with and finally crushed. It is no good trying to satisfy a tiger by feeding him with cat's-meat. . . .

"The loss of India would mark and consummate the downfall of the British Empire. That great organism would pass at a stroke out of life into history. From such a catastrophe there could be no recovery."

Churchill failed to rally the nation; his description of the India Act as "a monstrous monument of shame built by pigmies" aroused ridicule, not anger. He appeared to many Conservatives as a rabble-rouser, a troublemaker, a die-hard, a danger to Conservative unity, a political failure seeking an obviously unmerited return to prominence and power. He no longer received a sympathetic hearing in the House of Commons. Members even walked out when he rose to speak.

The Conservatives were so securely fixed in power that they could ignore all political outsiders. They spoke of the Labour Party with ridicule and contempt. Neville Chamberlain was particularly scornful of Labour suggestions and criticisms. He could see no sense and no merit in opposition activities. As the Labour Party had no chance of coming to power, why should their views be heeded? Lloyd George's attempts to form an alliance with the Conservatives for the 1935 election were treated with derision. A man whose "Party" had only four seats in Parliament was not a force to be considered. As Chamberlain noted: "L.G. will never support the National Government except on his own terms." Naturally, support of that nature was rejected.

In 1935 India seemed the issue after whose solution calm would return. Yet 1936 brought new alarms, neither domestic nor imperial, but European. Hitler moved his troops into the Rhineland, the part of Germany demilitarized in 1919.

For the next three years British politicians were forced to consider foreign policy to the virtual exclusion of all else. But just as the Government and the people both sought to avoid adventurous policies at home, so they looked with alarm at the prospect of foreign commitments. Baldwin reflected the pacifism and passivity of the nation when he refused to be hurried into an accelerated rearmament program. The fact that the strongest advocate of rearmament was the same Churchill who had taken such an extreme view over India weakened the appeal of the rearmament argument.

Churchill wished to show Germany that if she sought military dominance in Europe she would have to reckon with British hostility. He wanted Hitler to be told quite clearly that if he attacked France he would have to face British intervention. Above all, Churchill wanted these threats to be backed, not by bluff, but by armed strength. His alarms were dismissed as hysterical and his arguments as fallacies. He claimed that if Baldwin wished to alert the nation to the dangers he could transform passivity into awareness overnight. He also claimed that if Hitler were told firmly and precisely just where he must call a halt, this would have the required effect, and check the German advance.

There were a number of strong reasons for Conservative hostility to rearmament. Baldwin was afraid that the nation would reject an appeal for more arms; disarmament was advocated by any politician, Labour or Conservative, who wanted popular support. Chamberlain, who succeeded Baldwin as Prime Minister in 1937, feared that the whole economic structure of Britain, which he had guarded so carefully as Chancellor, would be shaken and even destroyed if money were drained away from social reconstruction in order to pay for guns or aircraft. As Chamberlain wrote in 1936: "If we were now to follow Winston's advice and sacrifice our commerce to the manufacture of arms, we should inflict a certain injury on our trade from which it would take generations to recover."

Chamberlain had yet another reason for disliking rearmament. He did not believe that a show of military strength was the way to avert war. He considered the threat of violence to be useful for only one task, to provoke violence. He refused to believe that Hitler wanted war with Britain. He hoped that in time of crisis war could be averted by diplomacy. In 1938 Chamberlain's skill was put to the test when Germany demanded certain areas of Czechoslovakia inhabited mainly by German-speaking people. Chamberlain did succeed, on his own initiative, in averting war. But Czechoslovakia suffered in consequence, and a number of Conservatives began to agree with Churchill that preparations should be made for war.

It was only in March 1939 that Hitler revealed his wickedness to the bulk of the Conservative Party. By occupying Prague he showed that his proclaimed desire "to bring only Germans within the German frontiers" was only a partial statement of his aims. Belatedly and slowly Chamberlain's Government began to rearm. It accepted and indeed initiated military alliances with Poland, Rumania, and Greece. It stood forth, as Churchill had for years been urging it to do, as the champion of endangered nations and the enemy of aggressors. When Hitler invaded Poland in September 1939 Britain declared war against Germany. The Conservative Party remained in power, strengthening itself by the inclusion of Churchill into the newly formed War Cabinet.

Many Conservatives began to feel that the demands of war made a coalition necessary. Some felt that Chamberlain, in spite of the skill he had shown in trying to keep the peace, was not the man to direct the war. Others resented Chamberlain's failure to have seen the German danger earlier, to have rearmed more rapidly, or to have dealt more sternly with Hitler during the Polish crisis. But Conservative unity was unshakable. The dominance that had been wrested from Lloyd George in 1922 and protected from Churchill in 1935 was not going to be discarded easily. Loyal Conservatives deprecated a coalition and insisted that Chamberlain was exactly the man they wanted as their wartime leader.

Some Conservatives disliked the blind, unconstructive loyalty of their fellow Party men. As one young Conservative M.P. caustically remarked: "If Chamberlain says that black is white, the Tories applaud him for his brilliance. If, a week later, he says that he was wrong, and that black is black after all, they applaud him for his realism." [1]

Gradually, as the war progressed, it was clear that a change of leadership was needed. Chamberlain seemed unable to direct the war with vigor or to arouse in the nation any military enthusiasm. Lethargy and even defeatism spread through Britain. The Germans, having conquered Poland, offered to make peace. Many, fearing a prolonged war, wished to accept the German offer. Then, in March 1940, Hitler invaded Norway. Britain tried to prevent this further conquest, but failed. Many Conservatives grumbled and some plotted against their leader.

On 7 May the House of Commons debated the war situation. The debate continued on 8 May. During those two days Chamberlain was attacked by Conservatives as much as by socialists. Lloyd George also denounced him and demanded that he resign from the premiership in the interests of the war.

On 8 May a vote was taken. Although Chamberlain still held a majority, it was greatly reduced. Eighty Conservatives abstained from voting, showing their lack of confidence, if not in their party, then in its leadership. More crucial, thirty Conservatives voted with the socialists against Chamberlain. Harold Macmillan was one of those thirty.

Following the German invasion of Holland and Belgium on 10 May Chamberlain resigned. A coalition was formed, with Churchill as Prime Minister. The socialists were given powerful positions in his administration. But Churchill became leader of the Tory Party and the Conservative dominance, both in government and in the country, survived. It was not until after the war, at the general election of 1945, that Conservative strength collapsed. The Labour Party came to power with an overwhelming majority. But in 1951 the Conservatives were returned to power, and for twelve years more were unchallenged.

[1] This Tory "rebel" was Harold Macmillan. In 1942 he became Churchill's Minister Resident at the Allied Headquarters in northwest Africa. In 1945 he was appointed Secretary for Air. When the Conservatives returned to office in 1951, he was successively Minister of Housing, Minister of Defence, Secretary of State for Foreign Affairs and Chancellor of the Exchequer. He became Prime Minister in 1957 and retired in 1963.

# ✩ 15 ✩

## HITLER AND THE FAILURE OF
## GERMAN DEMOCRACY

ADOLF HITLER had been through the worst of the Great War. He had been a regimental orderly, a corporal responsible for carrying despatches from headquarters to the battle zone. He had taken part in actions and drunk deep of the drama of war. In a letter to his old Munich landlord after the Battle of Ypres in November 1914 he wrote:

". . . a shell burst in the English trenches ahead of us. The fellows swarmed out like ants, and then we rushed them. We ran into the fields like lightning, and after bloody hand-to-hand fighting in different places, we threw them out of one trench after another. Many of them raised their hands. Those who wouldn't surrender were knocked down."

This particular action lasted for four days and nights. At the end of it Hitler was awarded the Iron Cross, second class. He had narrowly escaped death when a tent, which he would have been occupying but for the sudden arrival of a lieutenant colonel, was struck by a grenade. Most of those in the tent were killed. "It was," Hitler wrote to his landlord, "the most terrible moment of my life." The lieutenant colonel recalled, eighteen years later: "I came to know Adolf Hitler as an exceedingly brave, effective, and conscientious soldier."

And so, among the millions of men who served their countries, coming to terms with the ghastliness of the trenches and not expecting to survive, this one, like so many, sank his whole being into the terrible task of living with death. On 4 August 1918 his service and abilities were rewarded by the Iron Cross, first class, one of the highest distinctions to which a common soldier in the German Army could aspire. He had, it appears, while carrying despatches, come across an enemy officer and fifteen men (whether English or French has not been determined) and these he had captured. Hitler remained a despatch carrier to the end of the war. In October 1918 he was gassed and temporarily blinded. The legacy of that gas stayed with him always, noticeable in the strange hoarseness of his voice and in the effort he was forced to make in order to speak for any length of time. He was not a natural orator, but the continual challenge created by the gas seemed to draw out of him extraordinary powers of vocal persuasion and endurance. Thus, from the common holocaust, an uncommon man emerged, who had seen what men could do while at the same time grumbling and unenthusiastic. May he not have sensed to what even greater efforts they were capable if given a cause and a reason for enthusiasm?

Hitler was born in 1889. His father, an Austrian customs official, died when Hitler was fourteen. Two years later he left school, moved to Vienna, took up painting, and sought a place at the Academy of Fine Arts. He failed, and joined the mass of Vienna's unemployed, carrying suitcases for travelers at the Westbahnhof or selling his own postcard paintings for a few pence. Vienna was a dungeon for the young Hitler: inhospitable, offering no opportunities and unwholesome. As he later recalled: "Wherever I went, I began to see Jews, and the more I saw, the more sharply they became distinguished in my eyes from the rest of humanity. Particularly the Inner City and the district on the Danube Canal swarmed with a people which even in their exteriors had lost all resemblance to Germans." And so, through poverty and observation, Hitler came to nationalism. He was a German; for him Austria was nothing but a part of Germany. It was the Jews (whom he claimed he could recognize with his eyes shut, by their smell) who were the aliens. In 1913 he left Vienna for Munich, where he lived by selling his watercolors; then, when he was twenty-five, war came, and on 1 August 1914, standing excited among the great crowd in the Odeons Platz, he heard the proclamation announcing the declaration of war.

When the war ended Hitler joined the Munich District Army Command as a civilian. This military authority controlled all the troops stationed in Bavaria. Hitler worked in the political department of this army command, reporting on the strength of the various

20. Benito Mussolini. A young anti-German socialist who turned to fascism and brought to Italy dictatorship and alliance with Germany.

21. Mussolini with Joachim von Ribbentrop, Hitler's Foreign Minister. Italians were suspicious of German plans. In 1943 the Germans ruled in Rome.

22. Erich von Ludendorff and Adolf Hitler. They planned to seize power in Munich in 1923.

23. Paul von Hindenburg and Hitler in 1934. The old President poses for an official photograph with his new Chancellor. Later he protested against Hitler's anti-Semitic policies, but in vain.

24. (*above left*) Ramsay MacDonald, England's first socialist Prime Minister. 25. (*above right*) Neville Chamberlain. He flew to Hitler three times in 1938 to preserve peace.

26. Stanley Baldwin, a Prime Minister who restored conservatism but neglected rearmament.

27. (*above left*) Engelbert Dolfuss. He had too many enemies to outwit them all. In 1934 he was assassinated. 28. (*above right*) Kurt von Schuschnigg. When they met in 1938, Hitler refused to let him smoke. Austrian independence ended with his resignation.

29. Arthur Seyss-Inquart. A fervent Nazi, he was Chancellor of Austria for only two days. Later he ruled Holland for Hitler.

30. Thomas Masaryk. He created Czechoslovakia and in 1918 became its first President.

1. Eduard Benes. In 1938, at Munich, is friends and enemies joined ogether and destroyed his country.

32. Konrad Henlein. In 1938 Hitler exploited his fight for the autonomy of the Sudeten Germans.

33. Joseph Pilsudski, a Polish military hero who returned to rule as dictator in 1926.

34. Joseph Beck, Polish Foreign Secretary. All his subtlety could not keep Hitler away.

35. Clifford Norton, a British diplomat wh spoke the truth; but in 1939 there was wax in the ears of the men at the helm.

5. (*above*) Churchill, Roosevelt, and Stalin at Yalta in 1945. The two who joined the war in 1941 joke with the man whose wishes they overruled.

7. (*below*) Randolph Churchill and Joseph Broz Tito. The guerrilla leader and the Prime Minister's son together in Yugoslavia during the partisan war.

38. The Warsaw Ghetto uprising of 1942 failed. The Germans
killed all who surrendered.

political groups and on the loyalty of particular individuals who might help in the overthrow of the republican democracy. He joined one political group, the German Workers Party, perhaps because he had been ordered to spy on it. The group was tiny and Hitler suddenly saw that through it he might have a platform and influence. The party was about to die; Hitler brought it a new lease of life: "After long negotiations I put through the acquisition of three rubber stamps. I also succeeded in having our little invitations to meetings hectographed. . . ."

Thus came leadership: the voice that was to rouse a nation to violence, the speeches that were to spread hatred into every home, concerned with nothing more drastic than an office desk and invitation cards!

Hitler built up his little party swiftly and skillfully. He pushed aside all other leaders. Against one, who had printed a leaflet describing him as acting on behalf of "the Jews and their friends," Hitler brought a libel action. His opponent withdrew the pamphlet, accepted the Honorary Presidency of the Party, and allowed its statutes to be altered to give Hitler, as President, unlimited power.

In February 1920 the party published its program: the Twenty-five Points. The program was strongly nationalist and anti-Semitic. It also attacked capitalists and landowners. Hitler supported these latter points because they gained the party further support. But he repudiated socialism as his power grew, announcing dogmatically: "Whoever is prepared to make the national cause his own to such an extent that he knows no higher ideal than the welfare of his nation . . . that man is a socialist."

By 1923 the Berlin Government had virtually lost control over Bavaria. Even Hitler's little party had grown into a noisy organization, with a band of thugs to enforce discipline and beat up critics. The Bavarian Government, unable to rely on support from Berlin, did what it could to suppress the military and political groups which were clearly seeking its overthrow. Hitler's "Stormtroopers" were banned from Munich in January 1923. He thus turned by necessity to diplomacy and persuasion. This was Hitler's greatest skill, so fully developed between 1923 and 1939 that he could manipulate the passions and judgment not only of defeated and disgruntled Germans, but of cynical Frenchmen and confident Englishmen. In 1923 the diplomat won his first triumph by persuading four other nationalist groups in Bavaria to join with him in an attempt to overthrow another more powerful group which had seized control of Munich. Hitler was so successful that even Field Marshal von Ludendorff fell in with the ex-corporal's plans. The *Putsch* failed and Hitler was imprisoned for a year. But by his attempt to seize power in Munich he became more than a local political figure and leader of one of a number of little parties. After 1923 he was a national figure. He had learnt that attempts to seize power by force could be frustrated by counterforce, and that authorities could command more loyalty and obedience than rebels.

While in prison Hitler brooded over his failure and wrote his book, *Mein Kampf* (My Struggle), in which he set out, with disarming clarity, the lessons he had learned. Hitler had seen how effective were his powers of persuasion. He had persuaded others to join him in making a *Putsch.* Perhaps he could one day persuade the nation to accept him as their ruler. Perhaps he could also persuade foreign nations to accept Germany's claim for more territory and power. By the skill of his oratory, the directness of his argument, and the seemingly clear justification of his aims he might, without violence, come to power in Germany, and make Germany great in Europe.

Hitler achieved both these aims. His National Socialist, or "Nazi" Party began to grow as soon as he left prison in December 1924. Its band of thugs were organized on military lines, a private army complete with uniform and flags. The Nazi emblem was the swastika, at first a curiosity in the streets of Munich. Hitler nourished his party on promises of power. He offered a well-defined enemy, the Jews, visible in every city, easy to denounce and easy to beat up without fear of official reprisals. He also offered a variety of stimulating activities: youth groups, women's groups, a teachers' association and even a Union of Nazi Lawyers. For it was not only thugs who were catered for; the ambitious "little man" could be won over by being shown that if he voted Nazi he could step into the job which a Jew would be forced to vacate; the professional man would see his Jewish rivals, whether doctors, journalists, or teachers, driven into obscurity. Germany would assert its greatness at home and then denounce the restrictions placed upon it abroad. Even intellectuals found it hard to resist Hitler's appeal for "justice" to Germany in the international sphere: the union of all Germans and the return of the

colonies taken away by the Allied powers in 1918; the building up
of an army which, with defeat, Germany had been forced to abandon, and the recovery of national pride. This was simple, unsophisti-
cated nationalism. Hitler did not care for subtlety. He spoke as he
felt, catching the mood of the nation and shouting into the micro-
phone what others dared only to think to themselves. In *Mein
Kampf* he wrote:

"The Jew forcibly drives all competitors off the field. Helped by
his innate greedy brutality, he sets the trade-union movement on a
footing of brute force. Anyone with intelligence enough to resist the
Jewish lure is broken by intimidation, however determined and in-
telligent he might be."

And also:

[Democracy] "can only be pleasing or profitable to mendacious
crawlers who avoid the light of day, and it must be hateful to any
good, straightforward man who is ready to take personal responsibility. . . . None but a Jew can value an institution which is as dirty
and false as he is himself."

The more people listened to him and applauded when he spoke,
the more Hitler became convinced that he was the chosen leader of
the German people. Even after his failure to seize power in Munich
in 1923 he seems to have been aware of some inner force driving
him irresistibly forward. Many times in the course of his trial he was
asked by what right he, a man without origins, title, or virtually any
education, arrogated to himself the right to govern Germany, sweep-
ing aside all existing authorities. Hitler replied: "This was not over-
weening or immodest of me. On the contrary, I am of the opinion
that when a man knows he can do a thing, he has no right to be
modest. . . . In such questions there are no experts. The art of
statecraft is—well, an art, and you've got to be born to it. . . . My
standpoint is that the bird must sing because he is a bird. And a man
who is born for politics whether he is free or in prison, whether he
sits in a silken chair or must content himself with a hard bench . . .
the man who is born to be a dictator is not compelled—he wills;
he is not driven forward—he drives himself forward; there is nothing immodest about this. Is it immodest for a worker to drive himself towards heavy labor? Is it presumptuous of a man with the high
forehead of a thinker to ponder through the nights till he gives the
world an invention? The man who feels called upon to govern a

people has no right to say: If you want me or summon me, I will cooperate. No, it is his duty to step forward. . . ."

Hitler's opportunity came in 1930, when Europe was plunged into economic chaos. In Germany unemployment reached over a million in September 1929 and rose steadily in the years that followed, reaching five million in September 1932 and six million (its peak) by February 1933.

Hitler exploited the fears of those who thought that Germany was on the verge of chaos. He offered unity and discipline, recovery and resurgence. He also made a conscious effort to appeal to groups theretofore unaffected by nationalist propaganda. In March 1930 he produced a program for peasants: large farming subsidies, cheaper manure and electricity, recognition of the peasant's "vital role" in the community. In Nazi Germany, he asserted, even the peasant would be able to look with pride on his way of life.

To lift men from despondency to hope, to raise them from gloom to expectancy, to drive out pessimism and promise a golden future—how could the man who offered to do all this be rejected? Against the established parties who since 1918 had produced neither political stability nor economic advantages; against the disappointing institutions, Church, Army and bureaucracy, Hitler stood like a crusader. He offered to smash the castles of the established order, under which no one benefited; in his new order everyone would belong, everyone would prosper.

Hitler's triumph was one of technique as well as of inspiration. The appeals he made were of no political value unless he could put them across to vast audiences. He became a master of propaganda, exploiting to the full the new medium, wireless. His election campaigns were conducted as if men's lives depended upon them; exacting timetables were rigorously kept and airplane flights organized from one town to another. Massed rallies cried out slogans like military commands and filled the air with urgency. And above all was to be heard Hitler's voice, enticing, seductive, bursting suddenly into anger, the voice of the ordinary man, the provincial, the ill-educated fellow, the *Bierhaus* orator—penetrating into every home through the new-fangled wireless.

Hitler wished to become Chancellor of Germany, not by seizing power, but by legal means. In this he succeeded, though not without the accompaniment of violence. His private army, the S.A. (Storm-troopers) played an important part in cowing those who failed to be inspired by Nazi promises. The S.A.'s main function was to break up communist meetings and marches. It also attacked Jews and "pro-tected" Nazi voters at election time. The S.A. was Hitler's nation-wide organization, divided into twenty-one groups, and numbering over 100,000 men by 1931. Its Chief of Staff was Captain Ernst Roehm, three times wounded in the Great War and one of Hitler's earliest political collaborators. Within a year Roehm had raised the S.A. membership to 300,000, drinking up the unemployed, who, if they were willing to drill and march and obey, received in return a free uniform, free meals, and a free bed. The S.A. was not meant to seize power, but to impress on the politicians that Hitler must be taken seriously.

Hitler never obtained a clear parliamentary majority. At the height of his electoral success, in July 1931, he won only 230 out of 608 seats in the Reichstag. In April 1932, in the second election for president, the voting had been

| | | |
|---|---|---|
| Hindenburg | 19,359,983—53% | |
| Hitler | 13,418,547—36.8% | |
| Thaelmann | 3,706,759—10.2% | |
| (Communist) | | |

In January 1932 Hitler addressed the industrialists whose money he needed for his party and whose support was essential for his polit-ical success. He spoke for two and a half hours, winning over those who were previously hostile: ". . . And when people cast in our teeth our intolerance, we proudly acknowledge it—yes, we have formed the inexorable decision to destroy Marxism in Germany down to its very last root. . . . Either we shall succeed in working out a body politic hard as iron from this conglomeration of parties, associations, unions, and outlooks, from this pride of rank and mad-ness of class, or else, lacking this internal consolidation, Germany will fall in final ruin."

Hitler's appeals were successful: to the industrialist he promised greater profits and political security; to the soldiers a new army; to the "little man" quick promotion; to the unemployed a worthwhile job. Only communists and Jews were unwanted and uncatered for.

Hitler's election successes reflected his mastery of political propaganda and brought him respectability. Industrialists, noting that the communist vote had also increased, looked to Hitler as their savior from what seemed to be an imminent "red peril." Some of the largest industrial concerns took Hitler into their confidence, buying his support for their own independence by cash donations. Chief among his patrons was Fritz Thyssen, head of the Steel Trust, who as early as 1923 had given Hitler a substantial sum of money. At that time Hitler had had few backers. By 1930 the financial power of the I. G. Farben Chemical Cartel, the United Steel Works, and Conti Rubber were behind him. Not every seeker for power can attract at the same time the unemployed workman and the prosperous employer.

On 30 January 1933 Hitler was asked by President Hindenburg to become Chancellor of Germany, and accepted. He was not supreme; only three out of the eleven cabinet posts were held by Nazis. The Vice-Chancellor, Franz von Papen, was in Hindenburg's confidence, and regarded himself as the real power in Germany. It was Papen who had urged Hindenburg to make Hitler Chancellor, convinced that Hitler would then be his prisoner. Papen was mistaken: once Chancellor, Hitler was able to cast aside the intriguers and middlemen who had hoped to use his mass support for their own ends. He knew that power lay with him who grasped it, and, as Chancellor, he was able to grasp it firmly.

On 27 February 1933 the Reichstag building was burnt down. On 28 February Hitler promulgated a special decree "for the protection of the people and the State." The danger, he claimed, came from the communists, whom he at once charged with the Reichstag fire and with further plots to overthrow the state. The special decree enabled Hitler to legislate as he pleased. Under the guise of this emergency, his first autocratic measures were put into force. Freedom of the press, the rights of assembly and association, the privacy of the post and telephone, were "temporarily" abolished. The communists were hunted down and imprisoned.

Hitler ruled by decree, but this was only an emergency measure. Parliament still existed and would have to be called. Yet in it Hitler had no absolute majority. He still hoped to obtain an electoral majority, and elections were held in May 1933, heralded by vast demonstrations, S.A. processions, long exhortations from Hitler, and, for the waverers, open violence.

But despite this Hitler still failed to obtain an absolute majority for his party, receiving seventeen million votes against seven given to the Social Democrats, four to the Communists, four to the Catholic Center Party, and three to the Nationalist Party.

If Hitler added the votes of his Nationalist Party allies he could muster 340 seats, the other parties, 307. But Hitler wished to rule unhindered by the trappings of parliamentary democracy. To obtain full powers he needed to extend his emergency decree permanently. But to carry such an enabling act into law Hitler needed a two-thirds majority in the Reichstag. This, he saw, he could not get. But his abilities had not ceased on his becoming Chancellor. Having bid successfully for power, he bid again, this time for respectability.

On 21 March 1933 the Reichstag session opened. Hitler decided to hold the opening ceremony in the Potsdam Garrison church. The church contained the grave of Frederick the Great. It was the shrine of Prussian greatness. To it on that spring day came the marshals, generals, and admirals of the old empire, wearing their imperial uniforms; and with them the Nazi deputies in their brown shirts and swastika arm bands. Outside, the swastika flag hung side by side with the imperial emblems. This mingling of the old and new went further: into the church came President and Chancellor, and both spoke. Hindenburg said: "May the old spirit of this celebrated shrine permeate the generation of today, may it liberate us from selfishness and party strife and bring us together in national self-consciousness." Hitler declared: "Neither the Kaiser nor the Government nor the nation wanted war. It was only the collapse of our nation which compelled a weakened race to take upon itself, against its most sacred convictions, the guilt of this war. . . . In the last few weeks our national honor has been restored."

The enabling act was not yet passed, but after such a show of loyalty and patriotism, even foreign representatives at the ceremony realized that Hitler was master of his faculties, and of Germany. The enabling bill was laid before the Reichstag two days later, on 23 March 1933. Most of the Communist deputies had already been imprisoned, as had some dozen Social Democrats. Hitler spoke first, and moderately; the Social Democrat leader spoke next, opposing the enabling act. Hitler unexpectedly spoke again, less calmly, in answer to the Social Democrat challenge: "I do not want your votes.

Germany will be free, but not through you. Do not mistake *us* for bourgeois. The star of Germany is in the ascendant, yours is about to disappear."

The Catholic Center Party leader announced that the Center Party would support the Bill. Hitler had promised not to interfere with Church rights and had hinted at concessions to Catholics if they would support him. The Center Party were the party of compromise and compliance: they voted away their independence and with it parliamentary government. The votes were announced: for the Bill, 441; against, 94. The Nazis leapt to their feet in joy. Hitler had the power to rule unsupervised, unchallenged, and alone.

Hitler left few aspects of German national life unmolested. He destroyed the independence of the federal German states which since the unification of Germany in 1871 had preserved many traditional regional powers. Nazi governors were appointed for every state, with power to dismiss state officials, promote new laws, and if necessary dissolve the state assemblies. The governors' powers were themselves closely defined by Hitler: "They are not the administrators of separate states," he said in March 1934, "they execute the will of the supreme leadership of the Reich. . . . National Socialism has as its historic task to create the new Reich and not to preserve the German states."

The autonomy of the trade unions was destroyed as easily as that of the federal states. On 2 May 1934 the S.A. occupied trade-union offices throughout Germany. Union officials were arrested. For them, as for anyone else who henceforth dared to challenge Hitler's authority, a new fate was in store: the concentration camp. Here a new brutality was practiced; often sadists were put in command and given wide powers. The facts about the concentration camps were soon widely known, not only in Germany but abroad. On 10 January 1935 the *Manchester Guardian* devoted two columns to a description of concentration camp rules.

## NAZI CONCENTRATION CAMPS

### Official Regulations as Enforced at Lichtenburg

#### THE PENALTIES

1. *"Strenger Arrest,"* that is to say, confinement in a cell on bread and water with a hot meal once in four days. The "cells" vary in char-

acter from camp to camp—at Dachau they are of concrete, some of them being dark and having chains let into the walls so that prisoners can be chained up.

2. *"Strafarbeit,"* that is, hard labour, which means work of a particularly exhausting or repulsive kind, accompanied by "subsidiary penalties" (*Nebenstrafen*) such as floggings (*Prugelstrafe*), extra drills, tying to a post, a hard bed, less food, a ban on letters and so on.

3. *"Stockhiebe,"* or birching, which is often inflicted in the presence of other prisoners.

4. Death—either by hanging or shooting. (Fourteen prisoners in the Lichtenburg camp have either been killed outright or have died of their injuries.)

### THE OFFENCES

Amongst the offences for which these penalties are inflicted are the following:

No. 2: Sitting on a bed or lying in it without permission in the day-time—penalty, 5 days' confinement to cells.

No. 4: Reporting sick without reason—penalty, 5 days' confinement to cells and several weeks of hard labour.

No. 6: Making disrespectful or satirical remarks about an S.S. man or deliberately failing to salute—penalty, 8 days' confinement to cells, 25 strokes of the birch at the beginning of this period and another 25 at the end.

No. 10: . . . encouraging other prisoners to go on hunger-strike, or showing disrespect to the symbols of the National Socialist State—penalty, 42 days' confinement to cells or permanent solitary confinement.

No. 11: Talking politics, making speeches, forming groups with seditious intent, collecting true or untrue information about the concentration camps, conveying such information to foreign visitors, or smuggling it out of the camp . . . penalty—those committing these offences will be hanged as fomentors of sedition.

No. 12: . . . shouting or making speeches when on the march—penalty, instant death by shooting or subsequent death by hanging.

The concentration camps were quickly filled, as more laws made more activities illegal. On 14 July 1934 one of the many new laws was published, brief and succinct:

*Article 1:* The National Socialist German Workers' Party constitutes the only political party in Germany.

*Article 2:* Whoever undertakes to maintain the organizational structure of another political party or to form a new political party will be punished with penal servitude up to three years. . . .

It was against the Jews that Hitler acted most severely. From the very moment that he became Chancellor Jews were removed from government service, journalism, broadcasting, and teaching. Children were taught at school to mock their Jewish comrades. In many communities Jewish parents were refused special medicine for their young children. Hotels displayed signs: JEWS NOT ADMITTED; towns informed visitors on their approach roads: JEWS ENTER AT THEIR OWN RISK; and finally there came the proud boast of the "best" municipalities: THIS TOWN IS FREE FROM JEWS.

On 15 September 1935 the Nuremberg Laws were published. All the world could read them; they were the charter by which Jews were forced to live. Jews were deprived of German citizenship. They were forbidden to marry non-Jews. By 1938 they were not allowed to practice in the professions of law or medicine. Some of the most eminent and cultured Germans were thus reduced to the status of second-class citizens. Upon their abilities and desire to serve were poured the scorn and malice of a jealous, small-minded people.

Hitler was accepted by the Army because he promised to respect its traditions and hinted at a foreign policy that would involve eventual military action. But once in power Hitler relied heavily on his own S.A. The Army resented this neglect, and feared that the corporal who had struck at federal Ministers and trade unionists might soon turn upon generals. But Hitler was too astute to incur the army's enmity. If his own S.A. offended the generals, he would willingly curb its power.

Ernst Roehm had no desire to see a reduction in his importance; the S.A. was over four times as large as the Army. Roehm and his commanders wished to replace the army entirely and become the sole military force in Germany. Hermann Rauschning, one of Hitler's early associates, recorded a conversation he had with Roehm in 1933. Roehm told him (while somewhat flushed with wine): "Adolf is a swine. He will give us all away. . . . His old friends aren't good enough for him. Getting matey with the East Prussian generals. They're his cronies now. . . . Adolf is turning into a gentleman."

Hitler had indeed decided that the old army must take precedence over his personal creation. But "gentleman" was hardly the correct word: on 30 June 1934 Hitler struck at the S.A. with even greater violence than he had struck at the communists. Roehm and most of the other S.A. leaders were shot. The executions did not stop at the S.A.: Hitler took the opportunity to murder other enemies. A number of Catholic leaders were shot. The priest who had helped Hitler revise the proofs of *Mein Kampf* was found dead in a wood near Munich. Gustav von Kahr, who had helped defeat Hitler's 1923 *Putsch,* and was seventy-three, was found in a swamp, his body hacked to pieces. There were other vengeances; Hitler told the Reichstag that there had been "more than seventy-seven" victims: there were certainly a few hundred. The nation was treated to a lecture on morality: Roehm, a homosexual, had been surprised with his friends; Hitler, the guardian of the people's morals, had destroyed an ugly vice. The Blood Purge of 30 June was more than an example of Hitler's capabilities; it was an example of Nazi brutality, widely publicized at the time but soon, by most, ignored.

Hitler had shown his power. He turned next to construction. Under his ambitious gaze a new Germany was built, efficient and prosperous. The new Reich was the envy of foreigners. British visitors in particular, having seen the depressed areas in England and known the unpleasantness of labor unrest at home, admired Germany's discipline and drive. The German economy was advancing rapidly. Industry expanded and work was found for all. New styles of building and new industrial techniques emphasized the effectiveness of the German revolution.

Hitler had many visitors from outside Germany: he always enjoyed talking, and welcomed a chance to impress foreign statesmen and journalists. He seemed at times to despise the very Germans he was leading, to regard them as the somewhat stupid recipients of his wisdom. The English, he knew, understood the greatness of his achievement, and praise from England was praise indeed. He was prepared, too, to answer any adverse criticism. When asked by a group of Englishmen why he allowed the persecution of Jews he replied disarmingly: "Gentlemen, you can have no idea of the terrible things that would happen to the Jews if *my* protective hand were withdrawn." Lying thus, Hitler posed successfully, at home and abroad, as the moderate who stood between Germany and violence

Slowly and methodically Hitler built up the German Army, but when the British learned of this they did not take alarm. It was easy for anyone who sympathized with German aspirations to rationalize; to explain that Germany, as the only disarmed nation in Europe, needed an army for self-defense. Many Englishmen were aware of the humiliations which Germany had suffered in 1919; they argued that Hitler, for all his violence, was only trying to make Germany respectable again. Above all, it was thought, Hitler himself would soon be influenced by his growing responsibilities and become a calm, sensible, cooperative statesman. If Hitler were to become reasonable there was clearly no need to be frightened of a German Army. Such an army could, after all, act as an effective check to the ambitions of Stalin's Russia, the unknown power that might well be planning to dominate Europe. Hitler spoke frequently of the Bolshevik danger, and of his own role as guardian for a neglectful Europe. He also spoke continually of his desire for friendship with Britain, a country whose imperial history fascinated him. He considered the English a second master race. He knew that if he could win England's friendship, his survival was assured. How encouraging it must have been for him to find his English visitors so delighted with everything they saw in Germany: the new *Autobahn,* the smart soldiers, the enthusiastic young men and women in their summer camps, disciplined and working in the fields, singing with joy at their new-found national pride.

Lloyd George's reaction to Hitler was typical: "If only we had a man of his supreme quality in England today," he said.

Many Englishmen accepted the justice of Hitler's claim that he wished to incorporate within Germany's frontiers all Germans living outside them. Had not Britain, it was argued, helped to separate those Germans from their homeland at the Treaty of Versailles? And did not the principle of self-determination work in favor of Hitler's policy? Even Hitler's methods, though at times harsh, seemed in general praiseworthy. In July 1933 the London *Times* had told its readers: "Herr Hitler is certainly not devoid of ideals. . . . He undoubtedly desires to re-inculcate the old German virtues of loyalty, self-discipline, and service to the State. . . . Herr Hitler will win support which may be very valuable to him if he will genuinely devote himself to the moral and economic resurrection of his country."

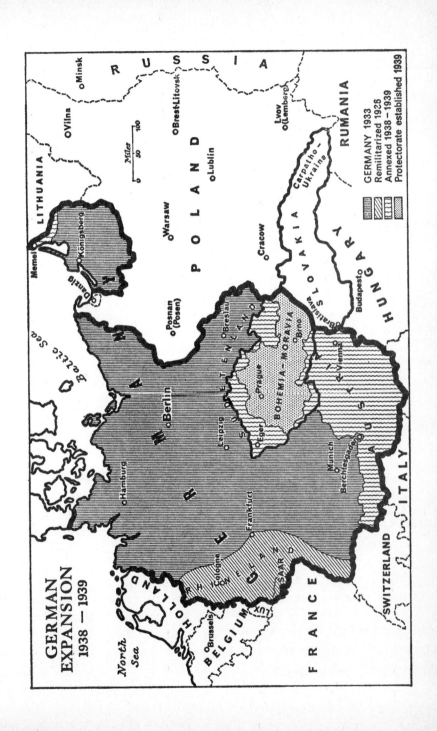

GERMAN EXPANSION 1938 — 1939

RUSSIA

oMinsk

oVilna

LITHUANIA

Memel

Königsberg

Danzig

Baltic Sea

oPosnan (Posen)

POLAND

oWarsaw

oLublin

oBrest-Litovsk

oLvov (Lemberg)

RUMANIA

Carpatho-Ukraine

oCracow

SLOVAKIA

Bratislava

Budapesto

HUNGARY

Breslau

SUDETENLAND

Prague

BOHEMIA-MORAVIA

Brno

Eger

oVienna

AUSTRIA

Leipzig

Berlin

GERMANY

Munich

Berchtesgaden

ITALY

SWITZERLAND

Hamburg

Frankfurt

RHINELAND

Cologne

SAAR

GLATZ

FRANCE

LUX.

BELGIUM

oBrussels

HOLLAND

North Sea

Miles
0    50    100

GERMANY 1933
Remilitarized 1926
Annexed 1938 – 1939
Protectorate established 1939

Hitler did not disappoint his foreign sympathizers. He knew the value of propaganda and had the supreme gift of being able to judge just what it was that was wanted of him. To those interested in economics he talked of Germany's economic recovery; to those interested in armies he talked of Germany's magnificent defense force; to those fearful of communism he pointed to himself and said—"Here is your savior"; to those concerned with keeping peace in Europe he discoursed at length upon his own war experiences and of how, in the trenches, he had learned for all time the lesson of the horrors of war.

Hitler boasted that he carried out his policies "with the confidence of a sleepwalker." His people delighted in their new leader and rushed to serve him. In the labor camps, where young men could work for the state, building roads or canals or clearing construction sites, intense patriotic fervor was created. Foreign visitors could not fail to admire the new spirit of Hitler's Germany: activity, urgency, optimism.

Who, in 1936 or 1937, could say what would be the outcome of all this feverish activity? Those who admired the new spirit of nationalism, self-discipline, and firm government could see no dangers for the rest of Europe in a strong Germany; those who disliked autocracy could still hope that the more brutal aspects of Hitlerism would not last long. As Winston Churchill wrote, on 17 September 1937: "I have on more than one occasion made my appeal in public that the Führer of Germany should now become the Hitler of peace. When a man is fighting in a desperate conflict he may have to grind his teeth and flash his eyes: anger and hatred nerve the arm of strife. But success should bring a mellow, genial air and, by altering the mood to suit the new circumstances, preserve and consolidate in tolerance and goodwill what has been gained by conflict."

A year later all such optimism was destroyed. Hitler annexed Austria in March 1938. In September 1938 he obtained the German-speaking areas of Czechoslovakia. Although the British Government approved of the union of Austria and Germany, and encouraged the Czechs to concede their disputed territory, Hitler's methods aroused hostility throughout Europe. Though his cause seemed just, his violent language was offensive. In March 1939 he occupied Prague; in July he demanded concessions from Poland. Again his cause seemed good: Danzig was an entirely German city artificially separated from Germany by the victorious allies in 1919. There were also Germans living in a compact mass on the Polish side of the Polish-German frontier. But Hitler acted with too much violence. Despite Britain's guarantee of Poland's independence, he was convinced that neither Britain nor France would fight for Poland. At first it seemed that he was right, that his genius for assessing the true nature of a situation was untarnished. He saw the British guarantee to Poland criticized in such differing organs of opinion as *The Times* and the *Daily Express*. Hitler sensed this division of opinion and convinced himself that Britain and France would not fight. On 1 September 1939 he invaded Poland. On 3 September Britain and France declared war. Hitler had made his first mistake: he underrated British hostility to his methods. In October 1939, having conquered Poland, he offered to make peace with Britain. He was prepared, he said, to guarantee the independence of the British Empire. He wanted to work in alliance with Britain, whose enmity, he insisted, he wished ever to avoid.

Hitler's peace offer was attractive. Some Englishmen wanted to accept it. Lloyd George was said to be demanding a secret session of Parliament and to be convinced that if they voted on Hitler's terms a majority of Members would accept them. But Neville Chamberlain refused the outstretched hand, convinced that Hitler was not to be trusted and that when it suited him to do so he would turn against Britain. Thus Chamberlain, the man of peace, who had believed Hitler's promises in 1938, put his face against defeatism. Britain's determination to fight until Hitler was defeated grew: in May 1940 Winston Churchill became Prime Minister and all chance of compromise with evil ended.

Hitler's plans failed: England, whose friendship he had sought, was now pledged to destroy him and his regime.

Using the same medium which Hitler had so fully exploited, the wireless, Churchill roused British courage to resist:

"These cruel, wanton, indiscriminate bombings of London are, of course, a part of Hitler's invasion plans. He hopes, by killing large numbers of civilians, and women and children, that he will terrorize and cow the people of this mighty imperial city, and make them a burden and an anxiety to the Government and thus distract our attention unduly from the ferocious onslaught he is preparing. Little does he know the spirit of the British nation, or the tough fibre of the Londoners, whose forebears played a leading part in the establishment of parliamentary institutions and who have been bred to value freedom far above their lives. This wicked man, the repository and embodiment of many forms of soul-destroying hatred, this monstrous product of former wrongs and shame, has now resolved to try to break our famous island race by a process of indiscriminate slaughter and destruction. What he has done is to kindle a fire in British hearts, here and all over the world, which will glow long after all traces of the conflagration he has caused in London have been removed. He has lighted a fire which will burn with a steady and consuming flame until the last vestiges of Nazi tyranny have been burnt out of Europe, and until the Old World—and the New—can join hands to rebuild the temples of man's freedom and man's honour, upon foundations which will not soon or easily be overthrown."

Confronted by such determination, by one country standing alone, but standing without fear or weakness, Hitler's shrewdness left him. The coolness, caution, and sense of occasion that had won him an empire disappeared. Hitler attacked Norway, Holland, Belgium, and France, sending his armies into every vulnerable nation, threatening Britain with invasion, promising Churchill and his people the same ill-treatment that he meted out to his other conquered peoples.

In 1941 he invaded Russia, his ally of two years' standing. In the same year he declared war on the United States, thus forcing upon himself the enmity of the world's least vulnerable nation. While the Allied nations combined to destroy him, Hitler succeeded in putting as many as six million Jews to death; Poles, Russians, and Yugoslavs were likewise massacred in great numbers in the name of a so-called racial purification of Europe. By this policy Hitler incurred the enmity of his old sympathizers, of those who had seen the justice of his demands and of those who had hoped to see him, as the years developed, grow more mellow and more tolerant. Such hopes had to be abandoned: the Allies finally determined to accept from Germany only unconditional surrender. By his own rash decisions Hitler found himself confronted by the combined forces of Britain, Russia, and the United States.

# ☆ 16 ☆

## AUSTRIA'S FRAGILE INDEPENDENCE

WITH THE SUDDEN and complete collapse of the Austro-Hungarian Empire in October 1918, the national minorities, Serbs, Czechs, and Poles, together with the Magyars of the Hungarian kingdom, cast off imperial allegiance and declared their independence. The course of the war had turned so severely against the Empire that there was no force, military or psychological, to hold the once cumbersome and now fragile fabric together. Habsburg appeals to unity fell on deaf ears in Prague, Budapest, and the borderlands. The Empire had collapsed: no proclamation of future reforms and no promise of a loose federal structure could restore it.

At the center of the chaos lay Austria itself, the German core of a predominantly non-German empire. Its neighbors had formed separate states: only the German-speaking Austrians remained, defeated and depressed, within the "empire." The Emperor Charles, without an empire to rule and with a hostile combination of Austrian nationalists and socialists demanding immediate union with Germany, issued his last proclamation on 11 November 1918. It marked the end of the Empire:

"Filled now as ever," the proclamation read, "with unchangeable love for my people I will no longer set my person as a barrier to their free development. I recognize in advance the decision which German-Austria will take on its future form of state. The people has now taken over the government through its representatives. I renounce any participation in the business of the state. Simultaneously, I relieve my Austrian Government of office."

The Austrian Republic was established on the following day.

"German-Austria" was in no sense the heir to the Habsburg Empire. It inherited instead the city of Vienna, whose size and prosperity had been dependent upon the whole Empire. To Vienna had come the produce of the Carpathian Mountains and the Transylvanian Alps, the intellectuals of Prague and Cracow, the ambitious bureaucrats and businessmen of every province, and with them the orientation of communications, the stimulation of commerce and the vast, detailed mechanism of government. Vienna had woven around herself an imperial coat of many colors. Suddenly the coat was torn to ribbons, leaving only a threadbare patch intact. The great city looked out upon small, pastoral provinces and upon a series of mountain-dominated valleys. Outside that narrow ring were potential enemies of every sort and of great strength. In the midst of the areas that had declared their independence lay the food, the coal, and the raw materials without which German-Austria could not live—and they lay in hostile hands, hands themselves desperate to grasp every possible semblance of strength and every symbol of independence.

The Entente Powers showed intense sympathy for the new nations that had sprung from the severed limbs of the empire—for Czechoslovakia, for Poland, for Yugoslavia, and for Rumania. But when the Entente looked at Austria it was hostile: Austria seemed the remnant of the enemy, German in speech, even if not in culture and outlook; one of the causes of the four years' agony; the nation that must be punished for its misdeeds. Thus it was that the Entente blockade, established to bring the war to a speedy end, was continued after the war. When the blockade was lifted after the Peace Conference the new nations, Austria's former partners in the Empire's trade, imposed their own barriers. The tariff replaced the machine gun, and men, instead of being shot down from the parapet of their trenches, starved in the streets of their capital. Austria could expect no sympathy from its neighbors. Indeed, it was dangerous to speak German in the streets of Prague in 1918 and illegal to take an Austrian newspaper into Yugoslavia, the new state built by the union of Slovenia, Croatia, and Serbia.

The Provisional Government of the Austrian Republic proclaimed Austria a part of the new German Republic. At that time all classes and parties in Austria seemed to regard union with Germany as an essential and obvious development. The nationalists in Austria had long given such a union a leading part in their program;

for them the Habsburgs were not German but multinational, and as such had always seemed a negation of the German spirit. For the nationalists, union with Germany would end the "two Germanies," the two independent imperial structures which had seemed, by their very existence, to weaken the potential power of a united German nation, a single "Germanity."

The Austrian Social Democrats had equally strong reasons for seeking union with Germany. They saw themselves combining with the strong socialist parties of Germany to bring about the final triumph of progressive socialism. Austria and Germany, once united, would discard the outmoded structure of capitalism and build a new egalitarian structure. For all Austria, Germany would clearly provide the raw materials, the outlet for domestic produce, and the opportunity for individual talent, which the new Slav states denied them. Vienna itself would cease to be a city without a country; inside Germany it would surely recapture its vivacity, its wealth, and its cultural dominance.[1] German-Austria sought union with Germany, not in order to conquer but in order to survive.

The name "German-Austria" was changed by order of the Entente Powers to "Austria." The left-wing socialist Otto Bauer had to resign the post of Foreign Minister when union with Germany, which he supported, was forbidden. He was succeeded as Foreign Minister by Karl Renner, who had become Chancellor of the coalition Government on the day of independence. Renner accepted the concept of an isolated, independent Austria. It was he who signed the Peace Treaty of Saint Germain, in which even the name "German-Austria" was formally abandoned. By the same treaty Austria was forbidden to join Germany. For Austria no appeal to "self-determination" was allowed: that ideal, which America had inspired, was applied to the Slav states but refused to the "Enemy Powers." Self-determination worked against Germany and Austria in three cases: the Germans in the Austrian South Tyrol were transferred to Italy, the Germans in the Sudeten region to Czechoslovakia, and the isolated groups of Germans in the cities of the former empire were absorbed into the new states of which those cities became part. The dictates of geography, the new nationalism of the Slavs, and the hostility of Britain, France, and Italy, all ensured that Austria should be isolated in Eu-

---

[1] After 1918 the Viennese described their capital as the *Wasserkopf;* a medical term used for a child born with an abnormally enlarged head.

rope, even from the Germans. The result of this isolation was a growing bitterness which in its turn led to the growth of autocracy and
violence.

Vienna, in 1919, was on the verge of starvation. The city was
saved by American aid. It has been estimated that but for the immediate response of the United States to Vienna's appeal, over one-
third of the city's population would have died of starvation. One
hundred and thirty thousand school children were sent abroad, to
spare them the worst of privation. Nevertheless, 90,000 of the 200,-
000 who remained were found to be undernourished. Food available
in the provinces was deliberately withheld from Vienna by the peasants.[2] The Habsburg Empire had commanded the loyalty of peasants and farmers; the old Emperor's portrait could be found in every
hamlet. But in the provinces the Republic was new and alien. The
names of its leaders sounded strange on peasant lips and the tone of
its official pronouncements jarred in their ears. They understood why
it was necessary to obey the Emperor, but to obey a socialist republican Government in Vienna was incomprehensible. Local patriotism was strong, supported by different dialects and the frequent
provincial intermarriage. With the collapse of the Habsburg power,
several of the provinces formed provisional governments which
sought to negotiate with the Government in Vienna over all questions of food supplies, requisitioning, and taxation. These provisional governments acted with great independence. The Tyrol declared, after a plebiscite in 1921, for union with Germany; the
Vorarlberg declared with equal firmness for union with Switzerland.
Styria was for union with Germany, though less decisively. The central Government at Vienna asserted its power and the Republic survived intact. But the forces for provincial disunion, and the forces
for union with Germany, were revealed.

From 1918 to 1938 Austrian politics were unsettled. Twenty
years was not enough to produce a stable form of government. The
will to stability was not absent, but the method of creating calm political development and general interparty agreement within coali-
tions was never discovered. The balance of the parties worked
against stability. In 1920 the dominance of the Social Democrats

2 It was possible to obtain the most precious items of food, such as a sack of
potatoes, if one was willing to offer the peasant something out of the ordinary—
jewels, a gold watch, or even a grand piano.

gave way to that of the Christian Socials, a Catholic, antisocialist party.

Karl Renner resigned as Chancellor in October 1920; in June 1921 Dr. Schober was elected. As Police President of Vienna he had learned a great deal about popular discontent. He sought security for Austria by a policy of external appeasement. He wanted Austria's neighbors to be won over to greater support of the Republic. He brought an end to the plebiscites which were producing pro-*Anschluss* results, realizing that such results were a prime cause of foreign alarm and hostility. No Austrian statesman during the interwar years made so determined and far-reaching an attempt to win Czechoslovak support. Under the Treaty of Lana, Austria received badly needed economic aid, in the form of a loan. In return, Schober bound Austria to respect the 1919 frontiers of Czechoslovakia. The pan-Germans in Austria were resentful, seeing this pro-Czechoslovak move as a further barrier to a revision of the Peace Treaty. Czechoslovakia was regarded as the power most interested in maintaining the postwar frontiers. The Austrians who looked forward to ultimate union with Germany had nothing but contempt for the new frontiers. Schober did not long survive his unpopular treaty. When inflation came in 1922 the pan-Germans and Social Democrats combined to outvote him. He was succeeded as Chancellor by Mgr. Ignaz Seipel.

Seipel sought political stability by ending the growing inflation. He did this by gaining international support for Austria. He persuaded Britain, France, Italy, and Czechoslovakia to guarantee a loan to Austria of 650,000,000 gold crowns. Austria gave an undertaking that, for twenty years at least, she would not give up her own independence. The four powers agreed both to respect and help preserve Austria's territorial integrity. These agreements were known as the Geneva Protocols. The pan-Germans in Austria were angry at Seipel's anti-*Anschluss* pledge. But they knew that without the loan the whole Austrian economy might collapse. The loan was successful: inflation ended, and Seipel's power increased.

Seipel's internal measures were designed to restore financial stability. They were ruthless and created much hardship. Nearly 100,-000 public officials were dismissed and the salaries of those that remained were cut. Unemployment and sharp social discontent followed. Seipel resigned in November 1924, being unprepared to grant a sudden but not unexpected demand for greater provincial autonomy. His successor, Ramek, was equally unsuccessful in resisting provincial pressure, and failed to improve the economic situation. His government was further discredited by a series of financial scandals.

Seipel returned as Chancellor in October 1926. His political power depended upon uniting a number of parties into an antisocialist coalition. Hostility to socialism became more important in Austrian politics than constructive legislation. Seipel made no concessions to socialist demands, despite the obvious need for social legislation. But antisocialist policies could not affect Vienna itself, which had been created a province in 1920, and whose own local government was entirely socialist and independent-minded. Seipel and his supporters, ruling Austria from Vienna, had to look on powerless while the Viennese socialists in their local assembly passed municipal legislation which changed the face of the capital. Banks and business houses were taxed to provide a social program of housing, education, and health, which in its turn increased the popularity of the Viennese socialist party. Private houseowners paid heavy taxes which went towards the cost of workers' flats, and put an end to slums in the capital.

The Austrian Army, or *Volkswehr,* had been controlled by the socialists immediately after the fall of the Habsburgs, and by 1927 had become a socialist party instrument. Outside Vienna other armies were created—local defense forces known as the *Heimwehr,* which were strongly antisocialist. Thus Vienna and the provinces found in their respective armies a further source of tension and conflict.

In 1929 the *Heimwehr* began to plan a *Putsch* against Vienna. The *Heimwehr* leader, Prince Ernst Rüdiger von Starhemberg, raised men and stockpiled arms without government interference. The socialists threatened to cut off all light, power, and water in Vienna if the *Heimwehr* attempted to seize the city. The former Chancellor Dr. Schober was again Police President of Vienna. In September 1929 he became Chancellor for the second time. The *Heimwehr* was confronted with a stern and experienced opponent. Schober, under pressure from the League of Nations, decided to legislate against the *Heimwehr* stockpiling of arms. But his Disarmament Bill was a failure. The *Heimwehr* refused to give up their arms. The Government was resentful but powerless; the provincial authorities sympathized with Starhemberg. In September 1930, Schober fell and Starhemberg became Minister of the Interior, in charge of the police. The *Heimwehr* saw its chance for a successful *Putsch*. But the plans of the *Putsch* leaked out and were published in full in the German press. As a result of the leak, moderates were alerted.

On 10 November 1930 Austria went to the polls. The socialist votes increased. The Christian Socials, led by a moderate, Ender, lost votes. Schober's moderate National-Economic bloc held the electoral balance. The *Heimwehr* tried to save themselves by seeking an alliance with Schober, who refused it. *Heimwehr* optimism waned. Schober became Vice-Chancellor and Foreign Minister. The Christian Social Ender became Chancellor.

The triumph of moderation came too late. Before Ender and Schober could take further measures against the *Heimwehr,* or inaugurate a progressive legislative program, economic disaster struck Austria and Europe. Schober had tried to plan ahead; he had sought by some master stroke to forestall the demands of the extremists whose cry was, as always, union with Germany. Schober knew this would be unacceptable to France. But he saw a whole spectrum of possibilities and chose what he hoped would be a middle way, drastic enough to satisfy Austrian extremists and mild enough to avert foreign hostility. Schober obtained German approval for his plan: on 21 March 1931 it was announced, in a joint Austro-German communiqué to the capitals of Europe, that a Customs Union was being negotiated between Austria and Germany.

Schober had made a terrible miscalculation. He had failed to consult any foreign government, even those who might have approved of his plan. The Austro-German Customs Union seemed a direct threat to the postwar frontiers of Europe. France, Czechoslovakia, and Italy made a joint protest demanding the retraction of the plan. Even the British Government, though no longer an absolute supporter of the postwar *status quo,* saw the Customs Union as a political threat and urged that the plan be submitted to the League of Nations Council. But France refused to wait for the cumbersome League system to work and therefore applied a private weapon of her own. Considerable sums of French money lay deposited in the Vienna *Creditanstalt* Bank. These sums were withdrawn. On 11

May 1931 the *Creditanstalt* informed the Austrian Government that it was unable to meet its financial obligations. The bank's Austrian creditors then began to withdraw their deposits. Germans and Hungarians with capital in Austria felt a loss of confidence; there was a run on their domestic banks. American creditors were alarmed and also withdrew credits. The great crash had begun.

Chancellor Ender appealed to France to redeposit French money in Austria. France was willing to do so only if the Austro-German Customs Union was renounced. Austria gave way on 3 September 1931, hoping by political capitulation to retain economic security. The international economic crisis spread meanwhile to other countries. In Austria economic disaster was averted by a French and British loan. But elsewhere foreign credit was withdrawn, long-term loans refused, and international trade reduced to a trickle. Lack of economic confidence led at once to political distrust among the nations of Europe. All sense of community was destroyed and each nation tried to fend for itself.

Internally every European government felt obliged to pursue a policy of discipline and hostility to economic concessions to the community. The citizen was required to sacrifice his personal hopes and ambitions for the more immediate, more rigid needs of his nation. The state began to assert its power as the sole effective instrument of national unity.

In Austria the position of the Christian Socials was threatened on both sides: by the Social Democrats on the left and by the *Heimwehr* on the right. The *Heimwehr,* encouraged by the growing success of the Nazi Party in Germany, grew more and more outspoken in its advocacy of totalitarian methods. A relatively little-known member of the Christian Socials, Engelbert Dollfuss, became Chancellor in May 1932, and joined parliamentary forces with the *Heimwehr* in order to avoid a dissolution of Parliament that might have given advantage to the Social Democrats.

In March 1933 this political stalemate seemed beyond solution. The economic crisis had affected the finances of the state-owned railways. On 1 March the railway management announced that it could not pay salaries except in small installments. It also declared itself forced to reduce pension rights for railway employees. The result was a two-hour strike. Dollfuss decided to exert his power. He ordered the army to occupy the railway stations. Strike committee

members were arrested, then discharged, jobless. The Social Democrats refused to call a general strike, preferring to appeal in Parliament for a vote of no confidence in Dollfuss. The railwaymen also
included right-wing *Heimwehr* supporters, so that the *Heimwehr*
vote was uncertain. Even the Christian Socials, though they would
not vote against Dollfuss, felt obliged to ask for the reinstatement of
the dismissed strike leaders. As men of all political parties worked
on the railways, no party could afford to ignore the railway interest.
Dollfuss took alarm, and, after receiving a narrow majority on 4
March, decided to bring parliamentary government in Austria to an
end. On 7 March 1933 he abolished the constitution by emergency
decree. He even prohibited the Constitutional Court from dealing
with complaints about the illegality of his action. When Parliament
tried to reassemble on 15 March it was prevented from doing so. A
few members managed to enter the building but were at once
ejected by Dollfuss's police. The Social Democrats were in a quandary. They had sought to avoid violence and had preferred parliamentary pressure to the more drastic instrument of the general
strike. Now Parliament was no more. Yet they still shrank from
calling a general strike, hoping still to reach a peaceful settlement,
and a return to parliamentary government, by negotiation with
Dollfuss. Karl Renner urged socialists to accept Dollfuss's fascist-
style Corporative State, even if they had to abandon organized
socialism. Renner hoped that the new state would become more
liberal if socialists supported it. But the support which the *Heimwehr* gave to Dollfuss was not a good omen for the Left.

Dollfuss tried to save Austria from those whom he regarded as
the state's enemies: the growing number of Austrian Nazis, who,
after Hitler's rise to power in Germany in March 1933, had become
outspoken, exuberant, and uncompromising, and the Social Democrats, whom he regarded as a disruptive and anti-Catholic force.
Dollfuss sought a compromise with the Austrian Nazis, which they
finally rejected in December 1933. His domestic legislation fell particularly severely upon the trade unions, who were to be controlled
in future by government nominees. The right to strike was abolished
for all workers in public enterprises. There was to be no place in the
new Austria for socialism. The Catholic Church supported Dollfuss's autocratic endeavors. On 21 December 1933 the bishops declared in their Christmas encyclical: "However small a state may be,

it needs a leader [*Führer*] . . . a master whom the others obey.
. . . The people, too, have to obey and to serve, not to decide according to their whims. . . . The frequently misinterpreted phraseology
about popular sovereignty is not only unreasonable but also unchris-
tian, and in the long run even atheist." Such was the message of
Christmas 1933: obedience to a man who had destroyed the constitution and made a mockery of Parliament.

In February 1934 the *Heimwehr*, unwilling to accept Dollfuss's
appeal to nonviolence, attacked the Social Democrats in Linz. In
Vienna the Social Democrats, fearing *Heimwehr* plots, declared a
general strike and mobilized themselves for their defense. Dollfuss
saw his chance to crush the Social Democrats and announced the
abolition of Vienna's autonomy as a province. Dollfuss could call
into action 50,000 men, of whom 10,000 were *Heimwehr* men; the
Social Democrats could muster only 15,000 to 20,000. Battle was
engaged. For nearly three days the workers in the courtyards of their
flats held out against superior forces. But once Dollfuss trained artillery on one of the workers' blocks of flats the battle was clearly lost.
In other provinces the Social Democrats were defeated more swiftly.
Dollfuss was completely successful, and after his victory promulgated a new, strongly antiparliamentary constitution "in the name of
Almighty God, from whom emanates all law."

As far as the *Heimwehr* were concerned, Dollfuss, by crushing
the Social Democrats, was making their own work easier. The
*Heimwehr* stood aside with equanimity to watch the guns go into
action against the Viennese workers. But it could not be so detached
when Dollfuss moved Austria further and further away from the
German camp, towards fascist Italy.

Dollfuss made Starhemberg Vice-Chancellor. When Dollfuss
went to Rome in March 1934 Starhemberg stayed in Vienna. On 17
March Dollfuss signed the Rome Protocols on behalf of Austria.
These protocols, of which there were three, created a pact for political
consultation between Italy, Austria, and Hungary, and inaugurated a
plan of intensified economic collaboration. Each of the three powers
agreed to respect the independence of the other two. Thus Mussolini
became Austria's patron, and the ever-increasing numbers of Austrian Nazis saw the possibility of union with Germany rapidly
recede.

A further blow to Austrian Nazi ambitions was the meeting between Hitler and Mussolini in Italy on 14 June 1934. As a personal encounter between the dictators it was not a success; Hitler was badly bitten by midges and in a truculent mood. He told Mussolini that "the Austrian Chancellor must be an independent person," and that Austrian Nazis should be taken into Dollfuss's Government strictly in proportion to the result of their electoral strength. But he pressed no German claims to patronage or control in Austria.

The Austrian Nazis felt abandoned by their German hero. An outburst of Nazi lawlessness was answered by Dollfuss with mass arrests and internments. Finally, on 25 July 1934, a group of Austrian Nazis, disguised as soldiers and police, attempted to seize power. They failed, as the Cabinet, whom they had hoped to arrest, was not in session. But they found Dollfuss in his office, and murdered him.

The death of Dollfuss did not benefit the Nazis; they had killed the head of state, but failed to seize power. Nazi risings in Styria, Carinthia, and parts of Upper Austria were suppressed within three days. The Government was reconstituted with Kurt von Schuschnigg as Chancellor.

Schuschnigg maintained Dollfuss's authoritarian constitution intact. But he was a gentler man, less eager to crush opposition and less willing to force matters to extremes. In October 1936 he called an emergency Cabinet meeting, at the end of which it was announced that all *Heimwehr* Ministers had been expelled. This dramatic action removed a source of violence from the councils of government. Schuschnigg thought next of restoring the Habsburgs, but was unwilling to face the international hostility which such a restoration would involve. He thought also of coming to terms again, as Schober had done, with the Czechs, but feared that this would only stir up pro-German feeling. In foreign policy he trusted in Mussolini's ability to warn Hitler away from Austria. In April 1935 the Stresa-front between Italy, Great Britain, and France promised greater international security for Austria. But with Italy's invasion of Ethiopia in the same year Britain and France disassociated themselves from Italian interests, and by implication from Austrian affairs.

It was impossible for Schuschnigg to ignore Germany by looking the other way, by imprisoning Austrian Nazis, or by relying upon Italy to support him. The number of Austrians who hoped for union with Germany never seemed to diminish, while Hitler himself appealed to all German-speaking people in his Greater-Germany policy. Schuschnigg's Austria represented calm and inertia; Hitler's Germany offered activity, a new sense of empire, the thrill of action and adventure. Nazism's appeal was to a nation on the move, anxious to assert its pride and power. Schuschnigg's regime could offer no such movement.

Schuschnigg tried bravely to resist the pressure of pan-Germanism. On 11 July 1936 he obtained a pledge from Hitler respecting Austrian sovereignty. In return Austria acknowledged itself "a German state." Mussolini was alienated by this Austro-German pact, lost interest in Austria, and preferred to come to terms with Hitler. Austria lay isolated, with only Schuschnigg's abilities guarding her independence. But the Austrian Nazis continued to plot, despite Hitler's apparent lack of interest. By January 1938 it was clear to Schuschnigg that a Nazi *Putsch* was imminent. He decided to confront Hitler with the evidence of the plot, in the hope that Hitler would remember his pledge in favor of Austrian independence and denounce the conspirators. Schuschnigg misjudged the situation. When he went to Berchtesgaden on 12 February 1938 Hitler not only told him that the conspirators were in the right; he ordered Schuschnigg to give a general amnesty to Austrian Nazis, to include some of them in his Government, and to suppress all evidence of a Nazi plot. Schuschnigg, isolated in Germany, could not challenge Hitler. But, returning to Austria, he determined to show Hitler that Austria could defend herself. On 9 March 1938 he announced that a plebiscite would be held on 13 March to decide in favor of Austrian independence.

Hitler could not allow Schuschnigg's plebiscite to go ahead. A majority for Austria's independence would be a blow to his pan-German cause. Hitler had no immediate aggressive plans, but he was not going to allow open anti-Germanism. On 11 March he demanded the postponement of the plebiscite and Schuschnigg's resignation. Schuschnigg, without allies at home or abroad, was forced to comply. On 12 March Hitler's army entered Austria, and from Linz Hitler demanded that Austria accept a pro-German Government, headed by an Austrian Nazi, Arthur Seyss-Inquart. Hitler seems to have wanted to see Austria linked to Germany within some loose federal structure, keeping an Austrian Chancellor and an Austrian

Government, but deferring to Germany in matters of foreign policy and overall economic interest. But once Hitler reached Linz he was amazed at the favorable reception; crowds cheered him wildly, seeing in his arrival the dramatic fulfillment of their pan-German dream. All the long-suppressed excitement of pan-Germanism was let loose. Even in Vienna, so Hitler was told, large crowds were demanding, not independence but *Anschluss*. Hitler seized his opportunity. On 14 March he entered the capital and proclaimed the total union of Austria with Germany. Even Hitler had been unable to anticipate the outburst of joy with which the *Anschluss* was greeted.

Those who opposed the *Anschluss* stayed at home, soon to be sought out by the police, and imprisoned, or cowed into silent submission. Hundreds committed suicide. Jews were at once singled out for ill-treatment.

After the *Anschluss* the Austrian Nazis proved Hitler's loyal supporters, fighting in his battles and even participating in his atrocities; and some of the worst Nazi outrages that were to come in the following years were carried out by Austrian divisions of the S.S.

Seyss-Inquart had been proclaimed Austrian Chancellor on 11 March; two days later he stood down for Hitler. He summoned his Cabinet and urged them to accept the *Anschluss*. At the same time he admitted to his colleagues that even he, good Nazi that he was, would have preferred to see "a certain measure of independence" preserved for Austria. Now he could save nothing. This two-day Chancellor represented the triumph of the Austrian Nazis and exposed the superficiality of their triumph. Austria was merged into Germany, physically and spiritually. Some Austrian Nazis courageously produced anti-Hitler pamphlets; then their printing press was raided and they themselves arrested. Dollfuss had crushed Austrian socialism; Hitler snuffed out Austrian independence, even the Nazi variety. Seyss-Inquart's career was advanced by Germany, not by Austria; he became ruler of German-occupied Netherlands in 1940, and was hanged after the Second World War, having been found guilty at the Nuremberg trials of crimes against humanity.

On 10 April 1938 Hitler held the plebiscite which he had refused to allow Schuschnigg to hold. The result was declared as 99 per cent in favor of Hitler and of the *Anschluss*. This result was clear, but the methods by which it was obtained were dishonest. The Social

Democrats refused to vote; Jews were not allowed to. For those who might have wished to vote for an alternative, no alternative was provided. Nevertheless the *Anschluss* was given a wide welcome. The Catholic Primate of Austria, Cardinal Archbishop Innitzer, had sent greetings to Hitler as he was advancing on Vienna, and even ordered churches to hoist their flags and ring their bells in honor of the event. Hitler met Innitzer in Vienna. The Cardinal promised Hitler that Austria's Catholics would become "the truest sons of the great Reich into whose arms they had been brought back on this momentous day." During the plebiscite Innitzer intervened decisively together with five other bishops, sending a letter to Hitler's deputy in Vienna which said: "On the day of the plebiscite, it is the obvious national duty of us bishops to declare ourselves as Germans for the German Reich, and we expect of all faithful Christians that they know what their duty to the people is."

Catholics were not the only people to be exhorted by their leaders to vote for Hitler. Karl Renner, first Chancellor of the Austrian Republic of 1918 and leader of Austria's moderate socialists, added his personal support for the plebiscite. Renner announced his hostility to the methods of the *Anschluss,* but his final verdict was approval: " . . . the *Anschluss* . . . is a historical fact, and I regard this as satisfaction indeed for the humiliations of Saint-Germain and Versailles. . . . The twenty years' stray wandering of the Austrian people is now ended. . . ." So ended also twenty years of independence marked throughout by uncertainty, turmoil, and political violence.

On the day before the plebiscite Hitler addressed 20,000 Nazis in Vienna: "I stand here because I flatter myself that I can do more than Herr Schuschnigg. I have shown through my life that I can do more than these dwarfs, who ruled this country into ruin. Whether in a hundred years' time anyone will remember the names of my predecessors here, I do not know. But my name will remain as the name of the great son of this country."

In this way iniquity triumphed over a cultured, bewildered people, who failed to solve their problems from within, and did not appreciate the wickedness that lay without.

## ☆ 17 ☆

# CZECHOSLOVAKIA: EUROPE'S FUTILE SACRIFICE

OF ALL THE NEW STATES set up after the Great War Czechoslovakia was geographically the most vulnerable. She stretched across a mountainous area of Europe in the most erratic manner imaginable. Within her boundaries lived Czechs, Germans, Slovaks, Hungarians, and Ruthenians. In the mining district of Teschen were a small but compact group of Poles. The conflicts of interest and temperament among these different groups created a difficult problem for the Czech government. The Czechs tried to organize and control these disunited groups and this attempt to bring peace and calm through legislation and supervision nearly succeeded. But the minorities were too large to accept the psychological inferiority of "minority status," even if they were not well enough united to agitate successfully for fuller autonomy or self-government. Nor did the Czech government feel able to make wide concessions, for it feared to weaken its newly won sovereignty.

Czechoslovakia was the product of the enlightened liberal theory of self-determination. President Wilson of the United States had given the state his blessing. Thomas Masaryk, President of Czechoslovakia from 1918 to 1935, was considered among educated Europeans the ideal democrat—wise, moderate, and far-seeing. But, like the Austro-Hungarian Empire out of which it had been born, Czechoslovakia was a collection of fragments, not a unity.

Czechoslovakia was created in 1918. The ancient territory of Bohemia, which was the last form in which the Czechs had known independence, had ceased to exist in 1620. Then, at the Battle of the White Mountain, Czech Protestantism had been forced to acknowledge the supremacy of Habsburg Catholicism. The Habsburg power grew and expanded, seeming to obliterate Bohemia beyond recall: the power that once stretched from the Adriatic, across the Danube, to the Elbe and the Oder, was submerged for 300 years. Only its memory remained; a legend half-remembered in the mouths of garrulous grandfathers, a grievance exciting the imagination of patriots, a map of antiquarian interest on the cartographer's desk. Who in Berlin, who in Breslau, who in Trieste—who even on the distant Dutch coast—remembered that once his ancestors had lived under Bohemian rule?

Czech patriotism grew slowly. In the nineteenth century all Europe was excited by the ideas of national sovereignty and statehood based on ethnic considerations. Bohemia was ruled from Vienna, but her own great city, Prague, later the Czech capital, flourished. It became a center for art and education, and nationalism thrived in its narrow medieval alleyways and courtyards.

On 26 July 1914 Austria-Hungary ordered mobilization. The first moves of the Great War had begun. It was not armies alone that were involved: within the Habsburg dominions the small nationalities saw their opportunity to surge forward to nationhood. The Russian Tsar, Nicholas II, fearful of the vast armies of Austria-Hungary, issued a manifesto promising the people of Bohemia their freedom, hoping to entice the Czechs away from the Austrian camp. The Austrian authorities took alarm. Thirty-five Czechs were executed for possessing a copy of the Tsar's manifesto. But Czech nationalists had seen that the future of their ideal—an independent Czech state—was bound up with the Entente Powers—France, Russia, Britain and (after 1915) Italy. If the Entente were to defeat Austria, the subject peoples of the Habsburg Empire expected to move forward immediately to nationhood.

It was not the Czechs alone who rejoiced. Their southern neighbors, the Slovaks, were equally enthusiastic about national independence. Czech and Slovak nationalists had often quarreled. Differences of temperament, conflicts of interest, and the desire to fight their battle single-handed, created constant disagreement between them. But two small Slav groups could not afford to squabble at a time of such great opportunity. Czechs and Slovaks realized that if independence came they would be more powerful together. Thus, as the war progressed, their leaders united. Unexpectedly and perhaps uncritically, the concept of Czechoslovakia was born: a single state for two related peoples.

Masaryk sought Entente support for a Czechoslovak state. In England he found two powerful allies. One, Wickham Steed, was foreign editor of *The London Times,* an outspoken critic of Habsburg rule and a competent, pugnacious propagandist. The other, Professor R. W. Seton-Watson, bombarded the academic world and the public with weighty books, persuasive pamphlets, and lectures. He urged London University to make Masaryk a professor. Masaryk gave his inaugural lecture on 19 October 1915. Its title was: "The Problem of the Small Nation in the European Crisis." Seldom had a small nation obtained so central a platform and so able a propagandist. Masaryk talked Czechoslovakia into existence; when he went to the United States he talked Czech and Slovak *émigrés* there into a declaration of unity, the Pittsburgh Manifesto, which in its turn persuaded Czechs and Slovaks in Europe to work together.

In Paris the Czechs set up a Czech National Council. Eduard Beneš, who supervised much of its work, has told the story of its activities in his *War Memoirs.* One aim dominated all else: to make the Czechs an important part of the Allied war effort. Beneš knew that if the Czechs could play a serious part in the defeat of the Austro-Hungarian and German empires, and if a sense of obligation could be created in Allied minds, the establishment of Czechoslovakia would be assured.

From the early months of the war Czech troops who deserted from the Austrian armies went over to Russia. A Czech Legion was created in Russia in August 1914, and joined the Russian front by the beginning of September. When Austro-Hungarian units were captured, Czech soldiers among them were transferred from prisoner-of-war camps to the Czech Legion. The Russian effort on the eastern front was made easier by the presence of Czech troops whose hatred of the Habsburgs was often more intense even than Russian hatred.

In 1917 Masaryk arranged for the transfer of 2,400 Czech troops from the eastern front to the western front. Britain and France were given a visible and effective example of the Czech desire to help the Allied cause. On 13 June 1917 the French Government recognized the Czech National Council and concluded an agreement with it over the transfer of troops. The Italians, seriously defeated by Austria at Caporetto on 1 November 1917, also hastened to recognize the Council, and encouraged Czech units to fight together with the Italian Army. Thus Czech troops bolstered the Allied war effort on three fronts. Masaryk estimated that 182,000 Czechs were involved in the war on the Allied side. This military support was decisive for the Czech cause. On 9 August 1918 the British Foreign Office issued a statement which raised the status of the Czech National Council from a small group of *émigrés* to a government: "Since the beginning of the war the Czecho-Slovak nation has resisted the common enemy by every means in its power. The Czecho-Slovaks have constituted a considerable army. . . . In consideration of their efforts to achieve independence, Great Britain regards the Czecho-Slovaks as an Allied nation."

Austria-Hungary, disintegrating under the double pressure of the Allied armies and the growing national unrest within her borders, could no longer maintain full imperial control. Her Ministers, in a last attempt to preserve some shadow of the Habsburg heritage, appealed to the minority groups to accept a federal instead of an imperial structure. The appeal failed: on 28 October 1918, amid the chaos of Austria's defeat, Czechoslovakia declared itself an independent state. Its leaders were in exile; but after nearly three hundred years the defeat of the White Mountain had been avenged.

Czechoslovakia was almost certainly the most democratic of the new postwar states. Within its borders a tolerance developed contrasting well with the harsher rule in Poland, Hungary, Rumania, and Yugoslavia. Minorities were not persecuted and left-wing political parties were not driven underground. But the Czechs were exuberant at their victory and would not allow minority groups to destroy their independence. What hostility to minorities there was, however, led to neither violence nor repression. The restrictions imposed—on the German-speaking minority in the Sudetenland, for example—were at times irksome, but never intolerable. Similarly, despite a left-wing attempt at a *coup d'état* in December 1920, the Communist Party was never banned. In almost every neighboring state to be a communist swiftly became a crime. In Czechoslovakia the communists polled over 900,000 votes in 1925. Then their influence declined. It was decline resulting from the common sense of the electorate, not from police pressure.

Czechoslovakia's foreign policy was conducted by Beneš, who was Foreign Minister from 1918 to 1935 and President (succeeding

Masaryk) from 1935 to 1938. Beneš looked to the League of Nations for support, trusting in the League to protect Czechoslovakia should enemies threaten, and giving the League much of his time and ability. He was elected to the League Council in 1923, and served as its chairman six times. Both France and Russia were willing to guarantee Czechoslovakia's frontiers. A Franco-Czechoslovak Treaty was signed in January 1924. Czechoslovakia had found a powerful and vocal ally. More important, there seemed no potential enemy. On 16 October 1925 the Locarno Agreements were initialed, and Germany, in return for guarantees of her frontiers, accepted the frontiers of her neighbors. The German-speaking minority in Czechoslovakia could not henceforth put their trust in an expanding Germany. They had, therefore, to accept their position within Czechoslovakia, as Germany had renounced her ambitions outside her Versailles boundaries. Few people in 1925 could foresee that French power would wane so quickly, or that Germany's self-restraint would be abruptly swept away and Locarno utterly ignored.

From 1919 to 1929 Czechoslovakia prospered. Her minorities were treated with growing sensitivity. Industry flourished and trade expanded. Ten years after the state had been founded, her people knew a contentment denied to their neighbors. Perhaps a second similar decade would ensure that the state should survive unmolested. But in 1929 the downward path began. The economic crisis which shattered the great nations could hardly leave the smaller ones unwounded. A gap was torn in the fabric of the new state that could not be repaired easily or quickly. And before the repair was done, the whole fabric had been destroyed. Even simple statistics tell a vivid tale. Foreign trade fell from 21 billion crowns in 1928 to 5.5 billion in 1933; unemployment rose from 80,000 in 1929 to 920,-000 in 1933.

It was the German minority who suffered most as a result of the crash. Its trade was almost exclusively with Germany. But Germany, itself in the grip of economic chaos, needed to protect its own products and trade with Czechoslovakia was therefore drastically cut. The German minority in Czechoslovakia was faced with economic ruin. Not Czech ill-treatment, but the sudden onrush of European economic collapse brought about the economic misery of the German minority.

The Sudeten Germans were discontented. But not all of them saw the answer to their misfortune in *Anschluss* with Germany. Before 1918 these German-speaking people formed part of the Austrian Empire. They had more in common with the Czechs than with the Germans. But after 1918 most of them had no common frontier with Austria. If they wished to be joined to a German-speaking sovereign state, it would have to be with Germany, not Austria. This many of them did not relish.

In 1933, with Hitler's coming to power in Germany, those Sudeten Germans who disliked Czech rule were presented with a cruel dilemma. If they were to be joined to Germany they would have to accept Nazi rule, with all the brutality and suppression which Nazism involved. The socialists and Jews among the Sudetens knew that they could expect only persecution and imprisonment from Germany; newspaper editors would be faced with censorship, artists and writers with the demands of an eccentric and crude state control of culture. This was not an inviting prospect. Many Sudetens therefore began to think in terms of greater privilege inside Czechoslovakia. They abandoned the once attractive idea of union with Germany. Now autonomy was their demand: they sought self-government in local issues, while leaving economic and foreign policy to the Czech Government in Prague. Local self-government was a reasonable demand. Most Czechs realized this and accepted the idea that sooner or later such concessions would have to be made.

An obstacle to good Czech-Sudeten relations arose in 1935 with the creation of a Sudeten-German Party. This party did not openly advocate union with Germany, but was so active in demanding local self-government that many Czechs feared this to be a cover under which lay extreme demands. Hence a mood of defiance grew up among many Czechs, who did not want to make any concessions, however small, for fear of encouraging the separatist tendencies which they thought they saw lurking in the Sudeten-German Party's inner will.

The Czechs also suspected that the Sudeten-German Party was financed in part by the Nazi Government. This was true. It did not necessarily mean that Hitler wanted to annex the Sudetenland, and it may only have meant that he was determined to cause trouble and dismay among his neighbors wherever he could. But nobody could be certain; the Czechs were not necessarily unwise in suspecting

Nazi German motives: lack of evidence was no proof of lack of intention.

The Sudeten-German Party's leaders were Konrad Henlein, Karl Frank, Kundt, and Sebekovsky. Their demand for local self-government was listened to sympathetically abroad. They came to dominate Sudeten-German politics. Their opponents, the Sudeten Social Democrats under Wenzel Jaksch, also wanted local self-government. But Jaksch was frightened by Henlein's overt Nazism. He feared that too large a measure of self-government would make Henlein master of the Sudetenland, and leave his own Social Democrats in a weak position, the victims of local coercion and local violence. Henlein's strength was his outspokenness. He demanded local autonomy with strident voice. Jaksch was less hysterical; hence his weakness.

Henlein visited Britain in 1937 and gained unofficial British support for his local self-government plans. Professor Seton-Watson introduced him to leading British politicians and journalists. Seton-Watson saw that most of Henlein's demands were reasonable. He also saw that they could be exploited by Hitler if Hitler so desired. Seton-Watson urged the Czechs to accept Henlein's proposals and thus forestall any attempt by Hitler to interfere. This was also the advice of Sir Robert Vansittart, head of the British Foreign Office. But both Seton-Watson and Vansittart warned Henlein that if his program expanded to include the annexation of the Sudetenland by Germany, they would not support him. Henlein promised Seton-Watson that his demands would never go beyond local self-government.

In August 1938 Hitler began to take an active interest in the Sudeten problem. He suggested in conversation with foreign diplomats that the Sudetenland ought to become part of Germany. One foreign diplomat in particular agreed with him. This was the British Ambassador to Berlin, Sir Nevile Henderson, who thought that Britain should take the initiative in advocating the incorporation of the Sudetenland into Germany. Hitler was naturally pleased to hear this view from English lips. But he made no official demands. He sat and waited, paid Henlein his subsidy, spoke angrily about how unpleasant the Czechs were, and encouraged the British to take his side.

Beneš tried to pursue an independent and conciliatory policy. On

4 September 1938 he called Kundt and Sebekovsky to his study. He asked them to present the Sudeten-German Party demands. "These I will sign," he said. But Kundt and Sebekovsky had brought no written demands. Like both Hitler and Henlein, they spoke vaguely of concessions without enumerating them. Beneš was persistent. He asked the two Sudetens to state their claims verbally. They did their best, demanding local self-government with the maximum of advantages to themselves. Beneš wrote their demands on a piece of paper while they were speaking. Then he signed it. "Here, gentlemen. I have agreed to all your suggestions." Kundt and Sebekovsky hurried to Frank, the deputy leader of the party. Frank exclaimed: "My God, they have given us everything!" This was true. But at this crucial moment other ideas were being mooted. In England on 7 September 1938 readers of *The London Times* learned that their paper favored the transfer of the Sudetenland to Germany. The news of this suggestion traveled rapidly through Europe. Hitler was encouraged by this and urged Henlein to demand annexation. Henlein was reluctant; this had never been his desire. He had told Seton-Watson the truth when he said that self-determination was his final aim. But even Henlein's views ceased to matter once Hitler had made up his mind that the Sudetenland should be German. On 12 September Hitler made his first public demand for the annexation of the Sudetenland.

The British Government, and many British people, thought that Hitler's demands were reasonable. Self-determination was a liberal principle which the British in general accepted. It seemed to point quite clearly to the rectitude of Hitler's demand. The British Government wanted to befriend Hitler and thereby improve Anglo-German relations. It imagined that if it could persuade the Czechs to give the Sudetenland to Germany, Hitler would be grateful. From gratitude would flow friendship, and close Anglo-German friendship would maintain peace in Europe. Czechoslovakia should be persuaded to make a small sacrifice, which would be Europe's gain: such was the British calculation which determined the subsequent course of events. Hitler demanded the Sudetenland. Neville Chamberlain accepted this demand and proceeded to put pressure on the Czechs to accept it also. While Hitler used the threat of a mobilized army, the British sent their Minister in Prague to influence President Beneš. Fear of the German Army and the arguments of the British Minister combined: Czechoslovakia agreed reluctantly to surrender

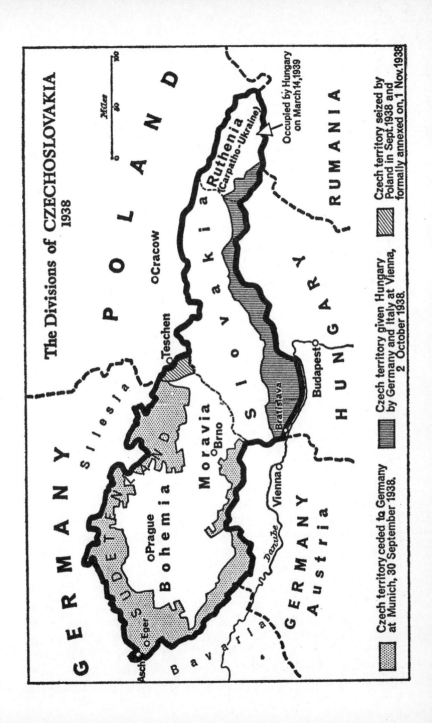

The Divisions of CZECHOSLOVAKIA
1938

Miles
0    50    100

GERMANY

POLAND

Ascho    Eger
S U D E T E N
oPrague
Bohemia
Silesia
Teschen
oCracow

Moravia
oBrno

S l o v a k i a

Ruthenia
(Carpatho-Ukraine)

Occupied by Hungary
on March 14, 1939

Bratislava

Budapesto

HUNGARY

RUMANIA

Vienna o
Danube
GERMANY
Austria
Bavaria

Czech territory ceded to Germany
at Munich, 30 September 1938.

Czech territory given Hungary
by Germany and Italy at Vienna,
2 October 1938.

Czech territory seized by
Poland in Sept.1938 and
formally annexed on,1 Nov.1938

the Sudetenland. The new frontiers of Czechoslovakia were drawn by Hitler and Chamberlain. The French and Italians then agreed to them. The Czechs were not consulted either about where the new frontiers should go or how quickly the areas involved should be transferred to Germany.

Such was the Munich Agreement: 2,825,000 Sudetens found themselves citizens of a dictatorial, brutal Germany; 820,000 Czechs, living within the Sudetenland, were also transferred to Germany.

Not all German-speaking Sudetens were delighted. The Social Democrats among them faced concentration camps or death. Wenzel Jaksch flew to London, seeking visas for his most endangered supporters. He was unsuccessful. The British Government did not understand that many Sudetens would lose much more under Nazi rule than they could ever have lost under Czech rule. The Jews among them automatically became second-class citizens; critics of Nazism became enemies of the state, hounded down and imprisoned or condemned to death.

The Sudetens were not consulted, as many people in Britain and France thought they ought to have been, about their transfer. Germany and Britain, the first avaricious, the second naive, made the decisions, both about the need for the transfer and the method of carrying it out. The only task for the Czechs and Sudetens was to obey. Many Sudetens lost their personal liberty: the Czechs lost their national independence.

From October 1938 to March 1939 the weakened Czechoslovak state maintained its sovereignty. But it could not resist the encroachments of German finance and the intensification of German intrigue. Beneš resigned after Munich. The new rulers were unable to avoid doing as Germany desired. In March 1939 the twenty-year cooperation of Czechs and Slovaks broke down. The Slovaks demanded independence. The Czechs, distraught, were powerless to resist. The Germans, watching Czechoslovakia break in half, swiftly and eagerly occupied Prague and declared a "protectorate" over the Czech districts of Bohemia and Moravia. The Slovaks, under a pro-Nazi government, were allowed to keep their "independence." Hungary, which had already gained a strip of Slovak territory at the time of Munich, annexed Ruthenia. Czechoslovakia was no more.

# ☆ 18 ☆

# POLAND AND THE RETURN
# OF WAR

THE FIRST great Polish kingdom had been created by Boleslaw the Brave, who, before his death in 1025, built an empire stretching from the Elbe to the Dnieper and from the Baltic to the edge of the Hungarian Plain. Separated from the Russian Slavs by Lithuanians, who at this time had taken control of the whole of western Russia, the Poles adopted Latin Christianity and were drawn into contact with the West. The Russians were converted to Eastern Orthodoxy, and came under the influence of Byzantine culture. In religion and in culture, Russia and Poland drew apart.

The Polish Empire fluctuated in size during the Middle Ages. Along the Baltic coast was established, by 1234, a strong German power, the Teutonic Knights, former crusaders who found in northern Europe the success that had been denied them in the Holy Land. In 1466, after twelve years of devastating war, the Poles succeeded in reducing the status of the Teutonic Knights to that of vassals of the Polish crown. By 1569 Poland reached its greatest territorial extent. In 1683 the Polish King, Jan Sobieski, led his troops to the relief of Vienna and so saved a greater part of Europe from Turkish domination. But Poland, despite its military prowess, lacked social or political unity. Its neighbors, Prussia and Russia, looked upon Poland as a potential victim for their armies. They needed only to combine to destroy Poland.

Russia and Prussia annexed part of Poland in 1772. A second partition in 1793 provoked a Polish revolt. The revolt was crushed, and in 1795 Poland was entirely absorbed by its neighbors. After the Napoleonic Wars the Russians allowed some autonomy to the

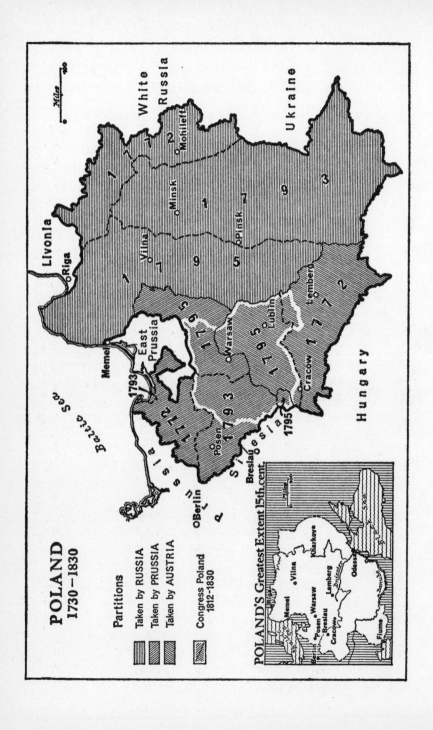

POLAND
1730–1830

Partitions

Taken by RUSSIA
Taken by PRUSSIA
Taken by AUSTRIA

Congress Poland
1812–1830

Miles
100

Livonia

White
Russia

Ukraine

Riga
Memel
Minsk
Mohileff
Vilna
Pinsk

1793
1
2
9
3
1
7
1
9
5

East
Prussia

Lemberg
Warsaw
Lublin
Cracow

Baltic Sea

Berlin
Posen
Breslau
Silesia
1795

Hungary

POLAND'S Greatest Extent 15th cent.

Riga
Memel
Posen
Berlin
Breslau
Cracow
Warsaw
Vilna
Kharkove
Lemberg
Odessa
Fiume

Black Sea
Danube
Dniester

"Congress Kingdom" of Poland, but a Polish attempt to win full independence in 1830 was brutally suppressed. "Congress Poland" became an integral part of Russia and Warsaw entirely subordinate to St. Petersburg.

Those parts of Poland ruled by Russia or Germany were rigorously controlled by their alien masters. Only inside the Habsburg Empire were Poles given certain privileges. They were allowed to dominate the Ukrainians, and Cracow, their capital town, became one of the cultural centers of Europe.

The Great War gave Poland its opportunity. In August 1914 Russia, to win Polish support, announced that it would bring both Prussian and Austrian Poland into Russia, thus uniting Poland territorially for the first time since 1772, even if under tsarist sovereignty. The Poles in Austria were not enthusiastic about this proposed change of masters. Inside Austria they were treated with some consideration; inside Russia they feared they would be coerced and suppressed. Joseph Pilsudski created Polish legions within Austrian Poland whose first aim was to fight against Russia. Pilsudski's ultimate aim was the liberation of Poland, independent from Austria, Prussia, and Russia alike. But in 1914 Russia was his major foe and his army thus won Austrian approval. The Emperor of Austria went so far as to draft a manifesto promising to set up all Poland as an autonomous kingdom within the Habsburg dominions. Though never published, the draft's existence was known to the Poles in Austria, and increased their hostility to Russia's promise. Meanwhile Russia's ability to act as a focus for Polish unity was destroyed: on 5 August 1915 the Germans entered Warsaw. The Russians retreated, burning Polish villages and destroying the harvest so as to deny it to the advancing Germans. Such Russian ruthlessness, though dictated by the needs of war, further alienated the Poles. Russia, driven from Warsaw, could not help them politically, nor could her repressive methods over many years be forgotten.

On 5 November 1916 Germany and Austria issued a joint proclamation proposing the establishment of an independent Poland and appealed to the Poles to fight on their side against Russia. The Poles distrusted this new patronage. But the proclamation had one important result. Until then Poland had appeared to be the concern of Russia alone. Suddenly she became a European concern. Because both sides wanted Poland as an ally, her existence was recognized

and ensured. In Paris a Polish National Committee established relations with France and Britain. Jan Paderewski, the world-famous
pianist, and a member of the Committee, went as its delegate to
Washington, to win American support for an independent Poland.

By the end of 1916 Poland was almost completely occupied by
Germany and Austria. Russia used every possible means to win
Polish loyalty in order to turn Poland against Germany. On 4 December 1916 the Russian Government declared as its aim the
restoration of "a free Poland in its ethnographical frontiers and in
indissoluble union with Russia." When the Tsar was overthrown,
Kerensky, head of the Provisional Government, proclaimed Poland
an independent state "in military alliance" with Russia. The Germans and Austrians were anxious to counter this propaganda. They
needed every able-bodied Pole they could muster to reinforce their
army. They needed the supplies that Poland could provide. On 1
September 1917 they therefore gave the Poles the right to administer justice in the Polish territories under Austrian control, and on 12
September they issued a patent establishing a Polish provisional
government. In November they appointed Pilsudski Commander-in-
Chief of the Polish Army, and on his arrival in Warsaw the Polish
Provisional Government invested him with supreme civil authority
and appointed him Chief of State.

Meanwhile the Polish National Committee had been active in
Paris. On 3 June 1918 France, Britain, and Italy agreed that "the creation of a united and independent Poland with free access to the
sea constitutes one of the conditions of a solid and just peace, and the
rule of right in Europe." In Washington, Paderewski was treated as
the accredited envoy of the new state. Some 20,000 Americans of
Polish descent volunteered to fight for the Entente Powers in France.
The Entente Powers recognized this army as "autonomous, allied,
and cobelligerent." Under General Haller, these legions rendered
important service to the Allied cause.

Throughout 1918 the Germans tried to devise some constitutional form for the new Polish Provisional Government which,
while persuading Poles to support Germany, would nevertheless
keep Poland subservient to Germany. But as the fortunes of the
Great War turned against Germany, and with Russia's sudden withdrawal from the war in October, Poland's initially nominal independence gained substance. On 11 November 1918, the day of the

Armistice, the independent existence of the Polish state was proclaimed.

In December Paderewski reached Poland from America. He persuaded the Allies to recognize Pilsudski as head of the Polish Government. The two groups that had fought for Polish independence combined. On 22 January 1919 independent Poland received its first foreign recognition, that of the United States.

The Polish-German frontier was settled at the Paris Peace Conference. The Polish delegation hoped to restore the frontier of 1772. The Peace Conference worked swiftly. A commission on Polish affairs was set up on 12 February 1919 and issued its report on 12 March. It awarded Poland the German city of Danzig and a broad corridor connecting Poland with the Baltic Sea. The commission reduced the territorial demands of the Polish delegation by a third. But Lloyd George still considered the commission's recommendation extravagant. Brooding over them, he decided to challenge the principle on which the new frontiers were based. On 25 March 1919 he sent a Memorandum to his colleagues, in which he wrote:

"I am strongly averse to transferring more Germans from German rule to the rule of some other nation than can possibly be helped. I cannot conceive any greater cause of future war than that the German people, who have certainly proved themselves one of the most vigorous and powerful nations in the world, should be surrounded by a number of small states, many of them consisting of people who have never previously set up a stable government for themselves, but each of them containing large masses of Germans clamouring for reunion with their native land. The proposal of the Polish commission . . . must, in my judgment, lead sooner or later to a new war in Eastern Europe."

The commission rejected Lloyd George's criticism. Its members interviewed Paderewski, who came specially from Warsaw, and then reasserted its belief that Danzig ought to be transferred from Germany to Poland. The controversy continued for some days. Finally Danzig was set up as a Free City under League of Nations supervision. The Treaty of Versailles, signed on 28 June 1919, contained, as the opening sentence of Article 87: "Germany recognizes, as has already been done by the Allied and Associated Powers, the complete independence of Poland . . ." But as a result of Lloyd George's hostility to Poland, Germany obtained a frontier drawn

POLAND
Minority Areas
1920-1939

Baltic Sea

ESTONIA

LATVIA

○Riga

LITHUANIA

GERMANY

Danzig

○Königsberg

EAST
PRUSSIA

○Vilna

○Minsk

R
U
S
S
I
A

White Russia

Ukraine

○Posnan
(Posen)

Warsaw○

P O L E S

○Lodz

○Brest-Litovsk

Lublin○

○Cracow

Lvov○(Lemberg)

CZECHOSLOVAKIA

Miles
0    50    100

HUNGARY

R U M A N I A

○ Polish communities

▥ German Minority

▨ Ukrainian Minority        ▦ Lithuanian Minority

▥ White Russian Minority    ······· CURZON Line

very much with German susceptibilities in mind. Danzig, instead of being absorbed into Poland, lay outside the Polish frontier, a vulnerable, insecure, unattached city, nominally self-governing under League supervision and Polish protection, but eagerly awaiting the day when Germany should be strong enough to demand its return to the German fatherland.

Poland's western frontier was determined by compromise: the eastern frontier was settled only by war. A Bolshevik invasion, which reached the outskirts of Warsaw in July 1920, was driven back. The Polish Army crossed the frontier which the British Foreign Secretary, Lord Curzon, suggested as Poland's eastern boundary, pressed on across Russian and Ukrainian territory and, in its moment of victory, concluded the Peace of Riga, which put under Polish sovereignty a vast area inhabited by White Russians and Ukrainians. Poland became a state of many minorities.

Polish treatment of its minorities was not good. Anti-Semitic activity was welcome to the Government whenever it distracted attention from anti-Government feeling. The Poles despised the Ukrainians and tried to assimilate them. Polish "colonists" were settled in Ukrainian territories. Polish Catholic priests were encouraged to convert the Ukrainians from their Eastern "heresy." The Ukrainians appealed to a Polish law of 1922 which recognized their right to self-government, but the Poles were reluctant to act upon their own legislation. Violence was the result. In 1930 crop-burning by Ukrainian extremists was answered by a "pacifying expedition" which set fire to Ukrainian villages, killed innocent peasants, and tortured men, women, and children. The horror of this "expedition" was felt in Paris and London. But despite European protests the Ukrainians were forced to accept further measures of restriction and repression.

Poland's domestic politics were confused and unsettled. A parliamentary system of government was set up in 1919, but did not last. There was a fundamental difference of outlook between Poles of Austrian, Prussian, and Russian upbringing. The peasant movement was divided between a tolerant group, willing to compromise, and a more radical, somewhat revolutionary section. The socialists too were disunited. Some wanted to welcome communism at the expense of national independence; others, moderates, considered self-determination the crux of socialism. The pro-communists soon formed themselves into the Polish Communist Party, openly pro-

Russian, and were quickly made illegal and driven underground.

Pilsudski, the President of Poland, disapproved of the 1921 Constitution which limited the President's powers to a minimum. He retired from public life and gathered around him at his country house all the opponents of parliamentary government. In 1926, with the help of the army which he had led during the war, Pilsudski marched on Warsaw and overthrew the parliamentary regime. The moderate socialists, who attributed their economic troubles to bourgeois-parliamentarian financial policy, put their trust in the new dictator. He was opposed by the governing middle-class party, and by the peasants. Pilsudski consolidated his power by gaining the support of industrialists and big landowners. He wooed the aristocracy and won them. The socialists became embittered, the peasants were confirmed in their opposition.

Pilsudski ruled Poland from 1926 until his death in 1935. Although Parliament survived as an institution, he drew to himself all the key powers of the state. He was always Prime Minister, sometimes War Minister, and always Inspector-General of the Army. Those who had served with him in the war were rewarded with high office. Those who had served with General Haller's legions in France were overlooked. Pilsudski himself sought unity and prosperity for Poland; his followers were often less high-minded. For them, Pilsudski's patronage was an excellent opportunity for self-enrichment.

Pilsudski's dictatorship became less and less benevolent. In the 1930 election eminent opposition leaders were arrested, imprisoned, and maltreated. The voters were terrorized by the police. In 1935 a new Constitution, hurriedly pushed through Parliament while opposition members were absent, increased Pilsudski's powers still further and curbed the legislative power of Parliament. Departmental administration became centralized. The Ministry of the Interior appointed prefects for the departments who could veto the appointment of mayors elected by the public.

Pilsudski died on 12 May 1935. Power remained in the hands of those whom he had favored: the "Government of the Colonels." Before the election in the autumn of 1935 the colonels reduced the franchise, as a result of which the opposition parties refused to take any part in the election.

The colonels' government was not entirely negative. Land reform was pushed forward and a public works program was inaugurated to relieve unemployment. The growing hostility of both left- and right-wing groups steered the colonels almost accidentally into a middle course. The openly Fascist National Radical Party, formed in 1937, though never outlawed as were the communists, became isolated, criticized, and lost entirely the official support which it had at its formation. The colonels shunned extremism, searching instead for a patriotic, national-based form of government. In this they failed. Internal dissension was too strong and the basis of their own power too narrow for them ever to win consistently wide support. Municipal elections in December 1938 gave the opposition parties 639 seats, the Government 383. The colonels were forced to adopt a conciliatory, unadventurous policy in order to survive.

Just as the colonels veered away from a pro-Nazi policy at home, so they took care to avoid a pro-German orientation of their foreign policy. But at the time of the German annexation of the Sudeten areas of Czechoslovakia they showed that principles were less powerful than self-interest. Poland claimed territory in the Teschen and Zakopane areas of Czechoslovakia. The Poles took advantage of Czechoslovakia's weakness to seize the disputed areas in October 1938. This crude action gave Poland a bad reputation in Britain and France. Yet after the German occupation of Prague in March 1939 the Poles accepted Britain's unilateral guarantee of Poland's frontiers, and committed themselves irrevocably to an anti-German policy.

The Polish Foreign Minister, Colonel Beck, had for many years sought to balance his country's allegiance between the different power blocs. Hostile to Russia, he had nevertheless avoided any firm commitment to Germany which might increase Russian hostility. Aware that Germany might one day cast avaricious eyes on parts of Poland, he studiously avoided any flirtation with anti-German powers. Aware that Poland and Hungary could easily combine to crush and divide Czechoslovakia, he still refused a firm alliance with Hungary for fear of antagonizing France, the friend and ally of the Czechs. Beck's cautious policy could not succeed with the growing hardening and brutalization of European politics. Once Hitler revealed, in March 1939, that he would continue his annexations in areas not predominantly German, Beck knew that he must soon commit himself to a pro- or anti-German policy. His mind was made up for him by Neville Chamberlain, who, fearing further German aggression in eastern Europe, decided to take up the cudgels in favor of the two threatened nations, Rumania and Poland. Chamberlain offered to guarantee Poland's frontiers against aggression. Beck accepted with alacrity: although as a result he could no longer juggle with the balance of power, he thought he was now secure against German encroachment, with Britain acting as Poland's patron and guardian.

Beck was mistaken: the British guarantee had been given hastily and without careful thought. The British Cabinet had not been consulted, nor had Parliament. Chamberlain was criticized from many quarters for having committed himself to the defense of Poland's frontiers. Germany, it was argued, had a just claim for the annexation of Danzig, and a good case for the revision of Poland's western frontiers in Germany's favor. Chamberlain was in part influenced by this argument. He still thought that Hitler could be won to moderation by concessions. An obvious concession to win German goodwill would be for the Poles to allow Germany to annex Danzig. Chamberlain tried to persuade the Poles to do this.

Chamberlain's attitude was challenged by Clifford Norton, Chargé d'Affaires in the British Embassy in Warsaw. Norton pointed out in every despatch he wrote that it would be both inexpedient and immoral to force Poland to make concessions. Such advice was unwelcome to the British Government. But Norton would not desist. In private letters to senior Foreign Office officials he reiterated his belief that Britain's best interest lay in upholding the guarantee to Poland in every particular.

Clifford Norton doubted British resolve. He feared that Chamberlain would find a way of wriggling out of his pledge to Poland. Hitler also doubted British firmness. He too believed that Chamberlain would not defend Poland if Poland were attacked. Hitler's conviction led him to press forward with his plan for the invasion of Poland in the autumn of 1939. Thinking that Britain would desert her new ally, Hitler went ahead with his anti-Polish plans unperturbed by thoughts of an Anglo-German war being the result.

Until the very moment of Hitler's invasion of Poland the British tried to make the Poles concede, or agree to the ultimate cession of Danzig.

Hitler, knowing this, could hardly be expected to foresee that, once he invaded Poland, British opinion would harden against him. Clifford Norton's minority voice became the voice of the nation. Hitler invaded Poland on 1 September; on 3 September Britain and France declared war on Germany. Neither gave immediate aid to Poland, despite Beck's plea that aircraft should attack Germany in the west and so divert Hitler's aircraft away from Poland. But Poland had the moral advantage of knowing that, for once in her history, she had friends and allies as well as enemies.

# ☆ 19 ☆

## THE GERMAN CONQUEST
## OF EUROPE

### THE DEFEAT OF POLAND

HITLER attacked Poland on 1 September 1939. The Polish frontier was geographically almost impossible to defend. The Germans outnumbered the Poles by nearly two to one. The Poles put too much faith in the power of infantry to hold back the Germans, who concentrated upon motorized columns and tanks, against which the Polish foot-soldiers and cavalry were useless.[1]

The Germans encircled unit after unit of the Polish Army, cutting off their retreat. German tanks destroyed railway installations. German aircraft harassed Polish lines of communication and immobilized railway junctions.

As the German armies drove into Poland from three directions the Poles appealed to their western allies, Britain and France, for assistance. They were particularly anxious for an attack to be made on Germany's western frontier to draw off some of the airplanes which were playing havoc with Polish communications. But it was not until two days after the German attack that Poland's allies declared war on Germany, and even then they were unwilling to take military action. On 6 September the Germans broke through the Polish frontier defenses and pressed towards Warsaw.

On 9 September Colonel Beck urged his Ambassador in London

---

[1] The German cavalry, on the other hand, not having armored vehicles to charge against, proved extremely effective. It could cross great tracts of land swiftly and without reliance upon the roads, where snipers lurked and refugees crowded, holding up motor transport.

to "put the position clearly before the British Government and ask for a more definite answer regarding war plans and help for Poland." The Ambassador hurried to the British Foreign Office but was received with neither enthusiasm nor promises of action. On 14 September the Germans surrounded Warsaw.

For seven days Poland's western allies had been silent: the Germans, who had hoped to avoid war with Britain and France altogether, discovered that war was not necessarily much of a burden. The French did indeed make small advances, crossing the French defenses, or Maginot Line, and occupying the territory between it and the German Siegfried Line. The French had over seventy divisions poised on their Maginot Line. They faced only thirty-two German divisions. But after their short and unchallenged advance they rested. They were unwilling to force the Germans into a war on two fronts.

On 19 May 1939 France had signed a military protocol to her Polish Treaty of 1935. In this protocol she pledged herself to a military advance by the sixteenth day of a German-Polish war. But on 17 September there was no movement from the French lines, nor did French aircraft try to draw off some of the German planes which were at that very moment swooping down upon columns of refugees fleeing eastwards, and bombing the center of major cities oblivious of their promise to bomb only military targets. On that day the Russians entered Poland from the east.

Western sloth has been emphasized by German generals as a crucial factor in their rapid success. General Jodl told his accusers at the Nuremburg Trial after the war: "If we did not collapse in 1939, that was due only to the fact that during the Polish campaign the British and French divisions were completely inactive."

There was some action in the western air: the British sent out airplanes to drop leaflets on Germany. Those leaflets told the Germans that their attack on Poland was wicked. The technique of dropping leaflets from the air had been developed in 1918, when the Austro-Hungarian army had been bombarded by British propaganda. It had been tried against tribes on Britain's Indian frontier who had been sent airborne appeals to their imperial loyalty, during the nineteen-thirties.

Leaflet-bombing was not a success. The first casualties it incurred were when British planes found themselves being chased. They were

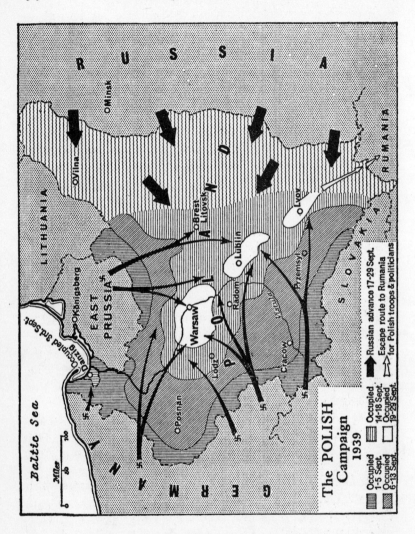

The POLISH Campaign 1939

Occupied 1–5 Sept.
Occupied 6–13 Sept.
Occupied 14–18 Sept.
Occupied 19–29 Sept.

Russian advance 17–29 Sept.
Escape route to Rumania for Polish troops & politicians

able to shoot down some of their pursuers. In retaliation they were themselves damaged. It was soon discovered that the "enemy" were Belgians. The leaflet bombers had accidentally flown over neutral Belgian territory and been vigorously challenged. The British Government apologized for its mistake. In future, it said, the leaflet bombers would avoid Belgian air space.

The official historian of the Royal Air Force has recorded that "it was everywhere remarked that while Poland bled and burned, we were bombarding the Germans with nothing more lethal than copies of Mr. Chamberlain's latest broadcast." There were other, more serious air attacks. The British were anxious to keep the German navy in harbor. The cost of doing so was high. Two German ships were slightly damaged, a submarine and a minesweeper sunk, and ten German fighters shot down at the cost to the British of forty-one bombers. One restriction on the bombers was not technical but political. They were forbidden by the Government to bomb German civilians. Again the official historian has recorded how "though the crews saw many warships they made no attack. Every vessel was in dock or harbor, where the fall of bombs would endanger the lives of civilians."

For three weeks the Germans pounded Warsaw with bombs. On 26 September their tanks penetrated into the suburbs of the capital. The German General Rommel opened negotiations with leading Polish parliamentarians and on 29 September the city surrendered. Rommel was so impressed by the bravery of its defenders that he allowed them full military honors: soldiers were set free after giving up their arms and officers were allowed to keep their swords.

By 28 September all Polish resistance was at an end. Some of her troops managed to cross into Rumania. Others surrendered to the advancing Russians. Some 66,000 were killed. German deaths totaled 10,000.

On 29 September Russia and Germany signed a treaty partitioning Poland. On 1 October Winston Churchill, who had been brought back into the British Government on the outbreak of war, broadcast to the nation:

"Poland has again been overrun by two of the great Powers which held her in bondage for a hundred and fifty years but were unable to quench the spirit of the Polish nation. The heroic defence of Warsaw shows that the soul of Poland is indestructible, and that she will rise again like a rock, which may for a time be submerged by a tidal wave, but which remains a rock.

"Russia has pursued a cold policy of self-interest. We could have wished that the Russian armies should be standing on their present line as the friends and allies of Poland instead of as invaders. But that the Russian armies should stand on this line, was clearly necessary for the safety of Russia against the Nazi menace. At any rate, the line is there, and an eastern front has been created which Nazi Germany does not dare assail. . . .

"I cannot forecast to you the action of Russia. It is a riddle wrapped in a mystery inside an enigma; but perhaps there is a key. The key is Russian national interest."

## FINLAND RESISTS RUSSIA

Russian self-interest did not cease with the annexation of eastern Poland. Within a month of the outbreak of war the Russians signed treaties giving them the right to garrison troops in Estonia, Latvia, and Lithuania. Stalin was anxious to deny the Germans further territorial advantages once they conquered Poland. He regarded his nonaggression pact with Germany as a necessary evil, designed to give Russia time to improve her defenses and create round her borders as large a buffer zone of occupied territory as possible.

The Russian frontier was most exposed where it bordered on Finland. Leningrad lay within easy reach of the Finnish border. Between Leningrad and the frontier was Kronstadt, the island fortress and naval base upon which the defense of the city depended. North of Leningrad was Lake Ladoga, which could be crossed by troops when frozen. The northern half of the lake belonged to Finland. If Finland came under anti-Russian control, Lake Ladoga could become the route for an assault on Leningrad from the rear. In the far north, on the White Sea, was the Russian port of Murmansk. Fifty miles further west was Finland's only Arctic port, Petsamo. Russia feared the destruction of her northern outlet, or the breach of its lifeline, the Leningrad-Murmansk railway.

The Russians opened negotiations with Finland early in October. They wished to lease Petsamo in the north and Hangö in the Gulf of Finland. They asked for alterations in the Finnish frontier such as would put Leningrad out of the range of an enemy and include all Lake Ladoga within Russian territory. The Finns were willing to give way on all points but one; they would not allow Russia to occupy Hangö. Such a move would give Russia complete control over the Gulf of Finland, and of Helsinki, the Finnish capital. The Russians refused to modify their demands and were convinced that they would quickly gain by war what they had failed to obtain by negotiation.

On 28 November 1939 Russia denounced her nonaggression pact

with Finland. Two days later she attacked at eight points along Finland's thousand-mile frontier. Helsinki was bombed.

As both Finland and Russia were members of the League of Nations, Finland appealed to the League. On 14 December Russia was formally expelled, but beyond verbal censure the League could do nothing. Finland was alone.

The Finnish resistance created wide sympathy: that so small a country could resist the onslaught of mighty Russia seemed incredible. Yet the Russians were beaten back everywhere except in the far north. They were unable to reach Viborg or to surround Lake Ladoga. They were driven back from Pudasjärvi, Lake Oulu, and Kemijärvi, and whole divisions were annihilated. The Finns were well equipped with skis and warm clothing. The Russians, expecting a rapid victory, had neither. They sent their infantrymen through pine forests ideal for ambush by the mobile Finns. Their tanks drove along roads too narrow for speedy turns. The Finns prepared a simple new weapon, a bottle half-filled with petrol, which exploded when hurled at the side or belly of the tank, where it was vulnerable to antitank weapons.

While Finland held Russia at bay the British discussed the possibility of sending aid. Such aid would have to pass through Norway, and the British Government were unwilling to make the violation of Norwegian neutrality which this would involve. Some thirty British aircraft were flown direct to Finland. Ten aircraft were sent privately from the United States. But soldiers were held back. The Finns informed Britain and France that they needed reinforcements of about 30,000 men in order to hold out beyond the spring. But before Chamberlain or Daladier could decide what their attitude would be if Norway refused transit for these troops, the Russians launched a second attack. For forty-two days they concentrated their artillery on the narrow front between Lake Ladoga and the Gulf of Finland. On 7 March they crossed Viborg Bay over the ice and on 8 March reached Viborg. Finnish resistance was broken; the road to Helsinki was open. The Finns called for an armistice and entered into negotiations with Russia. Finland had to grant Russia a thirty-year lease on Hangö; the frontier was altered so as to put seventy miles of Russian territory between Leningrad and the frontier; Lake Ladoga became a Russian lake; in the north the Russians obtained a small belt of territory, together with the lease of Petsamo.

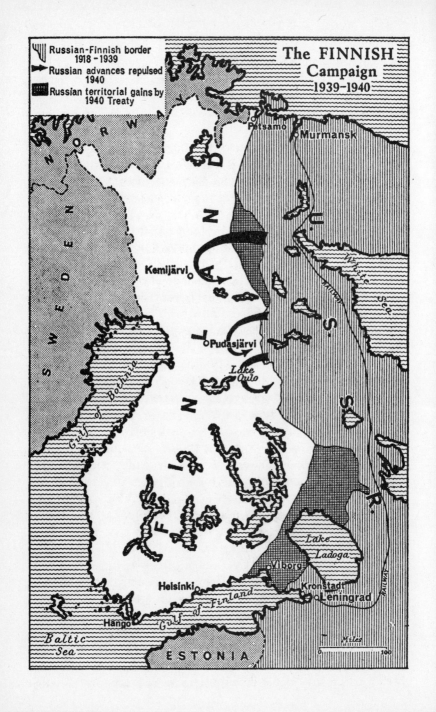

Six days before the Finnish surrender Daladier had decided, without consulting the British, to send 50,000 volunteers to Finland. The British, spurred on by this, decided to risk Norwegian anger and to send a military force to Finland's aid which would pass through Norway on 20 March. All this was too late; Finland had by then been forced to her knees.

The main effect of the Russo-Finnish war was to cast doubt on Soviet military strength. The fact that Russia had expected a swift victory and therefore neglected proper preparations was overlooked. It was argued in Britain that Russia's nonaggression pact with Germany was after all no loss to the West; that Russia would have proved a serious liability had she been an ally. It was argued in France that if Finland could resist for so long then the Russian Army must be ineffective; that it might be possible for France to take on Russia as well as Germany and, by attacking Russia's oil-producing territories, to weaken Germany though her eastern partner.

Hitler likewise argued that Russia was so weak that she could never withstand a German attack. None of these optimistic calculations took into account the special considerations of the Finnish war: Russian slackness, Finnish mastery of a peculiarly difficult terrain, and a winter extremely severe even for Finland's frozen north. Nor did Russia's critics pay enough attention to an obvious fact: Russia had won in the end. It is clear in retrospect that one of the most crucial aspects of the campaign was Russia's ability to bring such a massive force into operation so as to crush even the most determined resistance. Russia's action aroused great moral indignation in the West, for which there was much justification. It also aroused contempt for Russia's Army, which was less deserved.

## THE DEFEAT OF NORWAY

Having conquered Poland the Germans put out peace feelers towards the West. In October Hitler made a specific peace offer, involving the German retention of Poland, which was rejected. He had based his attack on Poland upon the assumption that the West would not declare war. This having been proved false, he was encouraged by Mussolini to believe that with the fall of Poland Britain and France would be willing to make peace. But although there was a widespread belief in both countries that a victory against the German war machine was impossible, there was also a growing spirit of defiance and bravado. It soon became unpatriotic to talk of a compromise peace, and treason to talk of surrender.

The defeat of Finland increased the western disadvantage. It also stimulated the western leaders to contemplate some adventurous enterprise that would catch the public imagination and weaken Germany.

In the first month of the war the British Cabinet had discussed the importance of Swedish iron'ore to the Germany economy. This ore was taken by rail from the Swedish mines at Gellivare to Narvik on the Norwegian coast. A special railway had been built for this purpose. From Narvik the ore was transported by ship to Germany. Apart from a small quantity that could travel to Germany through Lulea when, for the four summer months, the Gulf of Bothnia was not icebound, the German supply of this valuable ore was exposed to British sea power. "Nothing would be more deadly," wrote Churchill in December 1939, "not only to German war-making capacity but to the life of the country" than to stop the flow of iron ore for six months.

A British plan was prepared, on Churchill's initiative, to lay a line of mines south of Narvik inside Norwegian territorial waters. These mines would force the German ships to move away from the coast and out into the Atlantic. There, unprotected by Norwegian neutrality, they could be sunk. Churchill's plan was put to the Cabinet in September 1939. It was not accepted.

The Germans were more active in both plans and decisions. Hitler's Chief of the Naval Staff impressed upon him in October the need for a German occupation of Norway to forestall British action. In December Hitler made the acquaintance of a former Norwegian minister of war, Vidkun Quisling, leader of the Nationalist Party in Norway, a man anxious to instruct his fellow citizens in the advantages of Nazi rule. Quisling's political activities were at once linked with German naval plans.

In December 1939 Churchill learned that the Russians were sending an icebreaker to Germany from Murmansk. He rightly deduced that the Germans hoped to use it to keep Lulea ice-free in winter. In that way their ore supplies would be secure throughout the year. Churchill urged the rapid mining of the Norwegian coast. The Cabinet again rejected his request.

Unknown to the British, a German plan for the invasion of Norway was making rapid progress.

On 3 April 1940 Churchill resubmitted his proposal to mine the Norwegian coast and it was accepted. The mining was scheduled to start on 8 April. At the same time, in order to prevent any German retaliation, a small British force was to go to Narvik to control the port and the railway between Narvik and the Swedish frontier. Churchill sensed that this decision had been delayed too long: "Now after all this vain boggling, hesitation, changes of policy, arguments between good and worthy people unending, we had at last reached the simple point on which action had been demanded seven months before. But in war seven months is a long time." Chamberlain was less pessimistic. On 5 April 1940 he said:

". . . when war did break out German preparations were far ahead of our own, and it was natural then to expect that the enemy would take advantage of his initial superiority to make an endeavour to overwhelm us and France before we had time to make good our deficiencies. Is it not a very extraordinary thing that no such attempt was made? Whatever may be the reason—whether it was that Hitler thought he might get away with what he had got without fighting for it, or whether it was that after all the preparations were not sufficiently complete—however, one thing is certain: he missed the bus."

On 8 April, as planned, the British began to lay mines some forty miles south of Narvik. The Norwegian Government spent the morning drafting a letter of protest to the British Government. That afternoon two Norwegian warships were sunk off Narvik. Two hundred and eighty-seven Norwegian sailors were drowned: their attacker was a German ship; swiftly the Germans occupied Narvik. The British plan to follow up the minefield laying with the occupation of the port was thus suddenly and dramatically forestalled. That same afternoon it became clear that the German action was part of a larger plan. The Germans overran Denmark, and, by nightfall, attacked Oslo, the Norwegian capital. Two days later they occupied Oslo, Stavanger, Bergen, and Trondheim. It was clearly Chamberlain, not Hitler, who had "missed the bus."

The British, who had hoped to take the initiative in Norway, were now confronted by Hitler's superior planning and forced to alter their policy. A gallant naval attack on Narvik inflicted severe casualties upon the Germans but was driven off.

The Anglo-French Supreme War Council met on 9 April. Churchill drew the lesson from Norway's violated neutrality that other neutrals might find themselves similarly attacked without warning. He suggested that Belgium might be in that category, and was anxious for plans to be prepared for the occupation of Belgium by British and French troops. But Daladier argued that "such a threat might well cause a revulsion of public opinion in Belgium and might antagonize the Belgian Government against the Allies." Churchill was once more overruled. Bitterly he told the House of Commons on 11 April:

"The strict observance of neutrality by Norway has been a contributory cause to the sufferings to which she is now exposed and to the limits of the aid which we can give her. I trust this fact will be meditated upon by other countries who may tomorrow, or a week hence, or a month hence, find themselves the victims of an equally elaborately worked-out staff-plan for their destruction and enslavement."

The British failed to drive the Germans from Norway. Despite strong promptings from Churchill the general in charge of the British forces which were to attack Narvik again refused to take the risk of being repulsed.

The second British plan was an attack on Trondheim, which would cut off the Germans in Oslo from their troops in the north and provide a base for 50,000 men. As a preliminary 13,000 troops were successfully landed at Andalsnes, south of Trondheim, and Namsos in the north. Churchill would have preferred a second attempt to seize Narvik, but recognized the strategic superiority of Trondheim. Hardly had he thrown all his energy and enthusiasm behind the proposed naval assault on Trondheim than dissension arose among the British policy-makers. The Chiefs of the Naval, Air, and Military Staffs, together with their deputies, all opposed the plan on the grounds that adequate preparations had not been made for what was clearly "one of the most difficult and hazardous operations of war." They suggested that the landings at Andalsnes and Namsos should be followed up by an inland pincer movement of troops towards Trondheim. But they would not sanction a direct naval attack. The Trondheim plan was therefore abandoned.

Swiftly the Germans strengthened their position in Norway. The

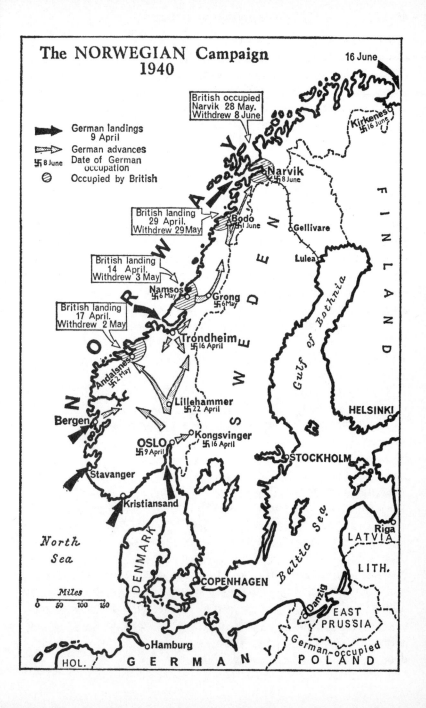

The NORWEGIAN Campaign
1940

16 June

German landings
9 April
German advances
Date of German
occupation
Occupied by British

British occupied
Narvik 28 May.
Withdrew 8 June

Kirkenes
16 June

Narvik
8 June

British landing
29 April.
Withdrew 29 May

Bodo
1 June

Gellivare

British landing
14 April.
Withdrew 3 May

Lulea

Namsos
6 May

Grong
6 May

British landing
17 April.
Withdrew 2 May

Trondheim
16 April

Andalsnes
2 May

Lillehammer
22 April

FINLAND

Gulf of Bothnia

HELSINKI

Bergen

Kongsvinger
16 April

OSLO
9 April

STOCKHOLM

Stavanger

Kristiansand

Riga
LATVIA

North
Sea

LITH.

DENMARK

Baltic Sea

COPENHAGEN

Danzig

EAST
PRUSSIA

Miles
0  50  100  150

Hamburg

HOL.    G E R M A N Y

German-occupied
POLAND

British were forced to withdraw from Andalsnes on 2 May and from Namsos on 3 May.

The failure of the Norwegian campaign aroused widespread anti-Government feeling in Britain. It was argued that Trondheim should have been attacked and that the troops had only been driven from Norway owing to the incompetence of the Government's plans. Chamberlain rejected the idea that a Conservative-Labour coalition was necessary to ensure the efficient prosecuution of the war. "We should do better," he insisted, "to occupy ourselves with increasing our war effort than disputing about the form of government." But because many people regarded the Norwegian failure as symbolic of a deeper malaise in the administration of the war, criticism continued. A division in the House of Commons saw thirty Conservatives voting against their leader. On 9 May Chamberlain made up his mind to invite the Labour Party to join his government. The Labour leaders said that they must consult their party conference, which was in session at Bournemouth. They hinted that the Labour Party would refuse to serve under Chamberlain. It was clear that the failure of the Norwegian campaign had depressed and angered the British people.

## THE DEFEAT OF FRANCE

With dramatic and overwhelming suddenness the Germans moved again. On the morning of 10 May their armies crossed into Holland, Belgium, and Luxembourg. Their objective was Paris.

On 10 May, confronted by the challenge of the new emergency, Chamberlain wished to remain Prime Minister, despite Labour Party opposition. But when his closest colleagues impressed upon him the need for a coalition government he gave way.

A new government was formed by Winston Churchill. On every front, in every capital, at every public gathering, the shadow of defeat was producing depression and gloom. Men talked of surrender and compromise. But with the appearance of Churchill as Prime Minister a new spirit of perseverance arose, at the very moment when the whole military power of Germany was hurled against the West.

Holland was the first to fall. Dutch security was based upon the ability to flood wide belts of land between their defenses and an advancing enemy. But the flooding was a slow process; some days were needed before the system could become fully effective. The unexpectedness of the German attack and the swiftness of the German advance were too much for this ancient and respected system.

As in Poland, the Germans planned intensive bombing raids on the major cities. On 14 May they began the systematic destruction of Rotterdam from the air. Having pulverized the city and demoralized its inhabitants they announced that they would turn their aircraft towards Utrecht on the following day. The Dutch High Command could not take the responsibility of condemning so many civilians to death; on 15 May Holland capitulated.

The British succeeded in destroying the oil tanks at Amsterdam. From The Hague they carried Queen Wilhelmina and her daughter, the future Queen Juliana, to exile and safety in Britain. During the four days of the German onslaught 80,000 Dutchmen were killed or wounded.

The French and British advanced into Belgium and took up positions along the Dyle and Meuse rivers on 11 May. The Belgians held the northern sector of this line, which the Germans failed to break; but on 14 May the Germans broke through the French defenses at Sedan. Reynaud, who had succeeded Daladier as Prime Minister in March, telephoned Churchill and greeted him with the words: "We have been defeated." By 17 May the Germans had driven their tanks forward almost to St. Quentin. Although the French and the Germans each had eighty divisions, and the French could add ten British and ten Belgian to their total, the balance of military power lay with Germany. Thirty strong reserve divisions waited behind the German frontier. In addition, eight German armored divisions confronted three French armored divisions. The British and Belgians had none. By the weight of their armor the Germans had destroyed Poland; they sought to do the same to France. They provided constant air support for their advancing tanks. Their supply operations, which provided the mechanized vehicles with their essential fuel, operated as efficiently as had been planned.

The German breakthrough from Sedan was followed by an attack upon the Belgian troops west of Maastricht. On 16 May the British and Belgians began to withdraw, abandoning Brussels and Antwerp

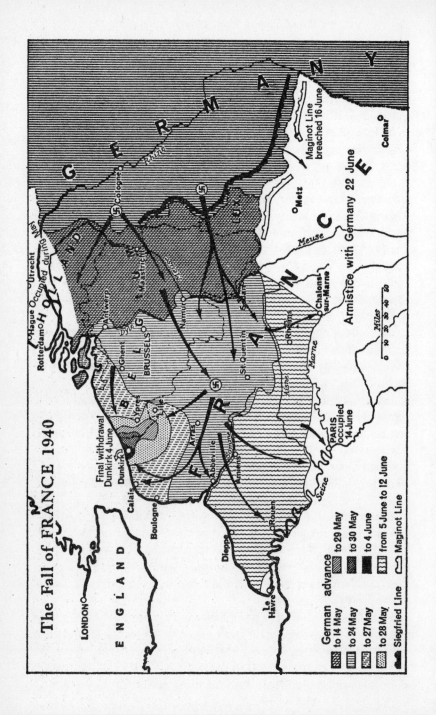

The Fall of FRANCE 1940

LONDON○

ENGLAND

○LONDON

Utrecht○
Hague Occupied during May○
Rotterdam○

H O L L A N D

Cologne○

G E R M A N Y

Antwerp
○Ghent
BRUSSELS○

B E L G I U M

Ypres○
Lille○

Dunkirk○
Final withdrawal
Dunkirk 4 June

Calais○
Boulogne○

Abbeville○
Amiens○

Dieppe○

Rouen○

Le Havre○

Scarpe
Somme
Aisne

F R A N C E

St.Quentin○

PARIS,
occupied
14 June

Seine
Marne

Meuse
Maas

Luxembourg
Metz○
Châlons-
sur-Marne○

Reims○

Maginot Line
breached 16 June

Colmar○

Armistice with Germany 22 June

Miles
0  10  20  30  40  50

German  advance

▨ to 14 May
▥ to 24 May
▦ to 27 May
▩ to 28 May
◫ to 29 May
▤ to 30 May
■ to 4 June
▒ from 5 June to 12 June

⌐◡ Maginot Line
▬► Siegfried Line

to the Germans. By the evening of 18 May the Germans had driven a wedge between the armies in Belgium and those in France. So bleak was the outlook for the Allied armies in France and so vivid the example of Rotterdam's destruction that Churchill telegraphed to President Roosevelt: "If this country was left by the United States to its fate no one would have the right to blame those then responsible if they made the best terms they could for the surviving inhabitants. Excuse me, Mr. President, putting this nightmare bluntly."

On 20 May Churchill launched "Operation Dynamo," whose objective was the evacuation of Allied troops from the French coast. That night the Germans entered Abbeville, their tanks having made possible advances of up to forty miles a day. On 21 May the British attempted to halt the German advance at Arras. They attacked, catching the Germans by surprise. But eighty-three British tanks could not hope to hold nearly 400 German tanks. The Germans counterattacked successfully. One of their divisions was commanded by General Rommel.

On 24 May the Germans entered Boulogne after a siege of thirty-six hours. The British and French troops who had sustained the siege were rescued by Allied ships. The Germans pressed eastwards towards Calais.

It became clear to Churchill that the Germans could, by driving sixty miles further along the coast, cut the British Army off from the sea, its only line of escape. Churchill resolved to hold Calais at all cost, and on 25 May ordered the garrison to hold out as long as possible. Upon their ability to check the Germans depended the fate of 220,000 English and 200,000 French soldiers being forced back to the Dunkirk beaches, twenty-five miles further east.

Brigadier C. N. Nicholson succeeded in maintaining the defense of Calais throughout 25 May. When the Germans, amazed at the pounding which the British had withstood, and anxious to press on towards Dunkirk, demanded his surrender, Nicholson replied curtly: "The answer is 'no' as it is the British Army's duty to fight as well as it is the Germans'."

At two in the afternoon Nicholson learned from London that "the eyes of the Empire are upon the defence of Calais" and just before midnight he received a telegram from Churchill: "Every hour you continue to exist is of the greatest help. . . . Government has therefore decided you must continue to fight. Have greatest admiration for your splendid stand. Evacuation will not repeat not take place and craft required for above purpose are to return to Dover."

"I could not help feeling physically sick after sending that telegram," Churchill recorded. Nicholson and his men held out until late in the afternoon of 26 May, the Germans subjecting Calais to an intense air bombardment all day. The ancient and beautiful city was smashed and its defenses broken. Nicholson was captured and sent with his men to a prisoner-of-war camp, where he died. The defense of Calais greatly inconvenienced the Germans and provided the British with a heroic saga.

In the tumult of war inefficiency and muddle often play as decisive a part as violence and death. Early on the morning of 27 May, *after* the Germans had occupied Calais, twelve British aircraft flew over the battered city dropping supplies of water to the troops they thought to be there still. A few hours later seventeen more aircraft dropped ammunition for the imagined defenders. Three of the aircraft were shot down. Their mission had been in vain.

On 28 May the King of the Belgians surrendered unconditionally to the Germans. He had consulted neither with his allies nor with his ministers. The Belgian Government, in exile in France, dissociated itself from its ruler's decision and declared its resolve to continue the war at the side of the Allies. But Belgian morale was broken. The King's action exposed the British and French armies, struggling desperately to withdraw to Dunkirk, to a further German onslaught from the east. That same day the Germans entered Ypres. The British were surrounded.

The evacuation of troops from Dunkirk was one of the most remarkable episodes of the Second World War: 338,226 men were transported across the English Channel between 27 May and 4 June 1940—a nine-days' miracle. These men were taken from the beaches by small boats while under heavy German air bombardment. In all, 861 ships, including many tugboats and pleasure steamers, took part in the evacuation.

The preparation of this armada had begun under "Operation Dynamo." Naturally it had then been secret. But once the evacuation began, secrecy was no longer essential. Innumerable private boats put out from the harbors of south and southeast England and crossed to Dunkirk. These little boats ferried men from the shore to the larger ships. Some 243 boats were sunk. But British fighter planes ensured that, however much havoc the Germans caused on the beaches, they nevertheless did not obtain mastery in the air. For every five German planes shot down only one British plane was destroyed.

On 31 May Churchill flew to Paris for a meeting of the Supreme War Council. The first question to be resolved belonged, so it seemed, almost to a previous war. Five days earlier, on 27 May, British and French troops had finally captured Narvik. It was at once agreed that the Allies could not afford the 16,000 men involved in the capture to be absent from France and the Council decided to evacuate Narvik on 2 June.

Reynaud then drew attention to the fact that although there were 220,000 British and 200,000 French troops in the Dunkirk area, ten times as many British had been taken off as Frenchmen: only 15,000 Frenchmen in fact. Reynaud insisted that "the French public might draw unfortunate conclusions" if this ratio were the final one. Churchill defended himself by saying that, as far as he knew, French troops "had had no orders to evacuate." One of the chief reasons he had come to Paris, he declared, "was to make sure that the same orders were now given to the French troops as had been given to the British." In this he was successful. When Reynaud suggested that for the final embarkation the British should go first Churchill intervened to say "that the evacuation should proceed on equal terms between the British and French, *bras dessus bras dessous.*" Churchill gave orders accordingly. When he was finally able to tell the French that of the 338,226 men snatched to safety from Dunkirk over 140,000 were Frenchmen, they were overjoyed. The Germans had failed to take the full advantage of their position. But they did capture 100,000 men, vast quantities of arms and ammunition, and many military vehicles.

On 4 June 1940 the Dunkirk evacuation came to an end. Churchill made a magnificent speech in the House of Commons which inspired the nation in its hours of doubt. He began on a pensive note: "We must be very careful not to assign to this deliverance the attributes of a victory. Wars are not won by evacuations." He ended with an inspiring appeal for courage and perseverance:

"Even though large tracts of Europe and many old and famous States have fallen or may fall into the grip of the Gestapo and all the odious apparatus of Nazi rule, we shall not flag or fail. We shall go on to the end. We shall fight in France, we shall fight in the seas and oceans, we shall fight with growing confidence and growing strength in the air; we shall defend our Island, whatever the cost may be. We shall fight on the beaches, we shall fight on the landing-grounds, we shall fight in the fields and in the streets, we shall fight in the hills; we shall never surrender; and even if, which I do not for a moment believe, this Island or a large part of it were subjugated and starving, then our Empire beyond the seas, armed and guarded by the British Fleet, would carry on the struggle, until, in God's good time, the New World, with all its power and might, steps forth to the rescue and the liberation of the Old."

With the completion of the evacuation from Dunkirk on 4 June 1940 the French were confronted with the possibility of defeat. Their armies lining the Somme and the Aisne had been able to rest somewhat during the German concentration against Dunkirk. But Germany was bringing forward the troops from Dunkirk, together with fresh, well-equipped reserves, against which the already battle-weary French could not hope to be effective.

Marshal Pétain, whom Reynaud had brought into his govern-ment to provide a figure symbolizing resistance and victory, had al-ready suggested to the French War Council that, if France found it necessary to make peace, she should not feel too strictly bound to defer to British wishes. In other words, since Churchill had made it clear that he would not contemplate surrender, that France should consider the possibility of making a separate peace.

On 5 June Reynaud reorganized his government, hoping to make it less defeatist. A regular officer, Charles de Gaulle, who had for many years urged the High Command to concentrate upon mecha-nized warfare, and who had been consistently ignored, became Un-der-Secretary for War and Defense. But it was too late to save France by political maneuver. On 7 June the Germans broke through the French defenses on the Somme and Aisne. On 9 June the government left Paris; two days later, faced with a German pincer movement from the Somme and the Marne and unwilling to see Paris suffer the fate of Rotterdam, the French army withdrew from the capital, which the Germans entered on 14 June.

On 10 June Reynaud appealed to Roosevelt: "Tell your people that France is sacrificing everything in the cause of freedom. We desperately need at once every form of material and moral help you can give us short of an expeditionary force. The fate of 90 per cent of the world's population is at stake and France, the advance post of democracy, is in mortal peril."

On 11 June, while the French armies were leaving Paris, the Supreme War Council met at Briare on the Loire. Reynaud pleaded with Churchill for British aircraft to come to France's aid. The morale of French troops, he said, "would be very high if they did not feel that they were dominated in the air." But Britain had lost large numbers of aircraft already, and had only sixty fighters and eighty bombers, at the maximum estimate, fit for operations. Churchill told Reynaud quite frankly that "it would be a fatal mistake" to denude the United Kingdom of its essential home defenses. "If the British broke up their fighter defence," he insisted, "we would be unable to carry on the war."

Churchill suggested that the solution of their difficulties lay with the French themselves. He urged that Paris should attempt to hold up the German advance just as Madrid had checked Franco's advance during the Spanish Civil War. The defense of Madrid had become something of a legend in the annals of war. But Churchill was told that orders had already been given for the army to leave Paris once its outer defenses fell.

Churchill then suggested that the Germans could be harassed in the occupied areas by some form of guerrilla warfare. This Pétain rejected on the grounds that it meant laying France waste, a "suicidal" policy which he refused to sanction.

Churchill returned to England on 12 June. The French Government moved to Tours. Thence Churchill returned on 13 June, landing only with difficulty as the Germans had bombed the airfield the night before. The streets were crowded with refugees; no one came to the airport to meet the British Prime Minister; no one in the town seemed to expect him. He made his own way through the streets and eventually persuaded a closed restaurant to open up and provide some lunch.

The Supreme War Council met that afternoon. Reynaud had to admit that for France the situation was desperate. He still hoped that America would come to France's rescue. But many of his colleagues were insisting that unless American aid were given immediately, France had no alternative but to surrender. Churchill tried to bolster Reynaud's morale by suggesting that the offer of immediate help from America was on its way—"perhaps even a declaration of war," he said. But Reynaud was not convinced. He said that the French might sing a less cheerful tune: "We cannot count on American help. There is no light at the end of the tunnel. We cannot abandon our people to indefinite German domination. We must come to terms. We have no choice." Churchill could offer no alternative. He reiterated that Britain would never surrender. But such determination could not help France. Churchill even suggested that if Britain were left on her own she would have to institute a blockade of Europe and that "famine and desperate suffering would ensue. . . . France . . . could not hope to be spared. . . . There might arise bitter antagonism between the French and English peoples." He could see only one glimmer of light for France, American intervention, and suggested that Reynaud must explain the position to Roosevelt "in its full brutal reality." Churchill returned to England; Reynaud and his government moved south to Bordeaux.

On 16 June the Germans breached the Maginot Line. At Bordeaux Pétain threatened to resign from the Government unless there were an immediate armistice. It was said that Pierre Laval, who had taken up rooms in Bordeaux, had encouraged this threat.

A second communication weakened Reynaud and his policy of resistance still further: he received a telegram from Roosevelt regretting that America could offer France no military help. Reynaud at once asked Britain if she would allow France to sue for peace.

Britain's consent to French armistice negotiations with Germany was at once followed by an offer from Churchill of the complete union of the two countries. No one in the French Cabinet knew whether the offer of union canceled the approval for an armistice. Reynaud's colleagues resented what appeared to them a theatrical and absurd proposal. It was even suggested that Churchill's intention was to relegate France to the status of a British dominion. Pétain described union with Britain as "fusion with a corpse."

Reynaud argued with his Council of Ministers on 16 June that union with Britain would enable resistance to be prolonged, pointing out that the *Declaration of Union* included the sentence: "The Union will concentrate its whole energy against the power of the enemy, no matter where the battle may be. And thus we shall conquer." But of Reynaud's colleagues only de Gaulle, who had played a large part in drafting the *Declaration of Union,* was enthusiastic. When the question of an armistice was raised thirteen members of the Cabinet supported it; Reynaud could muster only six in favor of continuing the war.

Reynaud resigned. Pétain became Prime Minister, and at once appealed for an armistice. The Germans continued to advance, capturing Belfort, Colmar, and Dijon. De Gaulle urged the Government to fall back with its army upon the French Empire, and to wage the fight from overseas. He was told that his plan was "childishness." A few Ministers sailed to Casablanca, hoping to form the nucleus of a French resistance government, but were sent back by the French authorities there, and abused on their return.

On 20 June the Germans bombed Bordeaux, caring as little for the skins of Pétain and Laval as they had for those of any of their opponents. This action persuaded Pétain to accept the German terms. At this moment of French humiliation, Italy, which had maintained its neutrality since September 1939, invaded France, occupying Menton on 24 June. To Mussolini's horror the French repelled an Italian attack in the Alps and inflicted heavy casualties upon the new invader. But France was already a defeated nation, and such defense was of no use. An armistice with Italy was signed on 25 June. That same day the cease-fire came into force between France and Germany.

By the terms of the armistice with Germany, France was divided into occupied and unoccupied zones. French troops were disarmed and demobilized. France was to pay for the cost of the German army of occupation. The French were to release all German prisoners of war, but French prisoners were to remain in Germany until a specific agreement was made about them. This provided Germany with a constant lever upon French obedience.

One of the terms of the armistice, upon which the Germans insisted, was that the French navy should be demobilized under German supervision. The British, anxious to avoid so strong an acquisition by the German navy, asked the French to sail their fleet to a British port. The Americans were equally anxious to prevent so large and sudden an increase of German power. The Secretary of State, Cordell Hull, telegraphed to Pétain warning him that if the French fleet were to fall into German hands, the French Government "would forfeit forever the friendship and goodwill of the United States Government."

Pétain was unwilling to break his armistice pledge. Admiral Dar-

lan, who commanded the French fleet, had promised Churchill at
Briare that he would never surrender his ships to the Germans. But
he feared that the Germans would march into the unoccupied zone
of France if he ordered the fleet to sail to a British port.

On 3 July 1940 the British took the only action left to them to
prevent the French fleet from falling into German hands. Those
ships in British harbors were seized. Those at Alexandria were immobilized under the threat of sinking; those off Oran were given
three choices—to join the British fleet and continue the fight, to sail
to a British port under British supervision, or to sail to a French port
in the West Indies, there to form the nucleus of an anti-German
force. Pétain ordered the admiral to refuse all three choices. The
British thereupon opened fire. The French ships, being at anchor,
could not retaliate. They were subjected to an intense bombardment.
One cruiser escaped; all other ships were destroyed or immobilized.
The French navy had ceased to be of value to Germany. The British,
who appeared to be on the verge of a fate as cruel as that of France,
had revealed that they had both the power to fight back and the
nerve to take terrible decisions. Churchill wrote:

"This was a hateful decision, the most unnatural and painful in
which I have ever been concerned. It recalled the episode of the
destruction of the Danish fleet at Copenhagen by Nelson in 1801;
but now the French had been only yesterday our dear Allies, and our
sympathy for the misery of France was sincere. On the other hand,
the life of the State and the salvation of our cause were at stake. It
was Greek tragedy. But no act was ever more necessary for the life
of Britain and for all that depended upon it. I thought of Danton in
1793: 'The coalesced Kings threaten us, and we hurl at their feet as
a gage of battle the head of a King.' The whole event was in this
order of ideas."

By ordering the destruction of the French fleet Churchill knew
that he had at one stroke strengthened the anti-British and pro-
German sentiment in France, and made it more difficult for de
Gaulle, who had set up a Free French movement under British aegis,
to rally colonial Frenchmen to his standard. The French were outraged, but Britain had maintained her command of the sea.

# ☆ 20 ☆

## GERMANY'S CHALLENGE
## TO THE WORLD

ON 21 JUNE 1940 Hitler arrived by car at the clearing in the forest
of Compiègne where, in 1918, the Germans had signed the armistice which ended the Great War. The *wagon-lits* in which the armistice had been signed was made ready to receive him. As he approached it he saw a block of granite set into the ground on which
was carved:

HERE ON THE ELEVENTH OF NOVEMBER 1918 SUCCUMBED
THE CRIMINAL PRIDE OF THE GERMAN EMPIRE – VANQUISHED
BY THE FREE PEOPLES WHICH IT TRIED TO ENSLAVE

Hitler now had the power to humiliate France, and to destroy that
"insult." He ordered the monument to be blown up three days later.
This was the spot he chose on which to dictate his terms. The French
delegates tried bravely to obtain modifications in the German demands. They were less successful than Erzberger had been for Germany on that very spot twenty-two years before. On the second day
of negotiations Erzberger had won concessions from France; on the
second day in the reverse role, France was told to sign, or to continue
the war. The Germans were never timid in their use of ultimatums.
The French signed, pleading for toleration in the coming settlement.
The *wagon-lits* was taken to Berlin, as a trophy of war. Ironically,
it was destroyed later in the war during an Allied bombing raid.

Hitler now ruled Czechoslovakia, Poland, Denmark, Norway,
Holland, Belgium, Luxembourg, and France. He had all the territory he wanted in western Europe. He had been more successful
than his advisers forecast; he could therefore afford the magnanim-

ity of allowing the establishment of an "unoccupied zone" in France, to be ruled by Frenchmen, with its capital at Vichy. His next desire was to consolidate his power in the East, and, in the fullness of time, to extend German dominance further eastwards, into the Balkans and the Ukraine.

Hitler needed British neutrality in order to concentrate upon these eastern ventures. He appealed to Churchill for a negotiated peace. Germany was willing, he said, to guarantee the integrity of the British Empire; she was willing to leave England intact; all she wanted was peace.

Many Englishmen saw the logic of Hitler's plea. Britain's allies had all been defeated while America stood apart, seemingly unperturbed at the advent of German mastery in Europe. In Norway Vidkun Quisling, in France Marshal Pétain, had become leaders of "neutral" regimes, accepting German hegemony in Europe and gaining in return a paper independence. Voices in England spoke softly for a similar solution.

Rumor had it that Lloyd George was willing to become a British "quisling"; counterrumor named Edward, former king, and since 1937 living in exile, as Britain's peacemaker. Such rumors angered Churchill, and frightened him. He took rapid action. Those who openly advocated surrender were imprisoned; senior government officials and military leaders were told:

"The Prime Minister expects all His Majesty's servants in high places to set an example of steadiness and resolution. They should check and rebuke expressions of loose and ill-digested opinion in their circles, or by their subordinates. They should not hesitate to report, or if necessary remove, any officers or officials who are found to be consciously exercising a disturbing or depressing influence."

Mediation was attempted by the Pope and the King of Sweden. But Churchill rejected all compromise. He insisted that, before peace negotiations could begin, Hitler must give guarantees "by deeds, not words" that independence would be restored to the conquered states.

Hitler was infuriated by Churchill's rebuff, yet nervous about attacking Britain. His military and naval advisers were urging him not to embark upon so dangerous a project. He himself talked incessantly of his desire to negotiate with Britain. For some time, on his direct orders, British convoys in the Channel which passed within ten miles of the German-held coast were not molested. If Germany destroyed Britain, Hitler argued, she would gain nothing: only America and Japan would profit from the collapse of the British Empire. But Churchill would not accept his offer of peace talks, and on 16 July 1940 Hitler drafted his Top Secret Directive "on the Preparation of a Landing Operation against England." It read:

"Since England, despite her militarily hopeless situation, still shows no sign of willingness to come to terms, I have decided to prepare a landing operation against England, and if necessary to carry it out.

"The aim of this operation is to eliminate the English homeland as a base for the carrying on of the war against Germany, and, if it should become necessary, to occupy it completely."

Hitler's lingering uncertainty is reflected in the phrase "if necessary to carry it out." Three days later he addressed the Reichstag. His speech was heard by Ciano (Mussolini's son-in-law and Italy's Foreign Minister), by Quisling, and by the German generals, as well as by the obedient deputies. Everyone was elated by the victory over France. Ciano jumped up and down, giving the fascist salute, whenever Hitler paused.

Hitler broke off his speech to award field-marshals' batons to twelve of the generals who were present. But the speech itself was far from bellicose. He appealed to Britain for peace, an appeal which, though abusing Churchill personally, contained none of the usual hysterical shouting. The master of Europe concluded: "In this hour I feel it to be my duty before my conscience to appeal once more to reason and common sense in Great Britain. . . . I consider myself in a position to make this appeal since I am not the vanquished begging favors, but the victor speaking in the name of reason. I can see no reason why this war must go on."

The British remained firm: they would not make peace with Europe's conqueror. Hitler, after the defeat of France, had visited Napoleon's tomb in Paris. Perhaps he pondered upon Napoleon's failure to conquer Britain. Certainly, as he began to plan the invasion of Britain, designated "Operation Sea Lion," his closest advisers found him hesitant, uncertain, and lacking in enthusiasm. His military and naval experts did their best to dampen what little enthusiasm he himself could muster. They knew that Germany, however expert at continental war, could not easily launch an invasion across the sea—

even across a mere twenty miles of sea. When Hitler asked whether he could invade Britain at the end of July 1940 his naval commander-in-chief countered: "All things considered, the best time for the operation would be May 1941."

Hitler deprecated delay. He ordered the bombing of England to begin at once, hoping to destroy British air strength and then, jumping his advisers' cautious timetables, to invade. But he was still nervous, and he began to hope that invasion would be unnecessary. He spoke openly to his generals of his intention to await a British surrender on the basis of his air bombardment alone. Invasion was set for 21 September 1940, but a clause in the directive stated boldly: "All preparations must remain liable to cancellation 24 hours before zero hour."

Throughout August the German air force tried to destroy British air strength. It was unable to do so: though outnumbered, the British pilots prevailed. British air space remained in British hands. The Germans decided to bomb towns rather than airfields. They thus lost forever the chance of mastery in the air. The bombardment of London began on 7 September. That night German bombs smashed into London's dockyards; a number of important railway junctions in south London were obliterated; London's East End became a holocaust of fire. Hitler was so impressed by the violence of his bombing that he postponed his invasion decision, hoping for a British capitulation. He even suggested to his entourage that revolution might break out in Britain, throwing a peacemaker into power. He was utterly mistaken: his bombing offensive ended all remnants of defeatism. And, by bombing cities and not airfields, he failed to destroy British air supremacy. Resistance became the dominant theme in Britain. The British pilots quickly found the measure of their opponents. On 15 September, a Sunday, more German bombers were destroyed than British fighters. The "Battle of Britain" was being won by the defenders. On 17 September Hitler took the unexpected decision of postponing Operation Sea Lion "indefinitely." Though his bombers continued to devastate the British cities, their losses mounted. At the same time British planes attacked German ships along the Channel and North Sea coast. Heavy losses were inflicted, not only upon the landing vessels of the now suspended invasion fleet, but upon the men who were to have sailed in it. Nor did British bombs fall only on the ports. On 23 August the first attack took

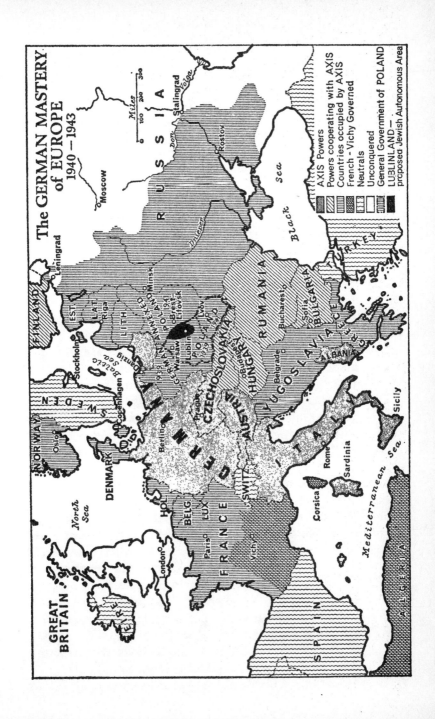

The GERMAN MASTERY
of EUROPE
1940 — 1943

Miles
0  100  200  300

AXIS Powers
Powers cooperating with AXIS
Countries occupied by AXIS
French - Vichy Governed
Neutrals
Unconquered
General Government of POLAND
LUBLINLAND — proposed Jewish Autonomous Area

GREAT
BRITAIN

North
Sea

NORWAY

Oslo

SWEDEN

Stockholm

Baltic
Sea

FINLAND

Leningrad

Moscow

Stalingrad

Volga

Don

Rostov

R U S S I A

Dnieper

Copenhagen

DENMARK

Danzig

EST.

LAT.
Riga

LITH.

Minsk

Berlin

G E R M A N Y

1939

Warsaw

LUBLIN

POLAND

Brest-
Litovsk

Lwov

Prague

CZECHOSLOVAKIA

Pripet

UKRAINE

AUSTRIA

HUNGARY

SWITZ.

HOLL.

BELG.

LUX.

London

Paris

F R A N C E

Vichy

Budapest

RUMANIA

Bucharest

Belgrade

YUGOSLAVIA

Sofia

BULGARIA

ALBANIA

GREECE

TURKEY

Black
Sea

I T A L Y

Rome

Corsica

Sardinia

Sicily

Mediterranean  Sea

S P A I N

A L G E R I A

place on Berlin and five days later the first German civilians in Berlin were killed by bombs. The war had been fought for less than a year, yet even Berlin was beginning to suffer. Germany had clearly failed in her attempt to force Britain to her knees without the need for actual invasion.

On 4 September Hitler had told a delighted audience in Berlin: "The babbling of Mr. Churchill . . . doesn't mean a thing to the German people. At best, it makes them laugh." But those babblings roused Britain to an intense fervor of courage and endurance. British pilots challenged the German bombers night by night. On 20 August Churchill told the House of Commons, while the air battle was at its most severe: "Never in the field of human conflict was so much owed by so many to so few."

It was not the pilots alone who sustained the Battle of Britain. Because it was clear that a powerful air force would be the instrument, not only of defense but also of victory, Churchill had appointed his friend Lord Beaverbrook, who had held ministerial office under Lloyd George in the First War, Minister of Aircraft Production. In August he was brought into the War Cabinet. He cut through the red tape of administration and struck out vigorously at inefficiency and slackness. Everything was thrown into the production lines; no moment was neglected, no supplies were wasted, no avenue of improvement left unexplored. This newspaper proprietor, hated for his politics and his power, transformed the aircraft industry. And on this transformation depended the Battle of Britain, and what lay beyond. Churchill's verdict on Beaverbrook was: "His personal buoyancy and vigour were a tonic. I was glad to be able sometimes to lean on him. He did not fail. This was his hour."

The Germans, having abandoned their plan to invade Britain, did not lessen the pressure of their bombing raids. On 29 December 1940 the City of London was severely damaged, though St. Paul's Cathedral survived the raging fires. But as the British air force grew, bombing became a hazardous affair for the Germans. They could no longer conquer, and even their powers of demoralization were waning. Between July and October 1940 at least 1,733 German aircraft were shot down. British losses were 915. In July Britain built 1,665 aircraft, of which 496 were fighters. These figures were repeated month after month. The Germans could not prevail.

Hitler's plans to conquer England had failed. He turned his eyes eastwards, hoping to find in Russia the victim that had been denied him in the West. In November 1939 Hitler had told his generals: "We can oppose Russia only when we are free in the West." Though such "freedom" was denied him by Britain's obstinacy, he acted as if he possessed it. In July 1940 he began to plan for the invasion of Russia, which he hoped to begin in May 1941. With the failure of the Battle of Britain he developed his plans further. But between January and May 1941 he was to be sadly disappointed.

Already the British had shown their strength, driving the Italian Army across the North African desert from Egypt to Benghazi. At Sidi Barrani in December 1940 over 40,000 Italians were taken prisoner; at Tobruk in January 1941, 25,000; at Benghazi, 15,000. Only with the arrival of German help did the Italians stand firm. The German armored corps was commanded by Erwin Rommel, veteran of the Polish and French campaigns.

The Italians had invaded Greece in October 1940. By mid-November the Italian Army had been driven back into Albania and the British had occupied Lesbos and Crete. Hitler was furious at Mussolini's inability to make war, and at his "skill" in drawing the British after him.

On 26 March 1941 the pro-Axis Yugoslav Government was overthrown by a popular uprising in Belgrade and an anti-German government set up. The Balkans were aflame with anti-German and anti-Italian activity. Hitler could hardly attack Russia with a hostile Balkans behind him. Hitler feared that the Turks too, although neutral up till then, might turn against him. He decided to redress the balance of Italian weakness.

On 6 April 1941 German aircraft bombed Belgrade without warning. Her citizens were subjected to the same terrible rain of bombs which had destroyed Rotterdam and reduced so much of London and Warsaw to rubble. The Croats in the north welcomed the Germans as "liberators," having kept their dislike of Serbian dominance alive since 1918. A "quisling" at once appeared in Zagreb, a former terrorist, Ante Pavelič, whom Hitler and Mussolini at once recognized as ruler of Croatia.

The Germans smashed Yugoslav resistance and drove on to Greece, held up for a while by a small British force, but entering Athens on 27 April. Greece was handed over to Mussolini, though Hitler made sure that Germany maintained control of vital towns. In

May the British were driven from Crete. In North Africa Rommel had come to Italy's aid, pushing the British back to the Egyptian border by the middle of April.

Hitler's plans to invade Russia in May had been disrupted owing to the Greek, Yugoslav, and African campaigns. The delay meant that the actual invasion gave Germany too little time to conquer Russia before the autumn rains, which would make the countryside impassable for tanks. But Hitler was determined to strike. He would not allow Mussolini's inefficiency to hold him back.

Hitler planned a new technique of conquest. In March he had explained to his generals: "The struggle is one of ideologies and racial differences. It will have to be conducted with unprecedented, unmerciful, and unrelenting harshness. . . . Commissars will be liquidated. German soldiers guilty of breaking international law . . . will be excused." On 22 June 1941 Hitler invaded Russia.

The German advance proceeded rapidly. In the north, helped by the Finns, Murmansk was besieged. The Baltic states were quickly overrun. On 1 October an offensive was launched against Moscow. Great slaughter was inflicted on the defenders; between Bryansk and Vyazma the Germans took 250,000 prisoners; they advanced to Volokolamsk, west of Moscow, and Tula, southeast of the capital. A state of siege was declared in Moscow, and foreign ambassadors withdrew in panic. In the south the Germans occupied the Crimea and pressed on to take Kharkov and Rostov. This rapid advance along a vast front was perhaps the most brilliant, and certainly the most spectacular, of Hitler's military achievements. Then, in December, with snow thick on the ground and the German front extended to the limits of its military capacity, the Russians counterattacked. Moscow was saved. Kalinin was recaptured. The Germans were deprived of a victory in 1941.

Russia, once at war with Germany, provided a rallying point for British enthusiasm. After being "alone" since the fall of France, Britain now had a fellow belligerent.[1] In September 1941 Lord Beaverbrook went to Moscow and, with the German armies in the full flood of their advance, pledged British support for Russia. The

[1] Britain's lack of a fighting ally was in part compensated for by Roosevelt's "Lend-Lease" policy, by which American equipment, which Britain could hardly afford to buy, was let out on loan for the duration of the war. "Lend-Lease" provided Britain with a great psychological boost. Churchill called it "the most unsordid act in the history of any nation."

Americans, though still neutral, did the same. On his return from Russia Beaverbrook wrote: "Russia is an ally, powerful and courageous. In her hour of need she is still indomitable. I am convinced that she will fight on through the winter and into the spring and summer. Before Moscow and Leningrad. If need be, beyond the Volga and the Don and the Urals."

On 7 December, while Russia held off the German armies, Japan attacked the United States of America. The European war was over, eclipsed by a wider "world" war.

Roosevelt declared war on Japan, but hesitated to declare war on Germany. Hitler acted where Roosevelt was hesitant. On 11 December 1941 he told the Reichstag:

"Roosevelt comes from a rich family and belongs to the class whose path is smoothed in the democracies. I was only the child of a small, poor family and had to fight my way by work and industry. . . . After the war Roosevelt tried his hand at financial speculation. He made profits . . . out of the misery of others, while I . . . lay in a hospital. . . . Now he is seized with fear that if peace is brought about in Europe his squandering of millions of money on armaments will be looked upon as a plain fraud, since nobody will attack America."

Hitler then announced that he had declared war on America. By his folly he thus brought America into the European war, a war in which he was doing so well; and brought to Europe a world war, for which neither he nor Mussolini were in any way equipped.

The tide of war now turned. For three and a half years Hitler battled against Britain, Russia, and America. His armies were thrown back from Stalingrad in January 1943 and driven from Lake Ladoga. In North Africa Rommel was defeated in May 1943. In the occupied territories bands of partisans began to disrupt German transport and terrorize their officials. In Yugoslavia Josip Broz Tito raised the standard of revolt in the mountainous terrain of Bosnia, and gradually won control of a large area. Among the British officers parachuted into Yugoslavia to help Tito and his partisans was Randolph Churchill, the Prime Minister's only son, who had also fought in the African desert.

Italy, which entered the war only when she saw France on the verge of defeat, and which had suffered the full force of British enthusiasm in North Africa, provided Hitler with a further shock, for in July 1943 Mussolini was overthrown. On 3 September 1943 British and American troops landed in southern Italy and five days later the new Italian Government announced that it was out of the war. Italy became a no-man's-land. But the Allies failed to exploit that opportunity. They overestimated the German ability to rush troops southwards, and took no chances. Hitler was already conceding the loss of Rome; but the Allied invasion fleet was too cautiously directed to move further north than off Naples.[2]

On 13 September Mussolini, whom the Italian Government had imprisoned in a hotel on the top of a mountain, was kidnaped by an Austrian Nazi, Otto Skorzeny, who landed an airplane on the mountaintop. On 15 September, at Hitler's bidding, Mussolini proclaimed a new "Italian Social Republic." Hitler persuaded him to surrender Trieste, Istria, and the South Tyrol to Germany. The German army took up positions in the former Italian occupied territories, and concentrated its power south of Rome to resist the Allied advance. Goebbels commented on Mussolini: "He is not a revolutionary like the Führer or Stalin. He is so bound to his own Italian people that he lacks the broad qualities of a world-wide revolutionary and insurrectionist." Now both Mussolini and his countrymen were under German domination.

Nineteen forty-three was a black year for Hitler. In July his third offensive in Russia was halted, then driven back. At sea the terror imposed on Allied shipping by his U-boats was broken, and German submarines increasingly fell the victims of radar and long-range aircraft. Throughout the year Allied bombers brought destruction to German cities. These Allied bombing raids were not entirely motivated by the demands of strategy. While the Americans concentrated on destroying German factories and supply depots, bridges and railway yards, the British formed a new, more compact target—German civilians. Starting in 1942, single night raids were made on the centers of selected cities. The aim of the raids was to create firestorms in the centers, burning the buildings and their inhabitants in one terrible rush of flames. German civilians began to suffer—and to suffer hideously—for the crimes of their leaders. As the fires raged fiercely, they sucked the air out of the ventilation tubes of the deep

---

[2] The American general, Dwight D. Eisenhower, who was criticized for failing to attack Rome, later explained that he was at this time short of troops, having sent seven divisions to Britain to prepare for the invasion of France.

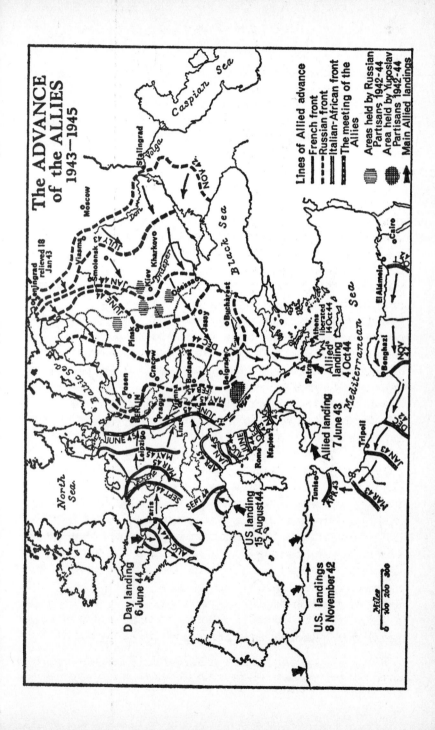

The ADVANCE
of the ALLIES
1943—1945

Lines of Allied advance
French front
Russian front
Italian-African front
The meeting of the Allies

Areas held by Russian Partisans 1942-44
Area held by Yugoslav Partisans 1942-44
Main Allied landings

Caspian Sea

Stalingrad

Volga

NOV

Moscow

Don

JULY 43

Leningrad relieved 18 Jan 43

Viasma

Smolensk

Kiev

Kharkov

JAN 44

JUNE

Dnieper

Odessa

Bucharest

Pinsk

Black Sea

DEC 44

Jassy

Belgrade

Budapest

Vienna

FEB 45

MAY 45

Cracow

Prague

Posen

Athens liberated 14 Oct 44

Allied landing 4 Oct 44

Patras

JUNE 45

Leipzig

MAY 45

APR 45

Linz

JUNE

DEC

Mediterranean Sea

Allied landing 7 June 43

JAN

Rome

Naples

SEPT 44

JUNE

Paris

AUG 44

North Sea

D Day landing 6 June 44

US landing 15 August 44

US landings 8 November 42

Allied landing 7 June 43

Tunis

APR 43

Tripoli

DEC

NOV

Benghazi

JAN 43

MAR 43

El Alamein

Cairo

Miles
0   100   200   300

concrete shelters, stifling and suffocating all who were within them. Goebbels noted in his diary on 26 July 1943: "During the night a heavy raid on Hamburg . . . with most serious consequences both for the civilian population and for armaments production. . . . It is a real catastrophe. . . ." And on July 29 he recorded a further tragic development:

"During the night we had the heaviest raid yet made on Hamburg . . . with 800 to 1,000 bombers . . . Kaufmann (the local *Gauleiter*) gave me a first report. . . . He spoke of a catastrophe the extent of which simply staggers the imagination. A city of a million inhabitants had been destroyed in a manner unparalleled in history. We are faced with problems that are almost impossible of solution. Food must be found for this population of a million. Shelter must be obtained. The people must be evacuated as far as possible. They must be given clothing. In short, we are facing problems there of which we had no conception even a few weeks ago. . . . Kaufmann spoke of some 800,000 homeless people who are wandering up and down the streets not knowing what to do. . . ." This killing of civilians by British bombs continued until February 1945 when, in one night, 135,000 Germans, mostly refugees fleeing westward from the Russian armies, were caught in the medieval city of Dresden, and burned or suffocated to death. Vultures, flapping away from the bombed area, grew so fat on the myriad corpses that they could not fly.

The Allied bombing reduced Germany's cities to rubble. On 6 June 1944 the British and Americans landed in Normandy. The second front was open; victory seemed certain. On 20 July a plot against Hitler in which many generals participated failed, but had wide repercussions.[3] A bomb had actually been placed within a few feet of Hitler; it had exploded, wounding Hitler, but not killing him. "I myself am entirely unhurt," he broadcast to the nation that night, "apart from some very minor scratches, bruises, and burns. I regard this as a confirmation of the task imposed upon me by Providence."

But Providence proved inconstant in her attentions. By the middle

[3] Among the military leaders who knew and approved of the plot was Field-Marshal Rommel. He had been severely injured on 17 July by low-flying Allied planes which shot up his car in Normandy. Hitler learned of his involvement in the plot and persuaded him to take poison. He was then buried with full military honors. It would have been impossible for Hitler to bring this popular hero to trial.

of August 1944 the Russians reached East Prussia and by the end of August had driven the Germans from Rumania. The Americans entered Paris on 25 August; the British took Brussels on 3 September and Antwerp on 4 September. The Allied advance was checked at one point only because it was so rapid and had outrun its supplies. The Russians continued advancing through Hungary. Hitler refused to believe that Russia was about to break through into Germany, shouting at his Chief of the General Staff, "It's the greatest bluff since Genghis Khan! Who's responsible for telling me all this rubbish?" By the end of January 1945 the Russians were only 100 miles from Berlin. Hitler pathetically asked Goering whether Britain might not take alarm at the Russian advance, and join forces with Germany. On 7 March 1945 the Americans crossed the Rhine. On 16 April they were in Nuremberg. On 21 April the Russians reached the bomb-shattered suburbs of Berlin. By searching for enemies outside Europe, Hitler had brought defeat to Germany and devastation to much of the Continent. He also brought the Russians, whom he had hated, wooed, and then tried to destroy, into half of Europe, giving them a power they had not sought and which, without his folly, they could never have obtained.

On 26 April Mussolini was killed by Italian partisans while trying to escape from Italy to Switzerland. On 30 April, with Russian shells exploding in the Chancellery garden, Hitler shot himself. A week later the German Army surrendered unconditionally.

# ☆ 21 ☆

## THE TRIUMPH OF
## BARBARISM

THE SECOND WORLD WAR was not dominated by the movement of troops or by the frequency of battles. The most significant aspect of the war was the cruel treatment of civilian populations. Soldiers in the battle zones were for the most part safeguarded by the recognized rules of war. On the western and African fronts prisoners of war were confined in special camps, given reasonable medical attention, and allowed such luxuries as Red Cross food parcels and letters from home. No poison gas was used in the battles. The opposing armies often admired each other's courage and initiative.

No such moderation was shown towards conquered civilians. The war became an excuse for cruelty on a scale previously unknown to history or fiction. The evils which the Germans encouraged were terrible and unprecedented. Nor were the Germans the only people whose behavior was so grotesque. Much of Europe succumbed to the lure of calculated violence.

The German conquest of Poland was the starting point of civilian terror. After parts of Poland had been annexed by Germany Hitler set up a separate General Government of Poland and appointed Hans Frank Governor-General. Frank had taken part in Hitler's Munich *Putsch* in 1923; in 1935 he became a minister in Hitler's Government; in 1939 he was appointed President of the Academy of German Law. He wrote in his diary: "On 15 September 1939 I was given the task of taking over the administration of the conquered eastern territories with the specific order to plunder the areas ruthlessly. . . . I was to reduce its economic, social, cultural, and political structure to a pile of rubble."

Frank obeyed his order with demonic zeal. He at once arrested all Polish politicians and intellectuals. Orchestras were forbidden to play Polish music. Schools were forbidden to teach Polish history. It became an offense to speak Polish in the streets of Warsaw. Camps were set up to which Polish men over the age of eighteen were sent to undergo forced labor, living without pay or privacy in crudely constructed barracks. Poland came under Frank's orders: he delighted in making the population frightened and subservient.

It was decreed that the cost of the German occupation should be borne entirely by the Poles. At the same time all raw materials, scrap metals, and machinery which could possibly help German industry were sent at once to Germany. It was laid down that nothing was to remain in Poland that was "not absolutely essential to maintain the existence of the inhabitants at as low a level as possible." At the same time a continual stream of forced laborers were sent to work in Germany. Poles were moved out of the best residential areas of the main cities, which were handed over to German administrators and emigrants. Hitler planned to make Warsaw an entirely German city, and Germany's eastern capital.

All Polish universities were closed down. All Polish newspapers were proscribed. Films, plays, and cabarets were banned. Wherever possible wirelesses were seized, and their possession made illegal. News and orders were transmitted by loudspeakers installed in town centers.

Particularly harsh measures were taken against university teachers. All professors were deported to German concentration camps in November 1939: seventeen, who resisted arrest, were shot. A year later Himmler recalled: "We had to harden our hearts at the shooting of thousands of leading Poles." It is not surprising that no Pole could be found to act as a minister in Frank's administration. Even in the four provinces into which the General Government was divided no "quisling" could be found. Poland was ruled by 40,000 German civil servants, who, in the worst of all imperial traditions, felt nothing but scorn and loathing towards their subjects.

The eleventh of November was Polish independence day. On that day in 1939 the Germans forbade all celebrations. But the Poles, after two months of occupation, were not yet cowed. A few defiant Poles put posters on walls in Warsaw telling their fellow countrymen to be brave. Frank at once gave the order that from every house on which a poster appeared one male should be taken and shot. His order was obeyed.

In mid-December the minimum age for compulsory labor was reduced from eighteen to fourteen years.

Late in December 1939 a German soldier was murdered in a village near Warsaw. It was said that he had raped a local girl. Frank did not trouble to make inquiries, or to hold a trial of those responsible for the soldier's death. He ordered an immediate reprisal. One hundred and seven male villagers were arrested, paraded in the center of the village, blindfolded, and shot. Their bodies were laid out in rows in the village square. The rest of the inhabitants were marched past. In future, they were warned, Germans were to be unmolested.

The policy of reprisals was callously extended; it became a "communal" offense even to insult a German verbally. Theft of German property, public criticism of German policy, even failure to give the Nazi salute, became offenses punishable by death. Sometimes reprisals were carried out immediately by military or S.S. units. Sometimes the accused were sent for trial. These trials, conducted by German lawyers and presided over by German judges, were a mockery of justice. The judges had been sent specially from Germany. They delighted in harsh sentences. They were supreme. One judge sentenced six people to death for harboring an escaped prisoner of war. One of the accused was a pregnant woman. The judge announced that, "in German fashion," he would exercise his prerogative of mercy. Five of the accused would therefore be released. Only the pregnant woman would be shot.

The Germans believed the Poles to be an inferior people. They were able to ill-treat them because they despised them. The Germans were not alone in feeling this way towards those whom they conquered. War provided the cloak under which many evils flourished. A determined individual could kill his neighbor and go unpunished. This acceptance of killing spread out from Germany to the occupied territories. In Croatia, the Nazi supporter Pavelič resorted to murder as a regular method of political activity. He was opposed by the communists, whose methods were equally harsh. The result was a prolonged and vicious civil war. In Quisling's Norway and Pétain's France German methods were similarly imitated or condoned. National rivalries, once conducted as newspaper polemics, were now pursued by means of the horsewhip and the machine gun. Europe lost its sanity and was plunged into five years of mounting horror.

The conquest of Poland, Czechoslovakia, Slovenia, France, and parts of Russia provided Germany with a vast supply of manpower which, it was quickly realized, could play an important part in maintaining German military and industrial strength. Indeed the prime purpose of conquest was often considered to be manpower. By October 1940 Hitler decided that any of his Slav subjects for whom hard labor was unsuitable, whether because of temperament or illness, were expendable. If they could serve no useful purpose for Germany, they could die. He made these points with extreme clarity when talking to Hans Frank and his officials on 2 October 1940. Hitler considered that: "the Poles are especially born for low labor. . . . They are lazy and it is necessary to use compulsion to make them work. . . . Poland should be used by us merely as a source of unskilled labor . . . all representatives of the Polish intelligentsia are to be exterminated. This sounds cruel but such is the law of life."

Hitler's concept of "the law of life" was understood by his subordinates, and acted upon. Any boy over fourteen and any man under sixty-five was liable to be deported to a labor camp in Germany. The actual deportation conditions gave a foretaste of what was to come: journeys lasting three days were spent in freight cars with no food, water, or sanitary facilities. The men reached their destination hungry and foul-smelling. On arrival in Germany they were forbidden to write to their relatives even to say that they had arrived safely. Nor was there any respite from terror once they were at work. Slackness was rewarded by severe beating, disobedience by death.

Most German industrialists could find a use for forced laborers. Krupp, the manufacturer of tanks, rifles, and ammunition, was no exception. The man he put in charge of his laborers' welfare has described the conditions in which they lived in a labor camp at Essen: "Its inhabitants were kept for nearly half a year in dog kennels, urinals, and in old baking houses. The dog kennels were three feet high, nine feet long, six feet wide. Five men slept in each of them." The men in that particular camp were French prisoners of war.

In all, seven and a half million civilian foreigners were sent to

Germany for forced labor in industry. Another two and a half million were employed on German farms. All were forbidden to go to church or to the cinema or to any public eating place. Sexual intercourse with Germans was punishable by death. Laziness too did not go unpunished. Refusal to work, whatever the cause of the refusal, was rewarded by "special treatment." To ensure that the factory owners should not be in doubt about the meaning of this vague phrase Himmler explained, on 20 February 1942, that "special treatment is hanging. It should not take place in the immediate vicinity of the camp. But a certain number of the laborers should attend."

Women were also employed as forced laborers. They too were subjected to foul conditions and rigid confinement. They too were employed by leading industrialists. Krupp's doctor described the women which the great industrial king employed: "They had no shoes. . . . The sole clothing of each consisted of a sack with holes for the arms and head. Their hair was shorn. The camp was surrounded by barbed wire." These people, however much they were ill-treated, were meant to be assets to Germany's industrial potential. Yet the brutality to which they were subjected naturally reduced their ability to do efficient work. Such thoughts did not bother their employers; the supply of forced labor appeared limitless. It was also cheap. If people could be acquired almost for a song, why should they be cared for? Himmler expressed the official viewpoint succinctly when he addressed his S.S. officials on 4 October 1943:

"Whether nations live in prosperity or starve to death like cattle interests me only in so far as we need them as slaves to our *Kultur*, otherwise it is of no interest to me. Whether 10,000 Russian females fall down from exhaustion while digging an antitank ditch interests me only in so far as the antitank ditch for Germany is finished."

The forced-labor policy had as its aim the strengthening of Germany's productive capacity. Though wasteful of human life, it was, in a perverted sense, constructive. Germany's industrial barons were building things. But the policy of killing civilian hostages had no such rationale. It was entirely destructive. Had its aim been to deter occupied civilians from murdering Germans it might have been defended by its perpetrators. But hostages were killed, not only as reprisals against the death of Germans, but for sabotage and indiscipline, and generally to create an atmosphere of terror.

In September 1941 the Chief of the German Security Police, Reinhard Heydrich, was appointed Acting Protector of Bohemia and Moravia. His rule was odious and he became known as "hangman Heydrich." On 29 May 1942 two Czechs, one of whom had been parachuted into Czechoslovakia from England, threw a bomb into his car. He was seriously wounded, and died on 4 June. The German leaders were determined to discourage any further assassinations. One thousand three hundred and thirty-one Czechs were shot at once in Prague; 3,000 Jews were transported eastwards, to be killed in a concentration camp. But as an extra warning a special reprisal was planned.

On 9 June 1942 the Germans surrounded the village of Lidice, which was totally unconnected with Heydrich's death. No one was allowed to leave. A boy of twelve who tried to run away was shot. On the following day all the males over sixteen were executed—172 in all. The women were sent to a concentration camp, where fifty-two of the 195 were killed. Four pregnant women were sent to Prague for their confinements. Their children were then killed.

There were ninety children at Lidice; eighty-three were sent to a concentration camp. Seven, who were under one year old, were selected by so-called racial experts as suitable to "become" Germans. They were given German names and sent to German families. With the inhabitants gone the village was burned down. The shells of the buildings were dynamited and leveled to the ground.

This style of reprisal was repeated many times, in Poland, Russia, Greece, Yugoslavia, and Norway. Finally, in June 1944, it was carried out in France. The Germans thought that some ammunition was hidden in the village of Oradour-sur-Glane. The men of the village were herded into a barn, which was set on fire. Those who broke out were machine-gunned and 190 were killed. The women and children were sent into the church. It too was set on fire, after its occupants had been machine-gunned. Two hundred and forty-five women and 207 children were killed. Nine men survived, having simulated death. One woman escaped from the church. The logic of reprisals had passed the bounds of sanity.

Although men, women, and children died as a result of the forced labor and hostages policies, the aim of these policies when first launched was not primarily to destroy. They represented, in a crude way, the "constructive" spirit of German domination; the employment and subjugation, the exploitation and terrorization, of subject peoples.

But a more evil spirit had been engendered in Germany by seven years of Nazi propaganda. The philosophical core of Hitler's writings and speeches was racial "purity." He insisted that Germany must be cleansed of all aliens and all racial blemishes. The conquered territories, he decided, must be similarly purged, to make impossible the contamination of German "purity" from outside. This racial extremism played a minor part in Nazi policy-making in 1933, when the chief problem had been the consolidation of power. But by 1935 German Jews were being barred from professional activity. By 1937 small numbers of Jews were being taken to concentration camps and cruelly tortured. In November 1938 an officially organized attack on Jews was launched; synagogues were burnt down and Jewish shops looted. Ten thousand Jews were sent to Buchenwald concentration camp. The aim of this pogrom was to frighten the Jews. But it also succeeded in alerting British, French, and American opinion to the reality of Nazism, and thus destroyed most of the goodwill that Hitler had created a month earlier at the Munich Conference. For a while the persecutions were relaxed. When a number of Polish Jews were murdered inside a synagogue during the German invasion in September 1939 the soldiers responsible were court-martialed and imprisoned.

It was indeed against Germans, not Jews, that the first "purification" measures took place after the outbreak of war in 1939. Hitler decided to eliminate "insane" Germans. His definition of insanity was a wide one. It included mentally retarded people for whom, in a less barbaric age, kindness and patience would have been prescribed. But Hitler had no desire to be kind to the German people.

In hundreds of towns, buses would draw up before the doors of the local mental hospitals. The inmates would be shepherded into the buses and driven away, whither no one knew. But a few weeks later relatives of the mental patients would receive a note informing them of the death of their aunt or cousin or nephew from pneumonia, or some infectious disease. They had been, said the note, cremated, at the state's expense. Often a small urn of the loved one's ashes would be sent to the bereaved family.

This innocent procedure concealed the systematic murder of the insane and mentally retarded. But the German people were not unaware of what was really happening. Nazi officials reported anxiously to their superiors that "many mistakes occurred. One family received two urns." Rumors spread rapidly. In one area a local doctor explained to his Nazi questioner that "families are refusing to send their sick to institutions, as they do not know whether they will ever get them back alive." The Bishop of Württemberg complained to the Minister of Justice that "the systematic extermination of lunatics, weak and frail compatriots . . . is reaching the proportion of a great danger and a scandal." Even children were aware of the hideous policy, explained the Bishop of Limberg. He had himself heard a child call to his companion: "You're crazy. You'll be sent to the baking ovens." The bishop was also worried because the cremating of some of the insane took place near the small town of Hadamar. Its inhabitants had approached him on a troublesome matter. They were, he said, "tortured with the ever-present thought of the miserable victims, especially when repulsive odors annoy them, depending on the direction of the wind." The "repulsive odors" of burning bodies were to enter the nostrils of many Germans before the war was over. A few, like the bishop, protested. But protests were dangerous things to make, requiring great courage, and seldom likely to succeed.

In 1941, because of the war with Russia, the German Army had to decide upon a policy towards Russian prisoners of war. In September 1941 the Chief of the Prisoner of War Department of the High Command, bearing in mind the danger of "contaminating" German soil with aliens, issued a special regulation: "The Bolshevik soldier . . . has lost all claim to treatment as an honorable opponent in accordance with the Geneva Convention. . . . Insubordination, active or passive resistance, must be broken immediately by force of arms. . . . Prisoners of war attempting to escape are to be fired upon without previous challenge. No warning shot must ever be fired."

A week after this regulation was issued Admiral Canaris, Chief of German Military Intelligence, protested. He urged that "it is contrary to military tradition to kill or injure helpless people." Canaris's objections were brushed aside. Wilhelm Keitel, Chief of the German Armed Forces, himself rebuked the admiral with a marginal note in purple pencil on his complaint: "These objections arise from the military concept of chivalrous warfare. What we are engaged in is the destruction of an ideology. Therefore I approve and back the measures."

The measure of which Keitel approved was carried out. Some 3,800,000 Russian soldiers were taken prisoner during the war, mostly in the course of the first great German advance from June to December 1941. They were subjected to incredible hardships. It became an offense punishable by death for a civilian to offer food to a prisoner of war. The Russian prisoners were marched vast distances without adequate rest or clothing; they were housed in camps which lacked any sort of amenity. They were treated like vermin, and, like vermin, were killed without hesitation. Sometimes there were protests, but of a curious sort. As the Gestapo chief, Heinrich Mueller, wrote: ". . . when marching, for example, from the railroad station to the camp, a rather large number of prisoners collapsed . . . either dead or half dead. . . . It cannot be prevented that the German people take notice of these occurrences."

To reduce the danger of civilian distress, Mueller ordered the shooting of all prisoners who looked as if they might not be able to survive "even a short march" to their prison camps. The Russians were deliberately starved to death, and, apart from 750,000 who were sent to Germany for forced labor, few of the 3,800,000 survived.

Behind the German lines the Russian people attempted to sabotage German administration, derailing trains and burning farm produce that was earmarked for Germany. These partisans sheltered in every village, and spread the spirit of resistance throughout the occupied territories. Against them the Germans employed the cruelest methods they knew, burning villages, shooting the entire inhabitants, and sending thousands of people to concentration camps. As Erich Koch, who was appointed ruler of the Ukraine, explained to his subordinates: "Gentlemen. I am known as a brutal dog. For that reason I have been appointed *Reichskommissar* for the Ukraine. There is no free Ukraine. We must aim at making the Ukrainians work for Germany, and not at making the people happy."

The German administration in the eastern territories was inefficient and clumsy. Contradictory policies were pursued simultaneously. Rival rulers quarreled over their respective jurisdictions. Hitler was bombarded with appeals from ambitious men anxious for greater authority. But he allowed the chaos to remain. He failed to see the value of an efficiently administered east. He failed to see the advantages which could be gained by a policy of moderation, by an appeal to the anticommunist feelings which still remained, or by an appeal to the anti-Russian feelings of Ukrainians, Latvians, or Estonians. He allowed a babel of authorities to destroy both the political and economic usefulness of occupied Russia. The only consistent policies were those which entailed the starvation of prisoners of war or the execution of partisans. But empires are not long sustained by brutality alone.

In the west Hitler put murder upon a more systematic footing. On 7 December 1941 he issued his "Night and Fog Decree." It provided a more "legal" basis for terror in the west than had been thought necessary for the eastern barbarians. Under the "Night and Fog Decree" anyone who was thought to be "endangering German security" was to be either executed immediately or else sent to Germany to vanish "in the night and fog" of the Reich. Their relatives were to be given no clue as to their whereabouts nor, when it inevitably occurred, of their death or burial place. All was to be silence and mystery. "Intimidation can only be achieved," Keitel explained in a subsidiary directive, "by capital punishment or by measures by which the criminal's relatives and the population do not know his fate." The victims of "Night and Fog" were not only those who had openly expressed anti-German attitudes, but also those suspected of harboring anti-German sentiment. Sometimes the subjects of neutral nations would be taken by "accident." In 1944 the German Foreign Office complained to the S.S. that "members of neutral countries had been 'turned into fog' by mistake." The Foreign Office were naturally anxious not to offend neutrals. But like many others they confined their protests to marginal memoranda.

The murder of Russian prisoners of war, of hostages, and of critics of Nazism in the west was a consistent operation. There was never a time when it was suggested that Russians should be released, or hostages imprisoned in tolerable conditions, or the victims of "Night and Fog" left unmolested in their place of exile: death was the object of all decrees. No such unanimity of purpose existed as far as German policy towards the Jews was concerned. As well as being the Germans' greatest imagined enemy, they were also their greatest embarrassment. There were so many of them; every conquest added more; by 1942 there were upwards of six million, whereas in 1939 there had been under a million.

With the conquest of Poland the Germans developed a plan for creating a Jewish territory to which all Jews in Poland, Austria, and East Prussia could be transferred. A part of the General Government of Poland was set aside for this purpose, with Lublin as its capital. Elsewhere towns prided themselves on being able to announce that they were "Jew-free." Eighty thousand Jews were sent to the Lublinland Jewish Reserve from the Polish territory annexed by Germany. In January 1940 a further 12,000 were sent from Vienna to their new homeland. The conditions of their transfer were indicative of the intensity of German anti-Semitic feeling: from Lublin station the first group of 1,200 Viennese Jews were sent on foot through a snow blizzard for fourteen hours. Seventy-two of them froze to death on the march. They were finally halted in a village where only barns and sheds were provided to house them. They had been allowed no luggage on their journey; they were given no supplies with which to establish themselves as a community. A further 150 died from exposure before the spring brought climatic relief.

Hans Frank, who wished to make as much of Poland "Jew-free" as possible, was anxious to get rid of the Jews altogether. He was not a supporter of the Lublinland Jewish state. He suggested to Hitler that all Jews should be deported to the French island of Madagascar, but Hitler was unenthusiastic. Frank then encouraged groups of Jews to cross into Russian-occupied Poland, hoping simply to export them. But the Russians protested against this "dumping," and the Jews were sent back.

Since he could not spirit his Jews out of existence, Frank made their life unpleasant. In December 1939 Jewish workers were deprived of the right to extra payment for overtime, and were made liable to two years' forced labor in special camps. All Jews between the ages of fourteen and sixty were liable to such labor and required to register. On 12 December 1939 it was decreed that "Ten years' hard labor shall be the penalty . . . for Jews who fail to appear promptly for registration."

The idea of a totally Jewish state was abandoned. At the end of 1940 Frank decided to push forward with a new policy. All Jews were to be confined in ghettos and deprived of all contact with

Poles or Germans. Ghettos were set up in Warsaw, Lodz, Lublin, and (after it was captured from Russia) Bialystok. To them were sent the Jews scattered about Lublinland and the Warsaw area. The ghettos were self-governing and potentially self-perpetuating communities. The Warsaw ghetto, which was the largest, was actually walled in, first by barbed wire and fencing, then by a brick wall. Jews leaving the ghetto were shot at sight. By October 1940 Frank had pushed 360,000 people into a space which normally housed 160,000. Even before the new people were brought in there had been serious overcrowding.

Conditions in the ghetto were terrible throughout 1941. Over 100,000 people were living on soup alone by the end of the year. Sometimes the soup had to be made from boiled hay. Potatoes were a rare luxury. Frank allowed each Jew thirty-three ounces of bread a week. A woman who stretched her hand through the ghetto wire to pull in a turnip was shot dead.

Forty-four thousand six hundred and thirty people died in the ghetto in 1941, over 10 per cent of the population. Fifteen thousand of them died of typhus, the rest mostly of starvation. The bodies of the dead were laid out naked on the pavements, their rags being too precious to commit to the vast communal grave. Collection of bodies was made as frequently as possible, but as over a hundred people died each day the death-carts were overworked.

The ghetto policy was not a success. When Hitler decided that some other solution was needed to the Jewish question than confinement and hardship, there were a number of suggestions from his keen subordinates. Frank's view was: "We must destroy the Jews wherever we come across them. . . . The Jews are particularly harmful gluttons. . . . We have at the moment 2.5 million Jews . . . perhaps 3.5 million; we cannot poison them, but we will nevertheless be able to intervene in ways which will somehow lead to successful annihilation." One of his suggestions was to cut off food supplies from the ghettos altogether. Another was to put the Jews to work at hard labor until they died from a combination of starvation and exhaustion.

The "final solution" of the Jewish question was worked out in the spring of 1942. Camps were to be set up in the Government General to which Jews from all the European occupied territories would be sent. These camps would provide a constant stream of forced la-

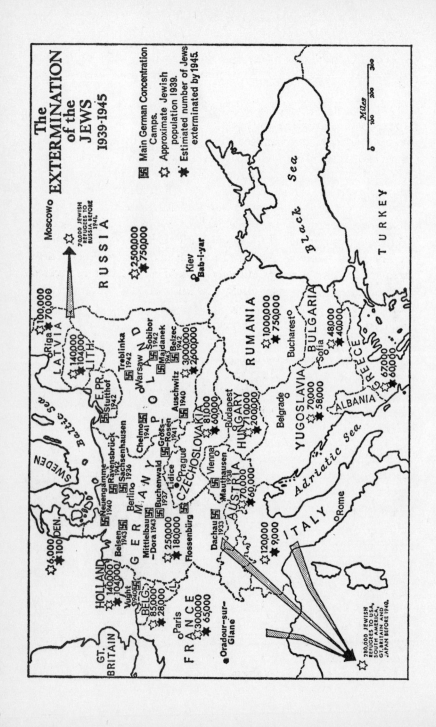

The
EXTERMINATION
of the
JEWS
1939-1945

卍 Main German Concentration Camps.

☆ Approximate Jewish population 1939.

★ Estimated number of Jews exterminated by 1945.

Miles
0   100   200   300

GT. BRITAIN

SWEDEN

Baltic Sea

North Sea

Moscow o

☆ 70,000 JEWISH REFUGEES TO RUSSIA BEFORE FALL.

R U S S I A

☆ 2,500,000
★ 750,000

o Kiev
Bab-i-yar

Black Sea

TURKEY

☆ 100,000
★ 70,000
o Riga
L A T V I A
☆ 140,000
★ 104,000
LITH.

卍 Stutthof 1942
E. PR.

Treblinka 1942
P O L A N D
o Warsaw 1942
卍 Sobibor 1942
☆ 3,000,000
★ 2,600,000
Belzec 1941
Majdanek 1941

卍 Chelmo 1941
卍 Gross-Rosen 1941
Auschwitz 1940

卍 Ravensbrück 1940
卍 Sachsenhausen
卍 Neuengamme 1940
卍 Berlino 1936

G E R M A N Y
卍 Buchenwald 1937
卍 Mittelbau—Dora 1943
☆ 250,000
★ 180,000
卍 Flossenbürg

☆ 6,000
★ 100,000
DEN.

HOLLAND
☆ 140,000
★ 104,000
Vught 1940
BELG:
☆ 85,000
★ 28,000

F R A N C E
☆ 300,000
★ 65,000
o Paris
● Oradour—sur—Glane

● Lidice
● Prague
C Z E C H O S L O V A K I A
卍 Mauthausen
o Vienna
A U S T R I A 1938
★ 70,000
★ 60,000

☆ 120,000
★ 9,000
I T A L Y
o Rome

卍 Dachau 1933

☆ 81,000
★ 60,000
H U N G A R Y
o Budapest
☆ 710,000
★ 200,000

R U M A N I A
☆ 1,000,000
★ 750,000
o Bucharest

Belgrade
Y U G O S L A V I A
☆ 70,000
★ 58,000

B U L G A R I A
o Sofia
☆ 48,000
★ 40,000

ALBANIA

G R E E C E
★ 67,000
★ 60,000

Adriatic Sea

280,000 JEWISH REFUGEES TO USA, SOUTH AMERICA, GT. BRITAIN AND JAPAN BEFORE 1940.

bor for near-by factories, some of which were specially set up to employ the new labor forces. But the main task of the camps was to murder the inmates and to eliminate the Jews from Europe altogether.

The largest camp was at Auschwitz. It was begun in November 1941. Twelve thousand Russian prisoners of war were involved in its construction. They were forced to work until they dropped from sheer exhaustion. They were not fed for three or four days at a time. When the buildings were finished only 450 remained alive. On 22 June 1942 the first trainload of Jews arrived, from Paris. A selection was made on arrival and over a third of them were sent that day to what they were told was a shower bath. It was in fact a gas chamber. Within a few minutes of the doors being sealed they were dead.

The "final solution" continued for just under three years. There were extermination camps in many parts of the German conquered territories, and in Germany itself. The knowledge of what was happening to the Jews was difficult to hide. The commandant of Auschwitz lamented that "the foul and nauseating stench from the continued burning of bodies permeated the whole area and all the people living in the surrounding communities knew that exterminations were going on." There was even competition among German firms to provide the ovens in which the bodies were to be burnt. One firm anxious to supply furnaces for an extermination camp near Belgrade wrote as follows:

"From the Didier Works, Berlin:

"For putting the bodies into the furnace we suggest simply a metal fork moving on cylinders. Each furnace will have an oven measuring only 24 by 18 inches, as coffins will not be used. For transporting the corpses from the storage points to the furnaces we suggest using light carts on wheels, and we enclose diagrams of these drawn to scale."

Another firm, C. H. Kori, claimed durability and faultless craftsmanship, having already constructed furnaces for Dachau and Lublin which had given "full satisfaction":

"Following our verbal discussion regarding the delivery of equipment of simple construction for the burning of bodies, we are submitting plans for our perfected cremation ovens which operate with coal and which have hitherto given full satisfaction.

"We suggest two crematoria furnaces for the building planned, but we advise you to make further inquiries to ensure that two ovens will be sufficient for your requirements.

"We guarantee the effectiveness of the cremation ovens as well as their durability, the use of the best material and our faultless workmanship. Awaiting your further word, we will be at your service."

These simple but diabolical machines did their work well. "Compared to this," wrote an official at Auschwitz, "the inferno of Dante seems a comedy." At their most effective the ovens dispatched 300,000 Hungarian Jews in forty-six days.

Of the 400,000 Jews in the Warsaw ghetto only 60,000 were left by the beginning of 1943, their fellow ghetto dwellers having been deported to the gas chambers at Treblinka. The remnant decided to risk the revenge of their tormentors and make a stand for human decency.

When the next call for deportees was announced the Jews took up arms and resisted. For four weeks they battled with the Germans. Juergen Stroop, Major General of Police, later reported on how the Germans had liquidated the Jewish rebels. His report, seventy-five typewritten pages elegantly bound in leather, was entitled "The Warsaw Ghetto is No More" and like so many of the diligently compiled German records it has survived.

On 19 April 1943 Stroop turned his artillery, tanks, and flame throwers upon the ghetto. "Hardly had the operation begun," he wrote, "than we ran into strong, concerted fire by the Jews." A tank and two armored cars were "pelted with Molotov cocktails." Every time a section of the ghetto was occupied, and large numbers of Jews captured, fortunes were reversed and "new battle groups consisting of twenty to thirty Jewish men, accompanied by a corresponding number of women, kindled new resistance."

Stroop finally decided to set fire to the whole ghetto, block by block. His daily bulletins tell a terrible story:

"The Jews stayed in the burning buildings until because of the fear of being burned alive they jumped down from the upper stories. . . . With their bones broken, they still tried to crawl across the street into buildings which had not yet been set on fire. . . . Despite the danger of being burned alive the Jews and bandits often preferred to return into the flames rather than risk being caught by us.

"During the day several more blocks of buildings were burned down. This is the only and final method which forces this trash and subhumanity to the surface.

"One hundred and eighty Jews, bandits, and subhumans were destroyed. The former Jewish quarter of Warsaw is no longer in existence. The large-scale action was terminated at 2015 hours by blowing up the Warsaw synagogue. . . . Total number of Jews dealt with: 56,065, including both Jews caught and Jews whose extermination can be proved."

The resistance of the Jews in Warsaw forms a heroic chapter in Europe's story. There is little corresponding heroism in German actions. By the horror of their occupation they introduced all Europe to barbarism. The catalogue of their crimes fills many volumes. Ghastly "medical" experiments on the living, terrible tortures on prisoners of war, the hurling of living children into the flames, the almost total destruction of European Jewry—these horrors are not forgotten in Europe, despite its postwar recovery, its prosperity, and its apparent lack of interest in the past.

Whatever Europe achieved in science, culture, or medicine, in technology or scholarship, between 1900 and 1939, more was destroyed in the six years of war than such achievements could easily compensate for. Neither economic recovery nor personal repentance could restore to life the victims of the "final solution." The fields and ditches in which their bodies lie are as much the symbols of Europe's "achievement" as any reconstructed city. When the Allied troops entered the concentration camps in 1945, the stench of dead bodies overpowered them. From that moment, the history of Europe became a permanent and terrible reminder of man's inhumanity to man.

# ☆ 22 ☆

## EUROPE IN ECLIPSE

IN 1939 there were four Great Powers in Europe: Germany, France, Italy, and Great Britain; and three outside Europe, Russia, the United States, and Japan. In 1945 there were only two Great Powers, Russia and the United States.

Germany and Japan had been defeated in the war and their territory occupied. France had been humiliated by her defeat in 1940 and by the formation of the Vichy Government dependent upon German approval for its powers. Italy, whose "greatness" had in large measure been the result of Mussolini's bombast, accepted with hardly a murmur the recognition that fascism had been a stupid and costly mistake.

The eclipse of Europe was swift, first revealed at the Yalta Conference in 1945 when Stalin and Roosevelt together overruled Churchill's objections to their plans for postwar Europe. Europe's eclipse was made clearer when India gained independence from Britain in 1947. It was emphasized further when France was driven from Indochina by force in 1954.

In eastern Europe the advance of the Russian armies brought a rapid end to all hopes of immediate independence. The Russians wished to set up states which would act as protective buffers between them and the West. In Rumania and Bulgaria communist governments were established as soon as the Russian armies had occupied the countries. Democratic parties were outlawed and leading socialist and liberal politicians imprisoned. The liberation of these eastern lands from German rule or control brought no relaxation of tension and only a small relaxation of terror. Stalin had developed in Russia such an effective system of state control, based on the secret police, the single party, the arrest of opponents, and absolute control of the Press, education, and employment that it was not difficult to establish communist dictatorships elsewhere. All he needed was initial military control. The nations of eastern Europe had been so stunned by German barbarism that their powers of resistance had sunk extremely low. In Hungary and Poland full communist control was established in 1947, in Czechoslovakia in 1948.

Thus Europe was divided in half, and over the eastern half there descended a darkness which covered many totalitarian sins. After 1956 the worst of communist repressions began slowly but steadily to disappear, and national autonomy, if not independence, showed itself once more. But for eleven years after the destruction of Nazism the peoples of half of Europe knew no measure of freedom or happiness.

Two countries vulnerable to Russian pressure were able to withstand it. Yugoslavia had not relied upon the Russian Army in order to drive out the Germans. Under Marshal Tito large areas of Yugoslavia had been liberated from German rule. Tito, though educated in Moscow, and a sincere communist, rejected Russian tutelage. In 1948, the year in which Czechoslovakia fell the victim to communist pressure and intrigue, Tito broke away from the Moscow web. He remained a communist, but gave Stalin no comfort. For over fifteen years Tito ruled Yugoslavia, and guarded her independence.

Finland had fought with Germany against Russia from 1941 to 1945, hoping to regain the territory which Russia had conquered in 1940. The Finns were forced, on their defeat in 1945, to pay reparations and to allow Russia to keep her earlier conquests. Four hundred thousand Finns in the Russian-occupied territories were given the right to choose Russian or Finnish citizenship. Almost to a man they chose the latter, and arrived in Finland as refugees.

The Finnish Government after the war was a coalition in which the communists, who were a minority party, held office. But whereas the communists in the Czech Parliament were able to push out their opponents, the Finnish communists were outvoted. A vote of censure in the Finnish Parliament in May 1948 resulted in the resignation of the leading communist minister. The Russians did nothing, and Finland's parliamentary democracy was assured. No doubt Stalin remembered the day in 1918 when he had issued the decree

EUROPE 1945-1948

Allied Control Zones of Germany & Austria
Ceded to Russia by Britain & America
Cities divided into 4 Occupation Zones
Annexed by Russia in 1945
States which became Communist between 1945 & 1948
Yugoslav gains from Italy
The Iron Curtain 1948
1937 Frontiers

FINLAND

Leningrad

SWEDEN

DENMARK

Baltic Sea

ESTONIA

Riga
LATVIA

LITHUANIA

Minsk

Danzig

EAST PRUSSIA
Polish Admin.

RUSSIA

American

HOL.

Bremen

Berlin

British

Russian

GERMANY

Polish Administered

POLAND

Posnan

Warsaw

FRANCE

French

American

Prague

Cracow

CZECHOSLOVAKIA

SWITZ.

British

Russian

Vienna

A U S T R I A

Budapest

HUNGARY

RUMANIA

Trieste
BRITISH & USA
OCCUPATION
1945-1955

YUGOSLAVIA

Belgrade

Bucharest

Adriatic Sea

BULGARIA

Sofia

ALBANIA

GREECE

TURKEY

Aegean Sea

Miles
0    100    200

Mediterranean Sea

granting Finland her independence. But more important was the fact that Finland represented no threat to Russian hegemony in eastern Europe. Russian troops had no need to be in Helsinki as well as Berlin.

Although Germany was totally defeated in 1945, peace came only slowly to Europe. Particularly unhappy was the Greek experience. When the British landed in October 1944 they found that the communist-led resistance movement was taking over control of the country as the Germans were driven out. The British persuaded the communists to join with the exiled politicians in the first government set up in Athens, but in December 1944 fighting broke out between British troops and the communists in the capital. After bitter fighting the communists were defeated, but allowed to survive as a political party. In the elections of March 1946 the extreme right was victorious. The communists were at once beaten up, arrested, and abused. In August they launched a civil war, and for three years were in complete power in northern Greece. Their arms were supplied across the borders of Albania, Yugoslavia, and Bulgaria, three communist states. Aid for the Greek Government came from an unexpected quarter. In March 1947 President Truman promised American aid to Greece. This gave Greece the means to combat the communists, though they were not finally subdued until 1949.

The two postwar powers, Russia and America, were agreed on one thing, the destruction of German power. They disagreed on how this was to be done, and on the territorial changes that ought to take place. Russia acted against American wishes in the East when she divided East Prussia between herself and Poland, and advanced the Polish frontier westwards to the River Oder, giving Poland the great industrial region of Silesia. The Americans were interested in a negotiated peace, and regarded all territorial changes as requiring sanction in a future peace treaty. The Russians considered that *de facto* frontiers should be regarded as legally binding. Certainly this view prevailed even with the Americans in regard to the return of the Sudetenland to Czechoslovakia, and the immediate annulment of the union between Austria and Germany.

As a result of these territorial changes detrimental to Germany, vast numbers of Germans were forced to flee westwards. Over ten million Germans were driven out of their former homelands. Many died during the journey, some were killed. The Germans have published many volumes enumerating the atrocities that took place against the expellees. But Europe was too stunned by the horror of what the Germans themselves had done over six years to take this complaint very seriously. Yet undoubtedly there was much injustice inflicted upon the Germans, many of whom, like the victims of Nazism earlier, were women ignorant of politics, or children too young to know the meaning of national fervor.

Germany was divided into four zones of occupation. Berlin, which was in the Russian zone, was similarly divided. Such heavy financial losses had been sustained by the victors, in particular Russia, Britain, and France, that the question of occupation was for a while of less importance to them than the question of their own internal recovery. And it was here that Europe turned to America.

American aid to the devastated continent in 1945 made the difference between starvation and survival. Churchill appealed to the Americans in August 1945: "Let them act up to the level of their power and their responsibility, not for themsleves but for others, for all men in all lands, and then a brighter day may dawn upon human history." American magnanimity was a powerful psychological stimulus for a Europe numbed by selfishness, violence, and the domination of evil. Confronted by this example, European economic and social reconstruction gained vigor and impetus.

The communist triumphs in eastern Europe alerted the West to a new danger, marked by an "iron curtain" which stretched through Germany, along the Danube and into the Balkans. The countries east of the curtain looked to Moscow for political, military, and economic guidance. They refused American aid which, for two years, had helped to keep them alive. They denied their inhabitants the right to travel to the West and barred the capitals of the East to all but a few diplomats and fellow travelers. They created the impression that Russia was preparing to use them for some further act of aggression. Against such a threat the West responded, led by America, and encouraged by Churchill who, though no longer Prime Minister, had, in the United States, on 5 March 1946, urged the defensive alliance of the English-speaking peoples.

On 17 March 1948 (after the communist seizure of power in Czechoslovakia) Britain, France, Belgium, Holland, and Luxembourg signed the Brussels Treaty, promising each other mutual assistance against aggression. A year later the Brussels Powers were joined by the United States, Canada, Italy, Portugal, Norway, Iceland, and Denmark in the North Atlantic Treaty. Thus was the West united for the purpose of defense. At the same time America developed her aid-giving agencies, the most notable being the Marshall Plan, which, over three years, provided twelve and a half billion dollars to Europe's depleted exchequers.

Europe's problems ceased to dominate international relations after 1945. In Asia and Africa growing nationalist movements attracted increasing attention. It was in the Far East that the most revolutionary change took place. Japan had sought the same mastery over Asia that Germany sought over Europe. On 6 August 1945 the Americans dropped an atomic bomb on Hiroshima; three days later a second atomic bomb on Nagasaki. Both cities were totally destroyed in a single explosion. On 14 August the Japanese surrendered.

With this new and uniquely powerful weapon used to such immediate effect, the United States established herself as the world's most powerful nation. Within ten years that power was shared in equal measure by the Soviet Union. Although two European Powers, Britain and France, developed their own nuclear weapons, they had not the means to do so on the Russian or American scale. They could imitate the giants, but they could not compete with them. Nuclear power became a standard of greatness beyond the economic ability of any single European state. It might also be argued that the exertions of six years of war had left Europe lethargic and unadventurous. Imperial possessions were surrendered swiftly and with a certain sense of relief; there was no desire to take up new burdens. The guarding, or tyrannizing, of the world could be left to others. Europe was weary of Churchills and Hitlers alike.

In 1945 most European politicians would have agreed to make Germany a permanently weak nation, deprived of all ability to wage war or to threaten the territorial integrity of her neighbors. But with the growth of East-West antagonisms, and the recognition that a cold war existed in which as much discipline and organization was needed as had been needed in the war which had just ended, Germany became of great strategic importance to the West. Fifty million Germans were in zones occupied by America, France, and Britain; seventeen million lived on the other side of the Iron Curtain.

The Germans became a key to the cold war. The memory of the Russo-German pact of August 1939 hung like a bad odor in the western air. Germany was needed in the western alliance. In February 1948 the four western occupying powers, together with Belgium, Holland and Luxembourg, announced that they would create a single constitution for western Germany. In June 1948 the Soviet Union, anxious to destroy western patronage of Germany, blockaded Berlin. The Western Powers organized an airlift through which the western zone of Berlin was provided with food, fuel, and other necessities of life. The blockade was ended in May 1949. It had brought together, almost as allies, the enemies of four years earlier. It destroyed what remained of western faith in Russian goodwill. It showed that German friendship was essential to Europe if the Iron Curtain was not to move further westwards.

In May 1949 the Western Powers approved the establishment of a Federal Republic in western Germany, with its capital in Bonn. Elections were held in August and Konrad Adenauer became Chancellor. West Germany became an equal among the European Powers. Her economy flourished, her cities were rebuilt, her industry expanded. She was allowed to create an army and, in 1954, she became a full member of NATO. Indeed General Adolf Heusinger, who had helped plan the destruction of Belgrade in 1941 and had become Chief of Operations of the German Army High Command in 1944, was appointed NATO's European commander. Thus Europe forgot her history in the face of new dangers, and allowed the hostility between Russia and America to determine her alliances, her friendships, and her organization. Though such activities were certainly in her immediate interest, providing a shield behind which she could shelter, they were also a recognition of her new and more lowly status. From 1900 to 1941 what happened in Europe at once influenced events in every part of the world: after 1941 Europe's primacy was shattered. Since 1945 the political developments of Europe have had to take their place alongside the problems of Africa, Asia, and America.

European developments were not of paramount importance in world affairs after 1945, yet they have not been insignificant. Germany, having put all Europe to shame for forty years and provoked retaliation, has for twenty years sought the path of parliamentary democracy, open discussion, and vigorous economic expansion. With the example of East Germany's totalitarian methods to serve as a constant reminder of the proximity of the past, West Germany is the leader of Europe's "miracle"—swift increases in productivity, substantial rises in the standard of living, and bold overseas trading and investment. This "miracle," though essentially materialistic, helped heal the scars of war, and outlined the patterns of future European progress.

Setbacks to the "miracle" have been frequent in the twenty years after 1945. But the problems which have worried western Europe since 1945 were more in the realm of social and political tensions inside each state than of national tensions between states. French fears of being ignored, German fears of being isolated, and British fears of losing the power of independent political action hindered European cooperation most before 1939. Since 1945 European governments have realized the importance of cooperation, and begun to work out the means to cooperate with their neighbors.

The many crimes committed in Europe and by Europeans between 1900 and 1945 cast a gloomy shadow over Europe's past. But they also serve as a warning. The weaknesses of democracy and the destructive powers of totalitarianism were both revealed with unprecedented clarity. If farsighted Europeans strengthen their democratic institutions, and refuse to succumb to the lure of totalitarian ones, they may yet defeat the pessimism of their fellow citizens and the skepticism of outsiders as to Europe's power of constructive and altruistic activity.

For forty-five years Europe led, shocked, and wounded the world. Since 1945, although her supremacy has gone, she has retained enough power to act, individually or collectively, as a good influence in international affairs. Russia and America are now the "giants"— but the "pigmies" can still play an important part as advocates of parliamentary democracy and as leaders of culture.

# BIBLIOGRAPHY

## CHAPTER I

Dickinson, G. Lowes: *Letters from John Chinaman* (Dent, 1900).
Hudson, Geoffrey: *The Far East in World Politics* (Oxford, 1939).
Joseph, P.: *Foreign Diplomacy in China 1894–1900* (Allen & Unwin, 1928).
Luard, Evan: *Britain and China* (Chatto & Windus, 1962).

## CHAPTER 2

Churchill, Winston: *The River War* (Eyre & Spottiswoode, 1933 edition).
———: *London to Ladysmith* (Longmans, 1900).
Marais, J. S.: *The Fall of Kruger's Republic* (Oxford, 1961).
Perham, Margery: *Lugard: The Years of Adventure 1858–1898* (Collins, 1956).
Pyrah, G. B.: *Imperial Policy and South Africa 1902–1910* (Oxford, 1956).
Ronaldshay, The Earl of: *The Life of Lord Curzon,* 3 vols. (Benn, 1928).

## CHAPTER 3

Ascherson, Neal: *The King Incorporated:* Leopold II of the Belgians (Allen & Unwin, 1963).
Duffy, James: *Portuguese Africa* (Oxford, 1959).
Langer, William: *The Diplomacy of Imperialism* (Knopf, 1951).
Moon, Parker: *Imperialism in World Politics* (Macmillan Co., N.Y., 1947).
Robinson, Ronald and Gallagher, John: *Africa and the Victorians* (Macmillan, 1961).

## CHAPTER 4

Berlin, Isaiah: *Karl Marx* (Oxford, 3rd edition, 1963).
Cole, G. D. H.: *Marxism and Anarchism* (Macmillan, 1957).
Joughin, Jean: *The Paris Commune in French Politics 1871–1880* (Johns Hopkins, 1955).
Lorwin, Val: *The French Labour Movement* (Harvard, 1954).
Mayer, Gustav: *Friedrich Engels* (Chapman & Hall, 1936).
Pelling, Henry: *The British Political Tradition: The Challenge of Socialism* (A. & C. Black, 1954).
Schorske, Carl: *German Social Democracy* (Harvard, 1955).
Treadgold, Donald: *Lenin and His Rivals: The Struggle for Russia's Future 1896–1906* (Methuen, 1955).

## CHAPTER 5

Kann, Robert: *The Multinational Empire,* 2 vols. (Columbia, 1950).
May, Arthur: *The Habsburg Monarchy 1867–1914* (Harvard, 1951).

Pribram, Alfred: *Austria-Hungary and Great Britain 1908–1914* (Oxford, 1951).

Redlich, Joseph: *Emperor Francis Joseph of Austria* (Macmillan, 1929).

Taylor, A. J. P.: *The Habsburg Monarchy 1815–1918* (Oxford, 1941).

Wedel, Oswald: *Austro-German Diplomatic Relations 1908–1914* (Oxford, 1933).

Wickham Steed, H.: *The Habsburg Monarchy* (Constable, 1913).

## CHAPTER 6

Albertini, Luigi: *The Origins of the War of 1914,* 3 vols. (Oxford, 1952–7).

Churchill, Winston: *The World Crisis,* vol. 1 (Butterworth, 1923).

———: *The Unknown War* (Butterworth, 1931).

Ludwig, Emil: *July 1914* (Putnam, 1929).

Schmitt, Bernadotte: *The Coming of War 1914,* 2 vols. (Scribners, 1930).

Seton-Watson, R. W.: *Sarajevo: A Study in the Origins of the Great War* (Hutchinson, 1926).

## CHAPTER 7

Blake, Robert: *The Private Papers of Douglas Haig 1914–1919* (Eyre & Spottiswoode, 1952).

Churchill, Winston: *The World Crisis,* vols. 1–4 (Butterworth, 1923–7).

Clarke, Alan: *The Donkeys* (Hutchinson, 1951).

Graves, Robert: *Good-bye to All That* (Cassell, 1929).

Pitt, Barrie: *1918: The Last Act* (Cassell, 1962).

Quigley, Hugh: *Passchendaele and the Somme* (Methuen, 1928).

Taylor, A. J. P.: *The First World War: An Illustrated History* (Hamish Hamilton, 1963).

Tuchman, Barbara: *The Guns of August* (Macmillan Co., N.Y., 1962).

## CHAPTER 8

Chamberlin, William: *The Russian Revolution,* 2 vols. (Macmillan Co., N.Y., 1935).

Churchill, Winston: *The Unknown War* (Butterworth, 1931).

Falls, Cyril: *The First World War* (Longmans, 1960).

Hoffman, General Max: *War Diaries,* 2 vols. (Secker, 1929).

Knox, General Sir Alfred: *With the Russian Army 1914–1917,* 2 vols. (Hutchinson, 1921).

von Ludendorff, General Erich: *My War Memoirs,* 2 vols. (Hutchinson, 1919).

Moorehead, Alan: *Gallipoli* (Hamish Hamilton, 1956).

Zeman, Z. A. B.: *The Break-Up of the Habsburg Empire 1914–1918* (Oxford, 1961).

## CHAPTER 9

Clemenceau, Georges: *Grandeur and Misery of Victory* (Harrap, 1930).

Gilbert, Martin: *Britain and Germany Between the Wars* (Longmans, 1964).
Keynes, J. M.: *The Economic Consequences of the Peace* (Macmillan, 1922).
———: *A Revision of the Treaty* (Macmillan, 1922).
Lloyd George, David: *The Truth about the Peace Treaties* (Gollancz, 1938).
McCallum, R. B.: *Public Opinion and the Last Peace* (Oxford, 1944).
Nicolson, Harold: *Peacemaking 1919* (Constable, 1933).
———: *Curzon: The Last Phase 1919–1925* (Constable, 1934).
Tardieu, André: *The Truth about the Treaty* (Hodder & Stoughton, 1921).


## CHAPTER 10

Clark, R. J.: *The Fall of the German Republic* (Allen & Unwin, 1935).
Coper, Rudolf: *Failure of a Revolution: Germany in 1918–1919* (Cambridge, 1955).
Epstein, Klaus: *Matthias Erzberger* (Princeton, 1959).
Eyck, Erich: *A History of the Weimar Republic* (Oxford, 1962).
Frölich, Paul: *Rosa Luxemburg* (Gollancz, 1940).
Gatzke, Hans: *Stresemann and the Rearmament of Germany* (Johns Hopkins, 1954).
Joll, James: *Intellectuals in Politics*. Contains an essay on Rathenau (Weidenfeld & Nicolson, 1960).
Pinson, Koppel: *Modern Germany* (Macmillan Co., N.Y., 1959).
Rosenberg, Arthur: *The Birth of the German Republic* (Oxford, 1931).
———: *A History of the German Republic* (Methuen, 1936).
Scheele, Godfrey: *The Weimar Republic* (Faber, 1946).


## CHAPTER 11

Beloff, Max: *The Foreign Policy of Soviet Russia*, 2 vols. (Oxford, 1947).
Carr, E. H.: *The Bolshevik Revolution 1917–1923*, 3 vols. (Macmillan, 1950–3).
———: *Socialism in One Country 1924–26*, 2 vols. (Macmillan, 1958–9).
Chamberlin, William: *The Russian Revolution*, 2 vols. (Macmillan Co., N.Y., 1935).
Deutscher, Isaac: *Trotsky, The Prophet Armed* (Oxford, 1954).
———: *Stalin* (Oxford, 1949).
Fischer, Louis: *The Soviets in World Affairs*, 2 vols. (Princeton, 1951).
Pipes, Richard: *The Formation of the Soviet Union* (Harvard, 1957).
Trotsky, Leon: *The History of the Russian Revolution*, 3 vols. (Gollancz, 1932–3).
Ullman, Richard: *Intervention and the War* (Oxford, 1961).
Wolfe, Bertram: *Three Who Made a Revolution* (Dial Press, N.Y., 1948).


## CHAPTER 12

Binchy, D. A.: *Church and State in Fascist Italy* (Oxford, 1941).
Ciano, Galleazzo: *Ciano's Diary 1939–43* (Heinemann, 1947).

Deakin, F. W.: *The Brutal Friendship: Mussolini, Hitler and the Fall of Italian Fascism* (Weidenfeld & Nicolson, 1962).

Fermi, Laura: *Atoms in the Family* (Allen & Unwin, 1955).

Finer, Herman: *Mussolini's Italy* (Gollancz, 1935).

Hibbert, Christopher: *Benito Mussolini* (Longmans, 1962).

Ludwig, Emil: *Talks with Mussolini* (Little, Brown, 1933).

Mussolini, Benito: *My Autobiography* (Scribners, 1928).

Salvemini, Gaetano: *The Fascist Dictatorship in Italy* (Oxford, 1927).

——: *Prelude to World War II* (Gollancz, 1953).

Smith, Dennis Mack: *Italy* (Mayflower, 1959).

Villari, Luigi: *Italian Foreign Policy under Mussolini* (Holborn, 1959).

### CHAPTER 13

Brogan, Denis: *The Development of Modern France 1870–1939* (Hamish Hamilton, 1940).

Cole, Hubert: *Laval* (Heinemann, 1963).

Joll, James: *Intellectuals in Politics*. Contains an essay on Blum (Weidenfeld & Nicolson, 1960).

Jordan, W. M.: *Great Britain, France and the German Problem 1918–39* (Oxford, 1943).

Micaud, Charles: *The French Right and Nazi Germany* (Duke University, 1943).

Thomson, David: *Democracy in France* (Oxford, 1946).

Werth, Alexander: *The Twilight of France, 1933–40* (Hamish Hamilton, 1942).

Wright, Gordon: *France in Modern Times* (John Murray, 1962).

### CHAPTER 14

Amery, Leo: *My Political Life: The Unforgiving Years 1929–40* (Hutchinson, 1955).

Beaverbrook, Lord: *Men and Power 1917–1918* (Hutchinson, 1956).

——: *The Decline and Fall of Lloyd George* (Collins, 1963).

Blake, Robert: *The Unknown Prime Minister: The Life and Times of Andrew Bonar Law* (Eyre & Spottiswoode, 1955).

Butler, David and Freeman, Jennie: *British Political Facts 1900–1960* (Macmillan, 1963).

Churchill, Winston: *The Gathering Storm* (Cassell, 1948).

Feiling, Keith: *Life of Neville Chamberlain* (Macmillan, 1946).

Gilbert, Martin: *Plough My Own Furrow* (Longmans, 1965).

Haxey, Simon: *Tory MP* (Gollancz, 1942).

Morgan, Kenneth: *David Lloyd George, Welsh Radical as World Statesman* (University of Wales Press, 1963).

Mowat, Charles Loch: *Britain Between the Wars* (Methuen, 1955).

Young, G. M.: *Stanley Baldwin* (Hart Davis, 1952).

## CHAPTER 15

Bullock, Alan: *Hitler* (Odhams, 1952).

Heiden, Konrad: *Der Fuehrer: Hitler's Rise to Power,* 2 vols. (Gollancz, 1944).

Hitler, Adolf: *Mein Kampf* (Hurst & Blackett, 1939).

Meinecke, Friedrich: *The German Catastrophe* (Harvard, 1950).

Rauschning, Hermann: *Germany's Revolution of Destruction* (Heinemann, 1939).

Roberts, Stephen: *The House that Hitler Built* (Methuen, 1937).

Wheeler-Bennett, J.: *The Nemesis of Power; The German Army in Politics 1918-1945* (Macmillan, 1953).

## CHAPTER 16

Brook-Shepherd, Gordon: *Dollfuss* (Macmillan, 1961).

———: *Anschluss* (Macmillan, 1963).

Bullock, Malcolm: *Austria 1918-1938: A Study in Failure* (Macmillan, 1939).

Gedye, Gerald: *Heirs to the Habsburgs* (Arrowsmith, 1932).

———: *Fallen Bastions* (Gollancz, 1939).

Gehl, Jurgen: *Austria, Germany and the Anschluss 1931-38* (Oxford, 1963).

Macartney, C. A.: *The Social Revolution in Austria* (Oxford, 1926).

von Schuschnigg, Kurt: *Farewell Austria* (Cassell, 1938).

## CHAPTER 17

Beneš, Eduard: *War Memoirs* (Allen & Unwin, 1954).

Grant Duff, S.: *Europe and the Czechs* (Penguin, 1938).

Krofta, Kamil: *A Short History of Czechoslovakia* (Williams & Norgate, 1935).

Mackenzie, Compton: *Dr Benes* (Harrap, 1946).

Ripka, Hubert: *Munich, Before and After* (Gollancz, 1939).

Seton-Watson, R. W.: *A History of the Czechs and Slovaks* (Hutchinson, 1943).

Thomson, S. Harrison: *Czechoslovakia in European History* (Princeton, 1953).

Wiskemann, Elizabeth: *Czechs and Germans* (Oxford, 1938).

## CHAPTER 18

Gilbert, Martin and Gott, Richard: *The Appeasers* (Houghton Mifflin, 1963).

Komarnicki, Titus: *Rebirth of the Polish Republic* (Heinemann, 1957).

Machray, Robert: *The Poland of Pilsudski* (Allen & Unwin, 1936).

Reddaway, W. F., editor: *The Cambridge History of Poland 1697-1935* (Cambridge, 1951).

Rose, William: *The Rise of Polish Democracy* (Bell, 1944).
Smogorzewski, Casimir: *Poland's Access to the Sea* (Allen & Unwin, 1934).
Zweig, Ferdynand: *Poland Between the Wars* (Secker & Warburg, 1944).


## CHAPTER 19

Bloch, Marc: *Strange Defeat* (Oxford, 1949).
Churchill, Winston: *The Gathering Storm* (Cassell, 1948).
———: *Their Finest Hour* (Cassell, 1949).
Derry, T. K.: *The Campaign in Norway* (Bell, 1952).
Ellis, L. F.: *The War in France and Flanders* (H.M.S.O., 1953).
Falls, Cyril: *The Second World War* (Methuen, 1948).
Jars, Robert: *La Compagne de Pologne* (Payot, Paris, 1949).
Reynaud, Paul: *In the Thick of the Fight 1930–1945* (Cassell, 1955).
Richards, Denis: *Royal Air Force: The Fight at Odds* (H.M.S.O., 1953).
Trevor-Roper, Hugh: *The Last Days of Hitler* (Macmillan, 1957).


## CHAPTERS 20 AND 21

Aron, Robert: *The Vichy Regime 1940–1944* (Putnam, 1958).
Farmer, Paul: *Vichy's Political Dilemma* (Oxford, 1955).
FitzGibbon, Constantine: *The Shirt of Nessus:* The Bomb Plot against Hitler in 1944 (Cassell, 1956).
Hersey, John: *The Wall:* The Warsaw Ghetto Rising (Hamish Hamilton, 1962).
Lochner, Louis, editor: *The Goebbels Diaries* (Hamish Hamilton, 1948).
Piotrowski, Stanislaw, editor: *Hans Frank's Diary* (Warsaw, 1961).
Reitlinger, Gerald: *The Final Solution* (Mitchell, 1953).
———: *The House Built on Sand* (Weidenfeld & Nicolson, 1960).
Rudnicki, Adolf: *Ascent to Heaven:* Poland under German Rule (Denis Dobson, 1951).
Shirer, William: *The Rise and Fall of the Third Reich* (Secker & Warburg, 1960).


## CHAPTER 22

Churchill, Winston: *The Sinews of Peace* (Cassell, 1949).
Feis, Herbert: *Between War and Peace:* The Potsdam Conference (Princeton, 1960).
Gavin, Catherine: *Liberated France* (St Martins, 1955).
Gimbel, John: *A German Community under American Occupation* (Stanford, 1961).
Moon, Penderel: *Divide and Quit:* India in 1947 (Chatto & Windus, 1961).
Zinkin, Maurice and Taya: *Britain and India* (Chatto & Windus, 1964).

# INDEX